Michaela Thomas is a Clinical Psycholo
founder of The Thomas Connection. M
busy people find balance over burnout, so ... ...ve, love and work in a more meaningful way. She is on a mission to show couples how to stay compassionate and connected even when feeling under pressure, using her online courses, workshops and therapy.

The Lasting Connection

Michaela Thomas

ROBINSON

ROBINSON

First published in Great Britain in 2021 by Robinson

1 3 5 7 9 10 8 6 4 2

A CIP catalogue record for this book
is available from the British Library.

ISBN: 978-1-47214-427-0

Typeset in Palatino by SX Composing DTP, Rayleigh, Essex
Printed and bound in Great Britain by Clays Ltd, Elcograf S.p.A.

Papers used by Robinson are from well-managed forests
and other responsible sources.

MIX
Paper from
responsible sources
FSC® C104740

Robinson
An imprint of
Little, Brown Book Group
Carmelite House
50 Victoria Embankment
London EC4Y 0DZ

An Hachette UK Company
www.hachette.co.uk

www.littlebrown.co.uk

To Robin – always & forever

CONTENTS

PART III Building a lasting connection with compassion

PART IV Maintaining your connection

Introduction

Hello and welcome – please take a seat on my sofa! My name is Michaela Thomas and I'm a Clinical Psychologist, Couples Therapist and the founder of The Thomas Connection. I'm married and have a young child. I'm short, I'm a dreamer and I like liquorice.

This book was written with passion and joy, as well as anxiety and doubt. Like most things in life, we can have mixed emotions about what we do, but anything worth having is worth working for. That's the mentality I've used in writing this book, as well as in my own marriage. Settle in – we've got some work to do.

Will you have a lasting connection?

As an experienced couples therapist, I can have a gut feeling about the health of a relationship. Although I use interviews and questionnaires to assess the quality of a relationship, it's not easy to predict whether it will last. After all, people and feelings are unpredictable. While I can map out the stumbling blocks facing a couple, and help them attempt to overcome those issues, I can't predict whether or not they will 'make it'. Sometimes the differences between two partners is irreconcilable; the pain and the damage done is too deep.

Often couples come to me after years of struggling, when they may be too exhausted to make the efforts needed for a repair. They've left it for too long before seeking help. However, you *can* teach old dogs new tricks – old habits in relationships *can* be changed, new patterns *can* be established, new wiring *can* be laid down in your brain, but you need to give yourself and your relationship that chance for change.

Who this book is for

This book describes the clinical methods I use with couples in therapy and in my course 'The Compassionate Couple' – a pioneering way of blending the research on romantic relationships, mindfulness, neuroscience and positive psychology with skills from three evidence-based psychotherapies: Behavioural Couples Therapy, Compassion Focused Therapy and Acceptance and Commitment Therapy.

Working through this book will help strengthen your relationship and encourage wellbeing for you as a couple. The book can be used as a stand-alone self-help guide or alongside couples therapy/relationship counselling. If your relationship is very distressed or you're on the verge of separation, then please seek out professional help as well (some couples might need someone objective to guide them through the exercises). If your relationship is not in an acute phase of distress, but you want to deepen your connection and make your everyday interactions smoother, learning to be more compassionate with yourself and your partner, then this book is for you.

I wrote this book with the intention of balancing theory and practice around romantic relationships, so you can both gain insight and know what practical steps to take. I didn't want to make it purely academic, but to make it easy to read (so you'll actually finish it!). It is not the definitive and perfect book on loving relationships, but if you're interested in focusing on *connection* in romantic relationships, then it's for you.

There are several aspects of this connection, depending on where you are on your relationship journey:

- You're happy with the connection with your partner and want to put things in place to protect that connection from dwindling.
- You're looking to strengthen the connection in a relationship where you're getting along OK, but needing to rekindle the spark as things have gone a bit flat.
- You're looking for help as your relationship is troubled, and hope to reconnect before the connection is fully lost.

- You're in a relationship where the connection cannot be repaired, and you're looking for a compassionate way out.
- You've ended a relationship and want to understand why the connection was severed.
- You're looking to find someone to connect with and want to understand your relationship patterns better before you enter another relationship.
- You're a professional helping people connect better to their partners and want to use this book as an aid.

Using the exercises in this book, you'll learn to develop compassion for yourself and your partner, to build a better foundation in your relationship. You'll explore how your respective life experiences impact on how you interact. You'll learn skills for more effective communication; negotiation tools when making joint decisions, ways of soothing yourself around arguments and jumping into your partner's shoes to truly *feel* empathy and be able to *show* compassion for the person you love. You'll learn what forgiveness is (and what it isn't), and use mindfulness and compassion skills to foster a deeper emotional and physical connection with your partner. If you follow the practices offered you'll notice an improvement in yourself as well as in your relationship, being able to be kinder to yourself and manage stressful times better, especially when the inner critic shows up.

The parts of this book – from theory to practice

Part I Here you'll gain insight into relationships – the difference between love and compassion, and what defines happy intimate relationships. It includes questionnaires around relationship satisfaction and 'make or break' factors. You'll explore what areas need most attention and how your attachment styles impact your relationship. I'll also illuminate the wider societal context we live in, of distraction and disconnection, and what may be getting in the way of a deeper connection in your relationship. You'll learn how love isn't enough for a lasting connection – you need compassion too.

Part II This part is based on my eight-week course 'The Compassionate Couple' (Compassionate Mind Training). You and your partner will learn how to give and receive compassion to others, but also to yourselves – using exercises in attention training and mindfulness, breathing, visual imagery and written work. Here you'll practise dealing with criticism towards both yourself and your partner. This skills training helps you cultivate a version of yourself which communicates well and acts with loving compassion towards your partner. This is the foundation you'll need to do the more specific couples work in a sustainable way, so spend your time here. You can do one chapter a week for eight weeks, and there are audio exercises to download to support your practice.

Part III Here we integrate your new Compassionate Mind Training skills together with specific exercises and tools from Behavioural Couples Therapy and Acceptance and Commitment Therapy. We'll practise communication, problem-solving, decision-making and activities to improve the mood in your relationship. You'll learn how to turn down the negatives such as criticism, hostility and friction, and turn up the positives such as acceptance, trust, collaboration and friendship. This will help deepen both emotional and physical connection, promoting intimacy and closeness. We'll manage high-risk situations, as well as practise forgiveness and embrace imperfection. We look at values you have as a couple, to help you flourish – focusing on thriving as well as surviving.

Part IV Here we map out the road ahead to continue a life worth living together using kindness and gratitude. We put together a compassionate tool kit for what you need in your relationship for years to come, also establishing a self-care routine for you – you cannot give what you haven't got.

These features in the book will help you on your journey:

'From the sofa' These real-life examples come from the sofa in my therapy room, and illustrate how others struggle with similar issues to you. All names and identifying information have been altered to protect confidentiality.

'Try this' Exercises to help you improve your relationship.

'Reflection & Connection' A moment to pause and sit down with your partner to discuss something, getting closer through sharing thoughts and feelings about what you've read.

'My story' I'm not a relationship guru with a perfect marriage. I'm a couples expert, yes, but also a human with a tricky brain, affected by my experiences just like everyone else. I've included my story to show you that we're all in this tricky life together, and I mess up too.

How to use this book

You can just read this book from cover to cover should you wish, but for it to help you go beyond insight and into change you also need to work through the exercises. Improving your relationship is a journey which takes time. There's no quick fix and changes will not happen magically overnight, so allow some time and space in your life to do this work. See it as an investment in yourself and your relationship.

All the worksheets and audio exercises are downloadable from the members section on www.thomasconnection.co.uk/thelastingconnection. These tools will support your practice in compassion, and you can find your username and password in the Resources section at the end of this book.

A word of caution

My role as a therapist is about helping couples make wise choices about their relationship, not about keeping them together at all costs.

This process may be painful for you. My job is not to shield people from feeling their emotions, but rather to be a companion on the road to where they need to get to. This book will clarify that destination, and make the journey as fulfilling as possible.

Walking that road includes sometimes tripping up, sometimes feeling exhausted and sometimes enjoying the sun shining on your face – highs and lows – so use this book as map and compass for your unfolding adventure. All I ask is that you go gently on yourself and your partner here – you've had a long journey getting to this point, and things will not change in a heartbeat.

I also care about you being *safe*. If you're worried about being at risk of domestic abuse or violence, please seek additional help. This book is not for you, as the risk of violence increases if the abused partner starts to voice discontent or starts being more assertive. If you're worried that you're going to be violent towards your partner, or already have been, this book is also not sufficient for you. Please look at the Resources section to find literature on compassion for anger and seek professional help immediately.

Pause – Purpose – Play

When it comes to relationships and creating a lasting connection with your partner, there are a few things which might help. I call my therapeutic process 'Pause – Purpose – Play'.

1 Pause

Pausing means we actively choose to slow down the pace of our busy lives and pay more attention to what matters. We become aware of our minds and bodies, learning to mindfully notice both our outer and inner world. Pausing helps couples who are getting caught up in strong feelings, defensiveness and retaliation, and promotes really listening to each other's perspective. Slowing down and taking the pressure off is also beneficial for couples who are competitive, striving or ambitious in other parts of their lives; overextending yourself will have a negative impact on your moods, wellbeing and relationship functioning. It also helps couples who have become complacent, lost track of their connection or are taking each other for granted to consciously reflect and find their sense of direction again. Press pause before you're forced to press stop (burning out) or even eject (leaving a marriage or relationship).

2 Purpose

When we've slowed down enough to spot the negative consequences of our behaviour, we can choose behaviours which will get us closer towards the meaningful life we seek. We can find our bearings, take out a map and compass and decide which direction to take, finding our *passion* and working towards it purposefully. This also means getting unstuck from unhelpful behaviours inhibiting connection, such as being inauthentic and not sharing our vulnerability. We use compassion as a way to act like the kind of partner we want to be.

3 Play

Having slowed down and found direction, we press the play button to move forward with intention. Building skills practice into everyday life and accepting life as full of both light and dark, we can then make space for fun and vitality. We can explore which adventures we want to go on with our partner, our hopes and dreams, and how we can increase positive exchanges and create rich memories to build a lasting connection. We can playfully connect with our desire and pleasure to achieve a fuller life with our partner.

I'm so glad you're here. Take a seat on the sofa and start on the first chapter of your new story together.

Warmest wishes

Michaela Thomas

PART I

Gaining clarity around loving relationships

- Understanding the foundations for long-lasting relationships and what causes the connection to break
- Learning the truth about how loving relationships develop over time and how love is not enough to keep the connection; you need compassion too
- Realising your emotional 'flammability' and what ignites a fire with your partner
- Outlining the stressors affecting you and your partner
- Assessing relationship satisfaction and what areas of your relationship need attention
- Setting an intention for the work to come

1 What is love?

The foundations of a lasting connection

Understanding what happens in your brain when you're infatuated versus in a long-lasting loving relationship will help you understand the difference between lust and love. From there, you can find out what elements make up a 'good' relationship and why love on its own isn't enough for a lasting connection – we need compassion too.

What makes a relationship last?

On a bus to a compassion retreat in Thailand, I got talking to a fellow psychologist about love and intimate relationships. I was jetlagged and about to fall asleep when she asked me what makes a relationship last. I replied, 'Basically, if you can own your own shit and tolerate your partner's shit, you've got a pretty good start.'

Since then, I've thought about the answer to this question and summarised it in a slightly more eloquent way.

> *Being satisfied and happy in a relationship isn't about finding someone without a journey of pain and hardship. It's about owning your own story and having the desire to understand theirs. We don't find a lasting connection, we build it. Relationships take effort and the satisfaction waxes and wanes like the tides of the ocean.*

Love is not enough for a lasting connection

Why, if it's possible to have a lasting connection, are divorce rates in the Western world around 40 per cent? There's no easy explanation, despite some marriage researchers claiming to be able to accurately predict whether a couple will divorce.

Being happy in your relationship isn't about always being massively 'in love'. Love is necessary, but not enough on its own. When you really love someone, you care for them and want them to be well rather than in pain or suffering, but this requires *compassion*: the foundation of a lasting connection. Let's explore how the care, clarity and courage of compassion can help your love survive and thrive.

The first core element of compassion in relationships is having a *caring commitment* towards your partner, wanting them to be well and safe. When you start to behave badly towards your partner, you've lost touch with your caring commitment. You're not acting in line with the values you might have around being supportive, loving, respectful or caring.

The second core element of compassion in relationships is *clarity* and wisdom. When you're 'drunk in love', you're neither clear nor wise. Infatuation clouds your judgement, giving you tunnel vision, and so you fill in the gaps of what you know with what you want to see in your partner. You might replicate old patterns from previous relationships without understanding why.

The third key element of compassion in relationships is *courage*, the strength to do difficult things for the sake of the relationship with your partner. Perhaps it's opening up to your partner, being vulnerable about feeling scared, lonely or abandoned. Maybe it's tolerating your own negative thoughts and feelings, like feeling hurt or jealous. Perhaps it's working on something challenging for you, from arriving punctually for your dates to controlling your angry outbursts. It takes strength to reliably show up for your partner when they need you, even if you've had a difficult day yourself.

> *Only love is not enough for a lasting connection*
> *– you also need the care, clarity and courage of compassion.*

What do happy couples do?

Marriage researcher John Gottman found, from studying hundreds of couples in his Love Lab, that happy and stable couples follow seven principles in their marriages.[1]

Satisfied couples . . .

- Know each other well, and keep getting to know each other
- Have fondness and appreciation for each other
- Turn towards each other instead of away, for emotional connection
- Respect each other's opinions, making decisions as a team
- Solve their solvable problems and manage conflict
- Overcome moments of feeling stuck in their perpetual problems
- Create shared meaning, being part of a family together

Gottman found that it wasn't that happy couples never argued or that they were 'perfect matches' (they argued about the same things other couples did and often differed in personalities or interests). Instead, the foundation of their relationship was a deep friendship, mutual respect and trust. The foundation of their happiness was being *attuned* to each other's needs and pains.

There are no quick fixes or magic bullets for achieving a lasting relationship. As Dan Buettner says in his work on 'blue zones' of human life longevity 'it takes doing the right thing and avoiding the bad thing over decades'.[2] You can't just be a bit nice to your partner for a while and think you've ticked the box.

I can't stress this enough:

Relationships take consistent effort.

Not all intimate relationships are based on commitment of the monogamous kind, so the principles around acting with compassion apply to open relationships or polyamorous couples too. Whatever your relationship structure, it's important to set it up with wisdom, establishing healthy boundaries around what's OK (or not), and to be courageous enough to ask for what you want with a caring, respectful attitude towards all those involved in the equation.

Your relationship 'garden' needs attention

Imagine that your relationship is like a garden: you can't just weed it once and think that's it. Soon the grass will be long, and the weeds, flowers and bushes will be fighting for space. It might be that you're happy with your garden being messy and overgrown, but if you want your garden to be a certain way, you have to cultivate it. Most of us forget about our gardens at times, taking the beautiful outdoor space for granted and neglecting it when we're busy with other things in life.

The same happens in relationships. Left on its own, a relationship will grow in all sorts of ways – some great, others not so. I'm here to help you roll up your sleeves and get stuck into the mud, so you can see the flowers bloom.

Choose to look after what you've got,
and it can last a long time.

Why does the connection break?

So *why* do so many marriages end in divorce? Do couples divorce because they didn't make wise choices when they picked each other, and married 'the wrong person'? Maybe some couples were never meant to be together?

Is it because people take the commitment of a long-term relationship too lightly, not valuing it enough to make the efforts needed to keep the connection strong? Do they start to take each other for granted and stop appreciating each other, maybe treating strangers and friends better than they treat each other?

Perhaps it's that they cannot cope when it gets tough, unable to repair a rupture in the relationship or to ride out a rough patch. Is there an expectation of love to be 'perfect' in today's society which makes us unable to tolerate when it's only so-so? Do romantic comedies have something to answer for in developing unrealistic expectations, only showing characters being completely infatuated with someone and not the calmer companionate love which follows? Were these expectations already embedded through the 'happily ever after' we're taught in childhood fairy tales?

All the above may play a part. I have certainly seen couples fit into each of these categories, meaning that my support for them has varied from couple to couple. Sometimes the focus is on working through a traumatic experience such as infidelity, to repair and rebuild the connection and allow the hurt to heal. Sometimes it's learning skills in how to strengthen the connection, as a way to protect the relationship and make it more resilient against any future ruptures. Sometimes it's about helping the couple to separate amicably and sever the connection completely. Couples therapy is about helping couples make wise decisions and choices about their connection to each other, whether it's worth it to keep working things out.

What was magnetic starts to repel you

The same things you fell for in your partner can, after a while, begin to really annoy you. Seeing your partner generously help everyone and always buy the rounds down the pub might initially have been appealing: thoughtful, selfless and kind. Years down the line, however, such actions might strike you as self-sacrificing and wasteful with money. There's a flip side to a positive trait or behaviour – generosity can become martyrdom. Being practical and solution-focused can seem cold or emotionless. Being creative and spontaneous can appear impulsive and short-sighted. Being organised and planned can seem rigid and dull.

Everything which can serve us well can also have drawbacks. The question is how you can build on your partner's strengths so that they complement your own and tolerate how their flaws interact with your own shortcomings. It's as if the magnet in your initial attraction has spun around, so that what initially drew you in now starts to repel you. It is possible to bridge those differences, using compassion to change what you can and accepting and tolerating what you can't.

Truly, madly, deeply – how love changes

Over time it's normal for romantic love to become less ecstatic and more comfortable, but that's not how love is often portrayed in films, poetry and love songs. In reality we go from experiencing fleeting moments of intense surges of lust and infatuation in the early stages, to a steadier flow of romantic and affiliative love as the companionship develops. We settle into a rhythm of deeper, meaningful love and connection: a lasting connection to be nurtured over time. If you can accept that this change is normal and to be anticipated, instead of seeing it as a failure, you'll take some of the pressure off the relationship.

Helen Fisher, anthropology researcher, expressed in her book *Why We Love* that there are three systems related to love: lust, romantic love and attachment. Using an fMRI scanner on people who described themselves as being 'in love', Fisher's research team mapped out which hormones and areas of the brain seem to be involved[3] (read Mona DeKoven Fishbane's book *Loving with the Brain in Mind*[4] if you're interested).

1 **Lust** is about the sex drive, associated with testosterone in both men and women, and can be experienced by a lone individual or linked to another person. The sex drive evolved in order for mankind to reproduce. In today's modern society, though, we don't just seek a partner for the purposes of reproduction, we also value the joy and motivation from romantic love, and the closeness and security provided by attachment. In Chapter 20 we explore lust and sexual desire in more detail.

2 **Romantic love**, or **romance**, is where we (from an evolutionary perspective) narrowed our efforts onto just one person, to find a mate. Falling 'in love' with someone means we think about them all the time and crave being near them as they become our 'special someone'. Dopamine, related to the brain's reward circuits, makes this phase of passionate love exhilarating and highly rewarding, to the point where you can become obsessive.

This pursuit of love isn't all a bed of roses, though. Thanks to the neurotransmitter norepinephrine, involved in your adrenalin response of fight or flight, your body gives you a pounding heart, sweaty palms, butterflies in your stomach and a dry mouth, to alert you to the potential threat of rejection. This phase is so addictive that you may grieve when it passes, thinking that love has been lost when your brain starts to stabilise and you move towards a closer bond (attachment).

3 **Attachment** is bonding with your 'special someone' long term, deciding to commit to each other even when the initial love craze has faded. The hormone most present in attachment is oxytocin, 'the cuddle hormone'. Through an evolutionary lens, attachment is part of the human survival strategy, as our babies are born helpless; we stay together for at least long enough to raise a child together, to ensure their survival. This strategy doesn't fit fully with modern society, of course: we can raise a baby in any family structure, without this focus on heteronormativity (the idea that heterosexual couples and reproduction is the norm).

These types of categories can become problematic if we take them too literally or use any evolutionary perspective as an 'excuse' for our behaviour. Just because you have an urge, it doesn't mean you need to act on it, or that your infatuation will be reciprocated. You need to understand what you've been through and take ownership for how you want to act using compassion, rather than giving excuses for your actions.

In summary, adrenalin is involved in our threat responses (also relevant during the early dating phase), dopamine propels us forward through our motivational pursuits and oxytocin helps us feel safe and soothed together. We'll look at what these chemicals do for your body and mind, and how they affect your relationship, in Chapter 6.

Keeping your love alive takes work

The fact that your love changes over the course of your relationship doesn't mean that it is doomed to be boring and unrewarding after a couple of years.

We *can* keep breathing life into our long-term relationships. You can have fun and laugh together until death actually does you part, but it takes effort and intention. We can have moments of passion and play, which you'll learn more about in Chapters 19 and 20, focused on your emotional and physical connection.

Common thoughts about loving relationships can also be their downfall:

> *'If I don't fancy everything about my partner, maybe they're not the right person for me.'*
>
> *'How can this relationship work out if we have issues after only a year together?'*
>
> *'You're not supposed to fight, not when you really are right for each other.'*
>
> *'If it's meant to be, it will work itself out, relationships shouldn't be this hard.'*

Whereas the initial infatuation can be an exciting time of getting to know each other and feeling really drawn to each other, the next phase is where the close connection can really be established. A strong relationship connection comes from consistently choosing each other, time and time again, even when we don't particularly *feel* in love. Choosing our partner and acting with love towards them is a conscious choice. The good news is that your feelings will often follow your behaviour – if you act with love, kindness and compassion towards your partner, your brain will also want to follow that path.

The myth of eternal happiness

It's easy to assume that you can achieve happiness as a couple and then stay happy forever, but happiness is not an emotional state you can control; the emotions involved are often fleeting and transient. Joy, excitement, satisfaction and infatuation are all blissful but short-lived. Like waves in the ocean, your emotions come and go. Long-lasting love isn't just built on feelings or emotions; it's also built on actions or behaviours linked to our values. That's why you're able to be a loving partner even if you don't feel 'in love' in that precise moment.

If you build your connection in your relationship on the 'drunk-in-love' sort of high and intoxicating feeling, you might interpret the sober reality of seeing your partner in the cold, hard light of day, with all their flaws, as meaning that the relationship 'isn't meant to be' and end it. This is just what infatuation, or the feeling of love, does to us – it makes us a bit stupid and impulsive, rather than wise and clear.

John Gottman[5] has shown that men and women are very similar in what they link their relationship satisfaction to (meaning that there is much less difference between the genders than suggested in outdated literature around men being from Mars and women being from Venus). How satisfied both men and women are with the romance, passion and sex in their marriage is determined to 70 per cent by the quality of the friendship with their partner. A sound friendship is a major determining factor in overall relationship satisfaction, across both genders.

You complete me perfectly

When doing research for this book, I found *three* couples' books (as well as several blog articles) using the phrase 'You complete me'. It's a quote from the romantic comedy *Jerry Maguire*. In her book *How to Be Human,* Ruby Wax quotes a monk who says, 'if you need someone to complete you, then you're making yourself less than you are and you'll always feel there is something missing'.[6]

This idea of someone else completing you is problematic because love is not about filling a hole within you with another person; nor is it about giving them everything they need. You're not a jigsaw puzzle with pieces that slot neatly together, with one particular 'partner piece'. Love can be found and lost many times over our lifespan; you don't *find* a lasting connection, you *build* it.

Having that lasting connection involves giving up on the struggle of getting the pieces to fit together perfectly and having the picture-perfect happy life. A successful relationship is about owning your own stuff and tolerating your partner's stuff, without trying to fix them or make them whole. Although your story is currently told together, the longest part of your partner's story may have happened before you entered it. So rather than focusing on chasing the 'happy ever after' ending, focus on how to keep telling the story, with all its twists and turns. You write it as you go along, and that's OK.

Relationships aren't easy

Odds are that you'll experience difficulties in your relationship at some point. This is the 'for worse' part; significant life stressors will impact on your relationship wellbeing.

Some of the things contributing to difficult times in a relationship include parenthood, loss, illness or financial strain. How you approach these inevitable hurdles will determine how much they threaten your relationship connection.

Some common themes in relationship distress are:

- I don't know what my partner wants from me
- I worry that my partner doesn't love me and will leave
- Life always gets in the way of us spending time together
- Since we had kids, we don't really have a sex life
- My partner isn't the same person I fell in love with
- We still love each other, but we can't seem to get along
- I'm so worried that I'm not good enough

According to Gottman's research, if there's a constant presence of negatives such as criticism and hostility, the relationship is likely to be distressed. Is a happy relationship one where nobody ever gets angry or experiences fears of being left? I think not. The answer lies in understanding that loving relationships trigger a full range of emotions, because *people* come with a full range of emotions, both positive and negative. If the underlying foundation of the relationship is positive, holding each other and the relationship in positive regard, it's possible to tolerate the negative emotions coming from living life together.

Can you now see how love on its own is not enough? Going through this life together, light and dark, you need a skill set: an approach by which you can turn towards your own suffering and your partner's, and be more attuned to them and to yourself.

Take a moment to pause here, and reflect on the following:

> *Which of these themes are present in your relationship right now?*
>
> *How would you describe your relationship and the quality of it?*

My invitation to you

Don't wait for the connection to dwindle, when the positives of your relationship have gone, and the negatives have taken hold. You need to see your relationship with your partner as we need to see our physical health. Our good health is something we take for granted until we don't have it any longer, thinking we're invincible until one day we get sick. It's easy to get complacent about looking after ourselves when we're well.

You can make wise choices around how to keep your body healthy, choosing to exercise more as *prevention*. If you wait until you're in pain or sick before you take action, you can't be surprised that you'll need to see a doctor or physiotherapist to find the *cure*. Of course, we can do everything 'right' and still get sick or injured. Much like in our relationships, there are simply no guarantees. You can do everything in your power and still love can be lost, but you can improve the odds of having a lasting connection by being proactive and looking after yourself as well as your relationship.

Your self-care is related to your health and wellbeing, and the *wellbeing of you* affects the *wellbeing of your relationship*. And the other way around.

Summary

- Love is necessary but not sufficient for a lasting connection; we also need compassion for a satisfying relationship.
- Compassion consists of a caring commitment, clarity and courage.
- You can't find someone to 'complete' you; you're not missing vital parts without another person present in your life.
- No relationship is happy at all times or can endeavour to pursue 'happiness' and stay there.
- Relationships take work and an acceptance of how infatuation and lust will settle down into a calmer, deeper love.

In the next chapter, I'll teach you how to use the compassionate mind framework as a way to build these foundations with your partner, by first exploring how flammable you are as a couple – whether you're highly combustible, or if you need to light a bit more of a spark.

2 Glowing embers

Becoming aware of how flammable you are as a couple

What creates heat and starts 'fires' in your relationship? Do you need to reduce your flame to a tolerable level, and cool down, or do you need to turn the heat up and be more emotionally expressive? Finetuning your flame will avoid burnout and result in those glowing embers where you can connect more deeply with your partner.

Flammability in relationships

Understanding what makes some couples work and others not is a million-dollar question. It's not one I can fully answer, but I do have a theory about 'flammability' – some couples are more flammable and so more likely to combust, while others are cooler and more likely to risk their fire fizzling out.

The highly flammable couple

Couples that are generally 'hot' might be highly explosive and have aggressive arguments, but also tend to be passionate and full of joy. There's simply a lot going on, a lot of heat generated as they struggle to regulate their emotions. They get on like a house on fire (pardon the pun) until they disagree – and then they REALLY disagree. These are the couples often dramatised on TV – but they aren't the only ones experiencing strains on their connection.

The cooler couple

These couples tend to get on fine day-to-day, not really arguing that much, but can go a bit flat and lack that certain spark. They might make good decisions and function well as a team, but they often state things like 'we've drifted apart', 'the sex has become a chore' and 'we're more like friends living together'. These partners might be controlling their emotions too much, or not daring to express how they feel in a disagreement. The fire in their relationship may have gone out through lack of attention, or maybe lust and desire didn't play a big part in their initial attraction.

Let's think together about how flammable you are, using the *fire triangle.*

Starting a fire

For a fire to start – for combustion to happen – three components are required: *fuel*, *heat* and *oxygen*.

The fire model of flammability in relationships

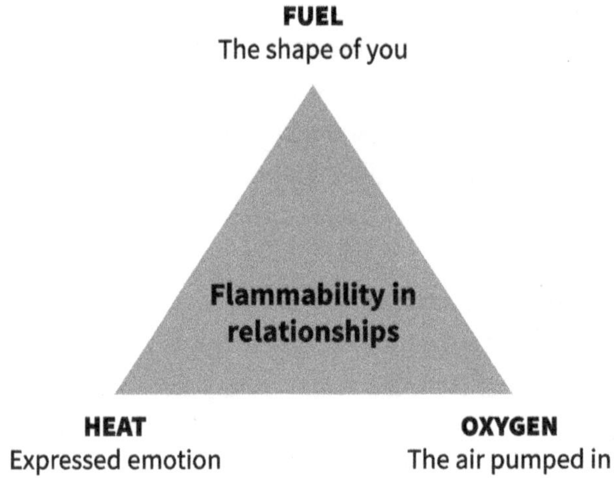

Fuel – the shape of you

Your connection with your partner is influenced by many complex factors which can all be fuel for the fire:

- Genetic makeup
- Temperament

- Personality traits
- Attachment style
- Legacy of previous relationships
- Learning history from the current relationship
- Upbringing
- How your parents modelled love and connection through their own relationship
- Societal norms and expectations around relationships

These factors make up the foundation of your relationship, the base. Your individual makeup and your unique strengths and weaknesses provide the *fuel* upon which the fire can take hold. We often feel 'lit up' in the presence of someone we fancy – that's when our fuel ignites with theirs. That fuel is what makes you both who you are, admittedly – but, if combined with heat and oxygen, may lead to a raging forest fire, burning out of control.

For example, someone who experienced their parents separating when they were young might be more flammable around making a serious commitment, reacting out of a deep-rooted fear of being abandoned or belief that things don't work out in long-term relationships. You can't wipe out that experience – and it's not your fault – but you can become aware of it. If you are open to how your personalities and emotional intelligences have been *shaped* – and so understand your 'fuel' – the material may still be flammable, granted, but will be much easier to handle. If you both discuss your feelings about past experiences, you can let go of them and move forward. *That was then, and this is now.*

If we take biology and genetics into account, we're drawn to people who might have a set of strengths and characteristics complementing our own, having something we lack. No wonder your fuel might react with your partner's. Being different is not what makes or breaks your relationship; it's what you do with those differences or incompatibilities that matters, and how you cope with the conflicts which arise.

Heat – expressed emotion

There's a misconception that being fiery is synonymous only with being passionate and full of vitality. The expression 'sparks fly' when a couple comes together gives us an image of passion, lust and compatibility. But sparks can fly in many different ways, and sometimes this fiery way of being generates more heat than a relationship can handle. Another common misconception is that couples who never argue are happier. Those couples can struggle to generate enough heat overall, being too controlled with their emotions, or scared to voice their opinions out of fear of conflict. It gets icy cold.

Having balance here is key. If you have to be on your toes at all times, constantly trying to avoid a major argument, because the rupture would be of volcanic proportions, you may have too much heat. What happens if one or both of you are having a hard time – does that bring you to frequently talking about breaking up? If you struggle to go through the 'downs of life' together without exploding there may be too much heat in your relationship. If your relationship has gone flat and you don't feel validated and warmly held by your partner, you may lack some heat.

So we need to make wise choices about controlling the *amount* of heat in our relationship, turning it up and down at the right times. High heat, or high expressed emotion, provides a breeding ground for conflict as the partners are more likely to have their threat systems activated and react with fight or flight. Low heat means a risk of the fire dying out completely, and partners feel disconnected and like they've fallen out of love. Later we will work on calibrating your heat to a level at which both partners can be comfortable – a level at which you can live and love.

Oxygen – the air pumped in

We need oxygen to breathe, and a fire needs oxygen to keep burning. If you cover a fire, the flames will die down. The same goes for relationships – if you don't have enough air coming in, the love will die down, feeling stifled. This can mean allowing a healthy amount of space in the relationship so as not to stifle each other, as well as being aware of what kind of air you're breathing into the fire. Pumping in helpful and nourishing air – care, kindness, empathy and trust – helps to nurture us and contributes to the survival of our relationships. Many couples get caught up bellowing the air of contempt, disgust, disrespect, rejection, criticism and sarcasm into the fire, turning the flames into a bonfire of relationship conflict. We need to identify how to breathe life into our relationships, using compassion and connection.

How flammable are you?

Think about your own flammability – are you and your partner generally a hotter couple where sparks fly, but you also fight with a fiery fervour? Or are you a cooler couple who are more measured towards each other, but have lost the spark day-to-day? There's no right or wrong here; lots of factors interact to determine the size of that fire. Don't let the fire consume you, but don't be afraid to carry some matches either. You need to nurture yourself and your relationship so that you can create fire at will, regardless of who you are as a person.

Let's take a closer look at something that fuels your personal fire: your attachment style.

Your attachment affects your connection

The closeness in your adult relationships is linked with the closeness you had with your caregivers when you were a child, and your life experiences. It's not predetermined that you'll be a certain way – it's more about how likely it is that you'll hit upon particular stumbling blocks depending on your own attachment style and that of your partner. It's the *combination* which makes your dynamic as a couple more or less flammable.

Secure attachment

The majority of people have a secure attachment style, which rests on parents responding to their emotional and physical needs most of the time – not perfectly, but good enough to also repair it when mistakes have been made. Securely attached children show when they're upset about their caregiver leaving them, and then either greet them happily on their return or, if they are upset, can work through those feelings of anger or sadness together with the adult. Adults who are securely attached enjoy being close with others and have the capacity for forming reliable, stable and safe relationships where they can express their emotions.

The good news A secure attachment from childhood is a great foundation for a deep and meaningful connection in adult relationships, but your relationships can still be strengthened by developing an understanding of how others – including, perhaps, your partner – may not have had the same experience as you. Not everyone has felt safe and secure growing up. Practising compassion for a non-securely attached partner will help strengthen relationships with anxious or avoidant adults too.

Anxious attachment

The anxiously attached adult may have grown up in an environment where they worried about whether their caregiver would come back. Perhaps they had a parent who was ill or who wasn't able to consistently show them warmth and affection. This child resists being left, as separation poses the threat of being permanently abandoned. As an adult, this manifests itself in frequently seeking confirmation from the partner – 'Are you sure you love me?' – and reassurances that the partner won't leave. It can also mean that the anxiously attached person avoids confrontation or conflict through not voicing their opinions or expressing needs. The long-term effect of this self-silencing can be resentment, bitterness and passive-aggressive digs. The partner who is frequently asked to give reassurance can feel suffocated and actually end up leaving, the very thing the anxiously attached person fears the most. This is especially true if the other partner is of an avoidant attachment style.

The good news This anxious and threat-focused way of behaving in relationships can be soothed by the safe presence of a securely attached partner making sense of the anxious person's experience; not feeding the insecurity through giving frequent reassurances, but giving warmth, support and love willingly when *not* asked for it. The anxiously attached person can also learn to soothe themselves, to turn down the heat and create their own sense of safeness without relying on others to make them feel secure.

Avoidant attachment

Adults with this attachment style often find it threatening to get close to and be vulnerable with others, possibly from having been hurt earlier in life. They like to 'keep options open', and may flirt with others. They might be with someone for a long time while still not feeling 'ready to commit' and reluctant to discuss life decisions such as moving in together, marriage or children, which would threaten their self-reliance. They may not want to experience emotions and will make concerted efforts to avoid them by walking out of arguments, shutting down or avoiding the topic. They have fears, blocks and resistances around receiving love, care and compassion, as their need for independence and autonomy is often greater than the need for closeness with others.

The good news The strategy of keeping their partner at arm's length has served the avoidantly attached partner well, protecting them from threat, but they miss out on a deep connection. It's possible to slowly lower the guard and start letting someone in, tolerating becoming vulnerable and less self-reliant. Practising being more compassionate with their partner's need for closeness and at the same time understanding why this is so threatening can help the avoidantly attached person feel safe, especially with a securely attached partner.

Disorganised attachment

Children who have grown up with caregivers giving inconsistent emotional support or being abusive may develop a disorganised attachment style. The child gets confused: the adult responsible for their safety is also someone who threatens their safety and survival. Adults with disorganised attachment styles can have an intense fear of being abandoned or lonely, with a reactive and flammable emotional style.

The good news Although relationships can be tricky with this attachment style, it's possible to learn how to get close, without getting too close or without rejecting a partner as a way to pre-empt rejection. You might need more support to be able to tolerate closeness and separation within relationships, for instance through individual therapy.

It's not your fault how you've been parented and what attachment style you have as a result, but you're accountable for being helpful rather than harmful to yourself and your partner.

Managing your attachment styles with compassion

Levine & Heller argue that anxiously attached and avoidantly attached shouldn't date each other, because of their different motivations (the anxious wants closeness and the avoidant wants independence).[7] I wouldn't go as far as that, but to make that relationship work, it's going to take a lot of good communication and balancing around your respective needs, to prevent a major sacrifice for either person. The relationship cannot cost you more than it's giving you – that isn't healthy. If you're bringing a lot of tricky fuel to the partnership, and there are high levels of expressed emotions, you'll need the air of compassion even more to manage your fire.

It's possible to become aware of these relationship response patterns through mindful compassion. The aim is for you to get to know yourself and your partner better and start to respond in a way which will help both of you to thrive within your relationship. However, you may unfortunately find that you've been staying in a relationship which is unsustainable and the most compassionate thing to do is to end it.

Reading about the attachment styles above – which one do you think you're likely to be?

Which one do you think your partner is likely to be?

How does that leave you feeling about your relationship?

Do you think you need to work on developing compassion for yourself, for your partner, or both?

Controlling the fire

If you take a breath before you speak, you can catch yourself from saying or doing things which are irrevocable. You might be able to prevent a fire starting, or get on top of it before it gets out of control. In some cases the metaphorical house has burned to the ground, but valuable lessons have been learned and the couple is keen on rebuilding the house or moving into a new home together.

You can also reduce your level of flammability by looking after your own vulnerability. If lack of sleep makes you irritable and reactive, help yourself by cutting down on caffeine and going to bed earlier.

Roasting marshmallows

In what sort of relationship climate do couples thrive? When they *constantly* argue? Or when they never discuss things they disagree on, so they *never* argue? What level of fire do we want in our relationship? As usual it's about balance and moderation – remember that it's on the glowing coals we can roast our marshmallows, not in the roaring fire.

Your marshmallows are the things you hold most dear in relationships – memories of good times, shared experiences, joint achievements, joy, team efforts, pride (perhaps in your children). So rather than fighting fire with fire, we learn to live with its different stages, from high flames to ashes, and to feed it with delicate hands so we can roast marshmallows once in a while.

Fanning the flames

You might be thinking that you want those marshmallows, but that there's no way your partner will work through this process with you. Please don't panic. Even if your partner isn't interested in understanding your relationship patterns and making changes, you can take ownership of how you act in your relationship, looking after the fire and breathing the right air into it.

Even if only you make improvements, the interaction between the two of you may be smoother. Compassionate acts can be contagious, so if you start to give out what you most want to receive, you may find that your partner reciprocates. If they don't you may be left feeling like you're making all the effort and not getting anything in return. Your partner may be sarcastic about your attempts for affection or mock the way you start to have a conversation. That will fan the flames, making things worse by adding insult to injury. If this is your experience, you'll probably need to seek further help.

The shame flame

We rarely speak to our partners the same way in public as we do in our own home, the car or on the phone. This is to do with *shame*. If we fear that others will judge us, or think negatively of us, we may experience shame. So, if we feel upset with our partner outside the supermarket, we may mutter 'We'll talk about this later!' to avoid creating a scene. That argument may be delayed until we get home; in some cases, that has given enough cooling down time to enable us to have a conversation about what sparked the argument. Or the moment has just passed, and it's no longer relevant, as the irritation was simply caused by hunger or stress. Shame can sometimes help the couple, as they're aware of how it looks to others when arguing. It might help them make more of a concerted effort not to shout or scream in view of others. Imagine how you would act if you were *shameless*?

Of course, shame is something which also fans the flames. Some couples fight very publicly; either one or both partners won't be able to contain the argument or turn down the heat on their emotions in that moment, and it 'ignites' into an explosion. When they realise others are watching, it's as if the shame flame lit within one partner gets passed on to the other, putting them down and blaming them. Shame makes us want to hide, but can also result in lashing out.

Not always what it seems

Think of those couples who may seem very functional at first glance – they are wonderful dinner party hosts, you see them walking hand-in-hand down the street, they settle a dispute calmly – great for them.

Keep in mind that things are not always what they seem, and couples who manage to behave themselves outwardly may not always do so at home, in their comfort zone. This poses another problem: if the comfort zone is filled with arguments it may not feel so comfortable any more. If your partner is Dr Jekyll during the dinner you have with friends, only to be Mr Hyde and scream at you once they've left, that's confusing and feels unsafe. You might come to see their outward behaviour as inauthentic and wait for their 'true colours' to come out once you're alone. Couples may start to avoid spending time alone together or start using other people as a buffer to keep themselves safe.

> *'If we're always out doing things, he can't shout at me for everything he thinks I'm doing wrong with the children.'*

> *'If I stay late at work and come back home after she's gone to bed, she won't get a chance to criticise me.'*

This withdrawal pattern is very common – we withdraw as a way to escape threat. If your partner shouts at you, it brings you into your *threat system*, with surges of adrenalin and the stress hormone cortisol. You feel burning hot, so to speak. You might then pull away, or keep busy to avoid feeling it. Your partner senses your avoidance and pursues you even further, wanting a resolution or apology or just a response (*the drive system*). You're now in a withdraw and demand pattern where neither of you gets any sense of feeling safe, relaxed or connected (*the soothing system*). Although it makes a lot of sense from a self-preservation point of view it means a breakdown of communication, and the avoidance further gets you on a downward spiral of disconnection.

Rest assured – we will explore these emotional systems in more detail in Chapter 6.

Bridging the gap

For most of us there is a gap between the way we behave and the way we'd like to behave. I'm going to challenge you now by asking:

What kind of person are you currently in your daily interactions with your partner?

If you think of the person in the example above, staying late at work to avoid their family, how would you describe them? Is that a person you would want to be, or wanted to be when you first met your partner? When you decided to be exclusive with them, moved in with them, married them, had a child with them, or any other form of commitment?

> *'Yes, I wanted to be an avoidant partner. A narky, sarcastic, fault-finding partner, who really goes for it in a fight. Or a partner who changes the topic as soon as it gets serious about our relationship. That is me. Spot on.'*

No, probably not. Rarely do people go into a relationship with the intention of inflicting pain on their partner. So, you didn't have the *intention* to be cruel or unkind to your partner, but somewhere along the line, you drifted. Perhaps you had a child, or your in-laws moved in, or you lost your job. These life stressors will impact on your relationship because they impact on *you*. You then drift away from the person you may have wanted to be in the beginning, the person who got asked for a second date. The one who was given a key to someone's house. The one who got asked to be someone's wife or husband. Would that date, key or ring have been given to the person you see shouting in the parking lot outside the supermarket? Possibly not.

That Mr Hyde hadn't come out then yet, perhaps. That dark side of you, a shadow self we all have. We're a bit more on our best behaviour at the beginning of a relationship. We try to navigate uncharted territory and get to know each other better. We ask questions, wait for the answer, laugh at funny anecdotes (because this is the first time we hear them), we smile, we joke, we're more present.

Now, I'm not saying that the early days of dating is what we should benchmark a sixty-year-long marriage against, for instance. I'm just saying that somewhere along the way, you lost track of you on your really good day. The you who would plan a date with nervous jitters in your stomach, hoping to impress this lovely person you've fallen in love with. Some people might call this *romance*. I call it *maintenance*. Making efforts for the person you love means you prioritise them and try to at least some of the time be 'you on a really good day', maintaining your love.

Focus on changing yourself

Back to the fires. It takes two to tango, but it can take only one person to start a fire. The flames can rise from the heat of the attack, and both people can keep the fire going with how they respond to the other person.

The same goes for effective communication. You can learn new skills yourself and practise more effective listening/speaking strategies with your partner, and you may find that they will respond better to you. But it's much harder to have effective communication with a partner who disengages.

You can develop skills in being more compassionate towards both yourself and your partner, and as a result it may shift your overall dynamic as a couple and your partner may reciprocate. But that's not guaranteed. You can't change your partner, but you can change yourself, giving out what you most want back and cultivating compassion for yourself and others.

Let's now take the temperature on your relationship satisfaction.

The Couples Satisfaction Index – CSI

This questionnaire was developed by the researchers Funk and Rogge to establish the level of relationship satisfaction a couple experiences.[8] Answer each question on your own, without your partner present, and ask your partner to do the same. Add up the scores for each question, the total score being a maximum of 161 points. The higher the score, the more satisfied each partner is with the relationship. A score below 105 would indicate that the relationship is distressed and needs attention. Remember that one partner could be more satisfied with the relationship than the other.

1. Please indicate the degree of happiness, all things considered, of your relationship.

Extremely Unhappy	Fairly Unhappy	A Little Unhappy	Happy	Very Happy	Extremely Happy	Perfect
0	1	2	3	4	5	6

Most people have disagreements in their relationships. Please indicate below the approximate extent of agreement or disagreement between you and your partner for each item on the following list:

	Always Agree	Almost Always Agree	Occasionally Disagree	Frequently Disagree	Almost Always Disagree	Always Disagree
2. Amount of time spent together	5	4	3	2	1	0
3. Making major decisions	5	4	3	2	1	0
4. Demonstration of affection	5	4	3	2	1	0

	All the Time	Most of the Time	More Often than Not	Occasionally	Rarely	Never
5. In general, how often do you think that things between you and your partner are going well?	5	4	3	2	1	0
6. How often do you wish you hadn't gotten into this relationship?	0	1	2	3	4	5

	Not at all True	A little True	Somewhat True	Mostly True	Almost Completely True	Completely True
7. I still feel a strong connection with my partner	0	1	2	3	4	5
8. If I had my life to live over, I would marry (or live with/date) the same person	0	1	2	3	4	5
9. Our relationship is strong	0	1	2	3	4	5
10. I sometimes wonder if there is someone else out there for me	5	4	3	2	1	0
11. My relationship with my partner makes me happy	0	1	2	3	4	5
12. I have a warm and comfortable relationship with my partner	0	1	2	3	4	5
13. I can't imagine ending my relationship with my partner	0	1	2	3	4	5
14. I feel I can confide in my partner about virtually anything	0	1	2	3	4	5
15. I have had second thoughts about this relationship recently	5	4	3	2	1	0
16. For me, my partner is the perfect romantic partner	0	1	2	3	4	5

	Not at all True	A little True	Somewhat True	Mostly True	Almost Completely True	Completely True
17. I really feel like part of a team with my partner	0	1	2	3	4	5
18. I cannot imagine another person making me as happy as my partner does	0	1	2	3	4	5

	Not at All	A little	Somewhat	Mostly	Almost Completely	Completely
19. How rewarding is your relationship with your partner?	0	1	2	3	4	5
20. How well does your partner meet your needs?	0	1	2	3	4	5
21. To what extent has your relationship met your original expectations?	0	1	2	3	4	5
22. In general, how satisfied are you with your relationship?	0	1	2	3	4	5

	Worse than all others (extremely bad)					Better than all others (extremely good)
23. How good is your relationship compared to most?	0	1	2	3	4	5

	Never	Less Than Once a Month	Once or Twice a Month	Once or Twice a Week	Once a Day	More Often
24. Do you enjoy your partner's company?	0	1	2	3	4	5
25. How often do you and your partner have fun together?	0	1	2	3	4	5

For each of the following items, select the answer that *best describes how you feel about your relationship*. Base your responses on your first impressions and immediate feelings about the item.

26.	INTERESTING	5	4	3	2	1	0	BORING
27.	BAD	0	1	2	3	4	5	GOOD
28.	FULL	5	4	3	2	1	0	EMPTY
29.	LONELY	0	1	2	3	4	5	FRIENDLY
30.	STURDY	5	4	3	2	1	0	FRAGILE
31.	DISCOURAGING	0	1	2	3	4	5	HOPEFUL
32.	ENJOYABLE	5	4	3	2	1	0	MISERABLE

How did it feel to complete this questionnaire? For you, and for your partner?

Perhaps you realise that your partnership is more satisfying than you thought, and you haven't been appreciating what's going well.

Perhaps there's a discrepancy between how satisfied each of you feel, with one person perceiving there to be a bigger problem than the other. If that's the case you need to start to really listen to each other.

Summary

- We've learned that who you are and how you've been shaped in life makes you more or less flammable when you come together with your partner.
- It isn't your fault if your fuel ignites together with your partner's, but you can still hold yourself accountable for changing and improving yourself, to strengthen your relationship.
- You can dial down the heat generated in your relationship by blowing in the air of care, kindness and empathy, rather than hostility and criticism.
- You can dial up the heat by blowing in the air of shared interests, desire and passion, to let go and enjoy yourselves more.

After looking at how much heat you generate together, we'll now start to think about connection and compassion in greater detail.

3 Connection and compassion

The antidote to disconnection is compassion

Why are we so disconnected in today's society? What does connection and compassion mean for us in our lives, and why do we need them in romantic relationships?

The meaning of compassion

The word 'compassion' comes from the Latin *com* (with) and *pati* (to bear, suffer), literally meaning 'suffer with'. The definition of compassion, as formulated by Professor Paul Gilbert, founder of Compassion Focused Therapy, is divided into two parts:

> *'a sensitivity to the suffering of self and others, with a commitment to try to alleviate it and prevent it.'*[9]

Essentially, it's about noticing and acknowledging the pain in yourself or other people, and being moved to the point where you want to do something about it. 'That really hurts – how can I help?' is a simple way of expressing compassion in action with your partner.

If we're connected to our partner will we feel each other's pain and suffering? It seems that way, from research around *attunement*. If one partner is telling a story of something painful, and experiencing negative emotions, the other will have elevated stress levels in their blood too.[10] This is linked with the human capacity for caretaking and compassion facilitated by the ventral vagus nerve, which has lots of oxytocin receptors (involved in attachment, bonding and care). The vagus nerve activates the parasympathetic nervous system to slow down the heart rate and calm the sympathetic nervous system (the fight-or-flight response) in both speaker and listener in a compassionate conversation. The listener emits little sighs of air when listening to their partner's painful story, brought about by the vagus nerve.[11]

Vagus nerve activation can also be used to restore the compassionate connection when couples get too heated. The air of compassion is thus both metaphorical and literal, as slowing our breathing has a positive impact on our threat response, taking us back to those glowing embers where we can really connect and care for each other.

Our need for connection and nurture

Connection and being there for each other is in our genetic makeup; we have an innate capacity to nurture each other as part of our survival strategy as a species. Human babies are born helpless and need their caregivers to enable them to survive, much like other mammals. Compare that to reptiles like sea turtles, where females lay their eggs in the sand and then move away. Their survival strategy relies on numbers – they lay lots of eggs so that a small percentage will make it into adulthood and reproduce.

If we truly connect to each other we can survive and thrive together, but our modern society and our brains hamper this at times. We've seen how challenging disconnection has been for people during the global COVID-19 pandemic. Regardless of culture or location on the planet, we humans belong together and don't like to stay apart.

Why we need compassion in life

It's time for a reality check about why we need compassion – because life is hard, full of challenges and suffering.

We're shaped by evolution

Evolution has left us with 'side effects' in how our brains function; we have the ability to plan and organise and be innovative, but we're also able to dwell on the past, worry about the future and beat ourselves up for who we are.

We're shaped by our genes

You didn't choose your parents and your genetic makeup. As we lead short lives of about 25,000–30,000 days, all we know with certainty is that we'll age and die. Our genetic makeup has an impact on the suffering we experience, in terms of illnesses or disabilities both you and your partner will encounter.

We're shaped by our experiences

We have limited control over much of what happens to us, for example where we were born and went to school, our social status and how our parents treated us. These social experiences affect your behaviour and value system, shaping your 'fuel' and affecting how much 'heat' you bring to a relationship in terms of expressed emotion, but also what capacity you have for breathing in that 'air' of compassion.

Why we need compassion in love

Here's the second reality check – relationships are hard too. During the lifespan of a relationship a couple may frequently struggle, naturally hitting upon pain points of disagreement and hurt. The expression 'love hurts' is quite accurate; researchers have seen in MRI scans that the pain centre of the brain lights up when we experience rejection – it physically *hurts* to be rejected by someone we care about.[12] Steve Hayes, founder of Acceptance and Commitment Therapy, says 'We hurt where we care'. If we didn't care about a person we love, we wouldn't experience that extent of pain when they hurt or reject us.

The many major life decisions we have to make can also be painful. Who will look after the children? Do we even want children? How will we work and earn money? How will we spend our time together and apart? Where will we live?

Previous generations of relationships had these decisions made for them. In heterosexual couples the man tended to be the breadwinner and the woman the home maker. Of course, some couples swapped roles within the relationship, but it wasn't the norm. Gay marriage was illegal, so homosexuality was seen as shameful and needing to be repressed, or outright converted.

What was the norm in the Western world fifty years ago feels strange and outdated today. Movements to liberate women mean they can financially support themselves through working and be independent enough to survive when leaving an unfulfilling relationship. The freedom to love regardless of gender identity or sexuality has been opened up through the LGBTQ+ movement, resulting in the widespread legalisation of gay marriage. This freedom has been fought for by previous generations, and the fight continues – we still need to close pay gaps and end domestic violence, discrimination from unconscious bias and hate crimes. Glennon Doyle's book *Untamed* illustrates how women enter or remain in hurtful relationships due to 'people pleasing' and pressure to be perfect, to be tamed;[13] and the Black Lives Matter movement of 2020 has shown us that we still have work to do for people of colour.

All this matters in loving relationships, as it's the context in which love occurs; we need change to make the world a more compassionate place. Some things haven't changed, however – we still fall in love, change and grow. We still get sick, age and die. The major stressors and pain points to a relationship are ongoing – infidelity, falling for someone else, growing apart, health problems, challenges at different ages and stages of our lives, going through grief and loss – the *relationship pain points*.

- Moving in together, moving house
- Getting engaged, getting married
- Trying for a baby or having fertility issues
- Becoming parents, sleep deprivation, role changes
- Physical or mental illness in one or both partners
- Emotional and sexual intimacy problems
- Identity crises and change in values
- Infidelity, both emotional and physical
- Financial constraints, unemployment
- Loss of a loved one
- Menopause/ageing challenges
- 'Empty nest', children moving out
- Retirement, old age, poor health

A few things make these pain points extra hard – our *tricky brains*, our *experiences* and our *emotion systems*.

Our tricky brains
They were built *for* us, not *by* us – and they get us into loops of thinking we didn't *choose*.

Our experiences
The social and genetic shaping of us and our partner is *not our fault*.

Our emotion systems
Evolution has shaped our emotions to protect us, but they're *hard to balance*.

Understanding your connection as a couple

Connection is a combination of the Latin words *com* ('together' or 'with') and *nectere* ('to bind'). When we connect to someone, we tie a bond together (suddenly the phrase 'tying the knot' makes a lot more sense!). Greek orthodox and Jewish wedding ceremonies, for example, include a physical binding as a way to connect two people.

How elastic is your connection?

The connection that binds you and your partner together can be compared to a rubber band. It can stretch and accommodate strains and stresses if it's kept soft and supple. If the rubber is allowed to dry out, it's more vulnerable and will not stretch very far before it snaps. If that happens you can still make efforts to reconnect – tie a knot in the rubber band to form the circle again. Even when you get over a hurdle, you'll still have the memory of the knot, knowing that your relationship is not perfect, but that it can be mended and you can find your way back to each other again.

So, in order to have a lasting connection, we need to look after the bond, the connection, by giving it frequent attention and maintenance. Of course, a knot can be unpicked and a binding unbound, which is why we have to make wise choices about whether we want to repair a rupture (tie the band together again) or leave it undone and go our separate ways. This wisdom comes from compassion, with yourself and with your partner.

We also need wisdom about the modern world we live in.

The pain of disconnection

It's important to be aware of the context in which we're trying to pursue love, meaning and happiness. In the individualistic Western world we often strive to pursue our own happiness and forget the wellbeing of others around us. In more collectivist cultures, such as in Asia, the group is considered much more than the individual. The messages all around us, however, encourage individualistic pursuit – collect more items, climb higher on the corporate ladder, be busier than others (and don't forget that you should look good doing it).

Kate Murphy, journalist and author of *You're Not Listening*, argues that our disconnection from each other comes from our reduced capacity for listening in a society which emphasises projection rather than absorption of information – we're so busy getting our voices heard that we forget to listen to the voices of others.[14] Sharing your content on social media or sending text messages on WhatsApp is not the same as connecting with someone.

> *How can we create longevity in relationships in a society which is all about disposable, expendable consumption and digital distraction?*

In a society where we are, in some ways, more connected than ever, we're also lonelier than ever. My single clients struggle to find love and happiness, feeling fed up with dating apps and endless let downs and rejections at the small swipe of a finger. We're so quick to judge and reject, based on the speed of processing of information – what's next, what's next? We're in an impulse-driven consumerist society, where stopping to pause and reflect 'takes too long'.

We're disconnecting – from each other and from ourselves; from what we think is meaningful and worthwhile. Next time you're on a train or a bus look around you at the other people – how many of them are staring at a screen? Mobile phones have been around for a while, becoming ever more sophisticated; today's smartphones can create whole worlds and communities, linking us up with social media and giving us the perception that we're less alone. But what happens when you're on that phone at the dinner table and missing what your partner is trying to say about her difficult day at work? What happens when you're reading your work emails and getting frustrated about something which needs to be done, while your partner is waiting for you to join movie night?

When connections are lost

Johann Hari, author of *Lost Connections*, emphasises the way we've disconnected from so many important things in our lives as a factor in the rise in mental health issues such as depression and anxiety.[15] He discusses how addiction comes about because we don't want to be present in our lives – it's too painful.

This is relevant for couples too. If it's too painful to be present in our relationship, we'll withdraw from it; if it's too painful to interact with our partner, we will avoid or numb that pain. The connection will then be severed or weakened. So, to strengthen the connection, we first need to make sense of the pain – what's hurting in the interaction with your partner? And what do you need to soothe that pain in a way which reconnects you to your partner, rather than taking you further away? We also need to consider how we have been attempting to resolve the issue with a broken connection: have we been adding more pain by being critical, shaming or controlling of each other? How can we let go of inflicting even more pain?

What causes couples to disconnect?

Modern couples in the West have many threats to their ability to connect with each other. Let's look at four of these:

Smartphone use

Many couples have important conversations over WhatsApp or other text messages, where emojis are supposed to replace genuinely expressed emotions and non-verbal communication. It's a recipe for misunderstandings. Some couples have more intimacy with their smartphone in bed than they do with their partner.

Work/life imbalance

Lots of professional couples spend far more time at work than with loved ones, leaving little time to connect with each other and family members. They struggle to settle their work/life balance, feeling a pressure to perform, which occupies time at work as well as thinking time at home, disconnecting them from being present with loved ones. The COVID-19 pandemic has highlighted what really matters to some couples, leading to a wish to spend their waking time differently, with less time working and more connection time together, while also having space for themselves as individuals.

Pressure to be perfect

The craze around self-improvement appears to be at an all-time high. We're told to shop only organic and eat more vegan food, to go to the gym to have 'perfect' bodies, and to cut down on single-use plastic. Although all these things are great, they can create pressure and preoccupy us in a stressful way. Perfectionism is on the rise, placing increasing demands on us, adding to the mental load in our brains.[16] If you're under pressure, so is your relationship.

Globalisation

People spend more time commuting now than they used to when working in their immediate community, meaning less time to connect with loved ones and, in a lot of cases, increased frustration (stuck in traffic, train delays, and so on). People live further away from their family of origin, sometimes even in different countries, meaning less support in everything from moving house to raising children.

> *Which of these disconnecting factors might affect your own relationship?*

The strains on your connection

There are many issues which could contribute to you two feeling less close, even disconnected, but not all issues bother all couples.

Use the scale below to rate how much each of these common problem areas bothers your relationship right now, by choosing a number from 0 to 10. The figure 0 means that this area doesn't cause any issues at all in your relationship, and 10 means it causes serious issues.

Doesn't cause an issue	*Causes moderate issues*	*Causes severe issues*
0	5	10

1	Emotional connection and affection	________
2	Joint activities, spending time together	________
3	Interaction with members of each other's family	________
4	Friendships outside the partnership	________
5	Finances	________
6	Sexual intimacy	________
7	Managing the home and day-to-day tasks	________
8	Work and career	________
9	Parenting and raising children	________
10	Communication	________
11	Trust and honesty	________
12	Religion and spirituality	________
13	Decision-making	________
14	Your own suggestion	________

> *What was it like to make this assessment? If you did it together, did you agree or disagree on which areas are most problematic in your relationship?*

How our brains make connection hard

You've probably already noticed that we have tricky brains. The safety-seeking motto of our brains is 'better safe than sorry', which doesn't help in relationships, as connection between partners is based on taking the risk of trusting each other and daring to be vulnerable.

The human species today really struggles because of how our brains have evolved. For simplicity's sake we will refer to the two parts of the brain as 'old brain' and 'new brain'. The tricky bit is how these two parts interact.

Figure 1.1 Interacting old and new brain functions

Irons and Beaumont, The Compassionate Mind Workbook *(2017). London: Robinson. Reprinted with permission.*

Old brain

This old part of your brain has evolved over hundreds of millions of years. For ease of understanding here we bunch together the protoreptilian brain (shared with reptiles) and the paleomammalian brain (or the limbic system, shared with other mammals). The main objective is to *survive and reproduce,* which includes navigating the dangers of the world to stay safe and protected from threat. The *old brain* controls your motives, emotions and behaviours.

Basic motives Avoiding harm, pursuing food, sex and status, and caring for others like our offspring

Basic emotions Fear, anger, joy, sadness, disgust and surprise

Defensive behaviours Fight, flight, freeze (shutdown), appease (submission)

New brain

The frontal lobes, or *neocortex*, are inherited from our primate relatives and have been evolving for about two million years. We share frontal lobes with other species, but they're highly sophisticated in humans, giving rise to our ability to plan and organise, problem-solve and innovate, and consider how others are feeling and thinking.

As humans we have the capacity to reflect on ourselves and how others might perceive us. Other mammals don't worry about self-image – pigs don't call themselves fat if they have put on a few pounds and don't worry about whether the other pigs will still be attracted to them. Monkeys don't fret about the meaning of life and dwell on what they did to another monkey yesterday. Wolves don't worry about whether they have anger management issues because they growled at other wolves. In short, other animals don't have the new brain capacity needed to reflect on themselves in the curious, judgemental or self-critical way humans do. And they most certainly don't do that with their partners.

The same part of our brains which has the imagination, planning and creativity to put people on the moon and find cures for life-threatening diseases also keeps us stuck in our own suffering. The ability to time-travel forwards and backwards in our minds means that we can keep a threat going long after the actual threat has disappeared. Sometimes we can get so stuck that we get caught up in *loops* of thinking, driving ourselves 'loopy'.

Rebuilding connection

The more we focus on the happiness of the other, rather than the happiness of the self, the happier we tend to be. We've just forgotten that in our individualistic and fast-paced society, so often creating toxic environments where we struggle to thrive. We have a built-in capacity for being compassionate to others. We also have a built-in capacity for aggression, hostility and territorialism.

How to make time for togetherness

Multiple experiments illustrate how mammals choose togetherness over aloneness, even choosing connection with their kin over food at times (in Harlow's monkey experiment a baby monkey chooses to sit on a soft mummy monkey structure rather than the cold, iron-wired monkey structure with a milk bottle).[17] Togetherness is dwindling in our society – people don't put the time, energy and dedication into making their togetherness a priority. 'Life is so busy; we don't really have time for each other.' But if our human togetherness BRINGS life to us (our parents made us through connection), and it KEEPS us alive (we rely on each other for protection and safety), how can we not put it at the forefront of our lives? One way to do that is to remind ourselves why we got together in the first place.

How it all began . . .

For many couples the beginning of the journey is sweet and full of butterflies. Casting glances at someone, wondering nervously if they like you back. When I ask couples to remember the initial connection they made with each other, their faces often light up. Reconnecting with your initial spark can help you remember and appreciate why you chose each other and to see those qualities in your partner even in the moments of darkness.

Reflection & Connection

Sit down with your partner and go through these conversation starters:

- How did we first meet?
- How did we first know we liked each other?
- Who pursued who? Or was it more a mutual 'it sort of just happened'?
- What drew me to you?
- What drew you to me?
- What did I appreciate about how you treated me?
- What of that initial connection has got lost along the way?

> *How did it feel to reflect on these early days together, to perhaps remember with fondness how you first 'fell' for each other, how your love developed?*

Summary

- Relationships are hard, because life is hard. Nurture the bond of connection in your relationship, or it may snap.
- Living in our modern society focused on individual goals can make it hard to make space for caring for others.
- In the digital age, we're hyperconnected yet lonelier than ever and this disconnection can partly be explained by the increased use of smartphones. We're always switched on, and on the go, being busy.

After looking at connection and disconnection, and why we need compassion in life and in relationships, we'll now think about what can further make or break your relationship.

4 Make or break

Are you in or are you out?

Here we look at what can make or break a relationship, stretching the connection to the point of snapping. There are also protective factors which can nurture and nourish the relationship bond. We explore how we all change, what threat does to a relationship and how having a compassionate motivation is more helpful than being competitive.

The 'make or break' list

The waxing and waning of a couple's connection is contextually dependent: what is going on around them will influence how close they feel to one another. Some of the factors which contribute to and threaten a lasting connection are listed in my *make or break* list.

MAKE	BREAK
Friendship and mutual respect	Hostility and disconnection
Gratitude/appreciation	Taking for granted
Empathy/compassion	Mindreading, assuming, emotional coldness
Accepting differences	Trying to change the other person
Adapting to change	Resisting change
Being attentive of each other	Ignoring each other
Self-awareness/taking ownership	Lack of insight into self
Making space for each other	Creating distance between each other
Raising complaints respectfully	Criticism and contempt
Ability to soothe and create safeness	Reactivity to threat, counterattacking
Caring for each other (compassionate goals)	Competing with each other (self-image goals)
Joint decision-making (deciding)	Major life decisions just happening (sliding)
Repairing a rupture, forgiveness	Burying past hurt, creating resentment

You can use the 'make' list to strengthen your relationship connection and become a 'master' rather than a 'disaster' at relationships. These terms were coined by John Gottman, a relationship researcher on what makes marriages work. He established that the way partners turn towards each other's bids for connection is crucial. For example, if your partner notices you sighing and asks you what's up, they have responded to your bid for attention in a helpful rather than harmful way. Imagine how that feels – then imagine how it feels if that doesn't happen, and those bids for connection are consistently ignored. What if they responded with something along the lines of 'Stop that huffing, it's really irritating'?

Gottman established four factors which can be deadly for a relationship connection (also on the list). He called them *The four horsemen of the apocalypse.*

The four horsemen of the apocalypse

Gottman found that couples were vulnerable for break up or divorce if they engage in these behaviours.[18]

- **Criticism** Harsh, hostile blaming, making personal attacks rather than specific complaints about the behaviour you dislike in your partner.
- **Contempt** Disrespectful sarcasm and cynicism aimed at demeaning or belittling your partner, assuming superiority. This pattern has often evolved over time, from raised complaints to global criticism to harsh contempt, thinking very negatively about your partner.
- **Defensiveness** When feeling attacked, partners defend themselves by either counterattacking or playing an innocent victim. This doesn't make the critical or attacking partner back down, and nothing gets resolved.
- **Stonewalling** The tendency to withdraw emotionally and physically, literally turning away and going quiet, not responding to the partner who is attacking or criticising. This avoidance strategy helps the person disengage from the conflict, but also disengages from the relationship.

These 'apocalyptic' behaviours are everything but compassionate. We need to develop wisdom about why they occur; to understand how we have an innate capacity for hostility and aggression, as well as for nurture and care.

Let's explore more what motivates you as a person and in your relationship, as a first step to help you either make or break your relationship.

Competitive vs compassionate motivation

When you're motivated by truly caring for your partner, you have engaged with your *compassionate motivation*. When you focus on beating them in winning an argument and showing them how you're right, then you have stepped into your *competitive motivation*. It's important to notice what drives your actions in your relationship.

Compassionate goals – driven by a caring motivation

- Be supportive of others (philanthropy, contribution, caring, giving)
- Avoid doing anything that would be harmful to others

Self-image goals – driven by a competitive motivation

- Get others to notice only your positive qualities (egotism, selfishness)
- Avoid showing your weaknesses and bad sides

> *Are you focused on caring for your partner, or showing them how you're right?*

Threat pulls you away from caring

Traditional couples therapy focuses a lot on communication skills. For many couples it's obvious that it isn't nice to call your partner horrible names and belittle them, and that it's more helpful to talk to them in a kind and respectful manner.

What often gets in the way is that things get too heated in the moment, leaving both partners feeling attacked and threatened. This is because of *threat system activation* – your inner alarm system goes off to alert you to danger if your partner speaks to you in an angry way. Stress hormones such as adrenalin and cortisol flood your body, and you're no longer able to see clearly about what is going on between you. If you focus on trying to defend yourself against your partner's criticism or contempt, it's understandable that you can lose track of that caring mentality. You'll simply get too 'hot' to follow your values around love and support, blocking your natural capacity for nurture.

In Part II you'll learn more about your threat system and how to soothe it through developing skills in compassion.

Feeling safe

In this book I'm proposing a framework for couples where the focus is on helping each person step into a version of themselves who is naturally nurturing, out of instinct and love towards their partner. It's very challenging for most couples to defuse an argument if they're overwhelmed by threat and negative emotions. You're going to fly off the handle if your stress levels are through the roof, and you're more likely to say things you later regret. Easing off the threat is crucial in order to be able to show up in your relationship in a way you feel happy with. Remember the fire analogy?

It isn't just about turning down the heat and soothing the threat, though. Feeling safe isn't just about an absence of something negative, being protected from threat and harm. It's also about a presence of something positive – a feeling of *being safe and connected*. Feeling psychologically safe is not only crucial to our survival as a species, it's also crucial for the survival of your relationship. This feeling of being safe can also lead to a joy, friendship and playfulness.

My course ('The Compassionate Couple') focuses on meeting compassionate goals, to strengthen the couple's connection through building mutual understanding, trust and safeness.

Do you feel that you and your partner have a sense of being protected from threat and harm?

Do you also feel that you have a sense of feeling safe and connected, feeling closely bonded together?

Create space, not distance

Does having space help us strengthen our connection? Does absence actually make the heart grow fonder? Creating some space and having time apart can help you reflect on who you are, independent of your partner, and help you grow into the person you want to be.

Too much space, on the other hand, means creating distance, where you're starting to build a life with your partner just on the periphery rather than having a life shared together. It's hard to build a sense of team spirit at your workplace if you hardly ever see your co-workers. The same applies in your relationship if, for example, your partner is asleep every night when you come in and leaves before you get up in the morning, or you spend all your social time with friends, never having the time or energy for your partner. You might feel like room-mates, living at the same address but not living a life together.

You need your lives to overlap and you need to spend time together for feelings of warmth to be generated. Psychology refers to this as '*the mere exposure effect*' – simply being in close proximity with someone increases your liking of them. It's sometimes referred to as the familiarity effect. How familiar can you be with someone you rarely see? How will you know what is important to them at a particular point in time? How will you know what stresses them out? How will you know what they want and need?

The term used in attachment-based theories of couples is *interdependence* – that we allow ourselves to be dependent on each other when needed, so we can truly also be independent in a healthy way. Amir Levine and Rachel Heller discuss this in their book *Attached*, understanding that it isn't a bad thing to 'need' one's partner or want to depend and rely on them. We need this connection for our emotional growth – it doesn't mean that we're deficient or not independent.

The seismic movement of change

Often I hear couples say, 'My partner isn't who I married', or 'You've changed so much, you're not the person I fell in love with'. This is absolutely true, in a physical sense of the word 'change'. We completely shed and re-grow outer skin cells many times in our lifetime. Likewise, your brain grows and develops throughout your life. So much like the caterpillar turning into the chrysalis, and then turning into the butterfly, humans change and evolve. Wouldn't it be rather sad if the person you're in a long-term relationship with hasn't grown and developed in all the time you've known each other? The question is thus not about whether or not someone changes in a relationship, but what partners can do to make space for change, adapting to it with curiosity and compassion.

John Gottman talks about building your 'love maps'. Unless you travel the seas and the lands of your partner, how will you be able to draw the maps? They become uncharted territory and you feel lost, not knowing your way around, and the connection to your partner is weakened. You drift apart. So, rekindling this connection is about making a conscious effort to keep getting to know your partner – asking them questions, listening intently and curiously to their answers, and spending time together. Consider our ageing process; you'll both grow older at the same rate, but you might not notice it until you come across a photo of your partner from a couple of years ago, and see a difference – a more receding hairline, or changes in body weight. These changes can be small and steady, but inevitable – and you need to accept and adapt to them.

We also go through patterns of change which are more dramatic, much like how tectonic plate movement can cause a volcanic eruption or earthquake. This level of earth-shattering change, where the person may feel an impulse to quit their job and move to Bali in solitude, can seem disastrous to that person's family. Other changes can be less disruptive, like a minor earthquake rattling the ground for a bit. Your partner decides they no longer want to eat meat because of the environmental impact – that will disrupt your daily cooking if you now have to accommodate a vegetarian or vegan diet. The bigger the magnitude, the more rarely does it occur.

If you make a vow to keep getting to know your partner, and keep drawing those maps to be mindful of any gradual changes, the continental drift may not reach catastrophic levels. You'll be aware of the changes happening in your partner, and in yourself, and be less surprised if there is a bigger event culmination.

Loving in the face of adversity

Some couples face more strains on their relationships than others, through no fault of their own. We know life is harder in areas of poorer economic growth and political unrest, and within communities of lower socioeconomic status and ethnic minorities. The two London boroughs with the highest vs lowest life expectancy – Kensington and Chelsea vs Tower Hamlets – may be only seven miles apart, but have a seven-year difference in life expectancy. If *life* is harder, then *love* is also harder. Imagine not knowing if you can afford the rent this month, or if you can buy new school uniforms for the kids. Imagine being in a low-income job with few prospects of progression. Imagine that your home has damp walls and a leaky roof. In these contexts, it's understandable that you struggle to show up as your compassionate best. You'll be in your threat system because of the risks to your safety and protection, which means it takes real effort to keep a relationship together. To love in the face of adversity is to show compassion for each other when you need it the most.

If you have weathered storms together you will realise that connection can come through both light and dark moments. Some couples face infidelity, sickness, poverty and existential crises and still find a way to make it work, by turning towards rather than away from each other.

Staying or leaving

If you're at a crossroads in your relationship, thinking about whether to leave or to stay with your partner, consider this:

Deciding NOT to leave is not the same as choosing to stay.

This is not just semantics: there's a real difference. If you have been communicating to your partner that you're at breaking point and want to leave, they will experience a whole range of emotions. They may feel angry towards you for wanting to go, as it may feel unfair or not warranted. They may feel scared or worried about what this will mean for them and the family. Will they need to move out of the family home? Are there children involved – how will it affect them? Your partner may even worry about YOU – if they think you're in a bad place, they might worry that you'll do something self-destructive or not be able to cope. They may feel a deafening sense of sadness, confusion and betrayal at the uttering of the 'D' word (divorce).

Decisions regarding separation or divorce should not be taken lightly. There are serious ramifications. If you have told your partner that you want to leave you cannot unsay those words; even if you change your mind and stay the hurt has already been caused. You *can* repair and rebuild, though – having said that you want to leave or have a divorce does not mean that you have no other option but to go through with it.

Staying with intention

If you decide together that you want to work on this relationship, to try to reconnect and restore what you had, be aware that you may be doing that in a climate of betrayal. It's a long road back once the threat of leaving has been uttered. Staying with your partner is not the same as just deciding it was a bad idea to go. Staying with your partner and working it through is an active choice, taking courage and strength, but also compassion, empathy and kindness – you're both hurting here! There is no 'winner' in the scenario where two people have loved each other and had a meaningful connection, and then one person wants to leave: both will be hurting.

Having a lasting connection partly means that you choose each other time and time again, doing so with intention to stay rather than to just *not leave*.

Leaving with compassion

For some partners the most important self-reflection made is the realisation that the connection needs to be severed.

If you choose to leave your partner, try to make that decision with compassion. We look at this in more detail in Part II, where you'll learn the skills needed to understand why you're in so much pain, and also how much pain this is going to cause your partner. In some ways it's more important than ever to be able to hold each other's feelings in mind and understand one's own triggers when going through a separation or finalising a divorce, especially if there are children present. Ending a relationship can be a lot more amicable with the right understanding of what happened and why you couldn't put the pieces back together.

Setting your intention

If you have decided to try to work on improving your relationship connection, it's important to establish why you're committing your time and effort. Because this may hurt – you're bound to experience some negative emotions. *'If it hurts, we're in the right place.'* You may even want to give up on the work altogether at some point. Reminding yourself of the original intention can help you stay on track.

Try this

Setting an intention for the work to come

1 Why am I choosing to work on the relationship?

2 What could be the potential costs to me and my partner from this process?

3 What could be the potential benefits to me and my partner from this process?

Some people find it helpful to set a little mantra or sentence to encourage them throughout the process.

> *'We have been through hard times before,*
> *we can do it again.'*
>
> *'There is still love left.'*
>
> *'I don't want to lose what we have.'*
>
> *'We promised each other "for better, for worse", now we're in the worse.'*

If you're married, you may find it helpful to look at the vows or commitments you made on your wedding day. What did you promise each other? Revisiting your vows can help you navigate a rough patch, as well as strengthen an already good patch.

If you're not married, what other commitments have you made to each other? Maybe living together? Sharing finances? Having children together?

If you aren't in a rough patch, but rather want to enhance, deepen and strengthen your connection with your partner, setting an intention is still very important. It's easy to drift away from working on things which don't hurt and desperately call out for our attention. If you're getting along fine day-to-day, it's easy to forget the importance of working on your connection. Pause at this stage and really focus on your *why*. It will keep you motivated and on track.

If you're not able to make the decision about whether to stay or to go at this point, don't worry. These things are not a perfect 'paint by numbers' exercise; we have to feel our way around it as we go along. Read on, start the exercises of training your compassionate mind and see how you can best direct this part of you to your relationship, your partner and yourself.

Summary

- Factors which make or break a relationship include criticism, contempt, defensiveness and stonewalling.
- We all go through natural changes in life – we need to keep getting to know each other to keep the connection strong.
- Deciding to leave is not the same as choosing to stay.
- Setting an intention for the practical skills training to come can help you remember why you're doing this.

You're now ready to start the work of tending to your relationship garden.

PART II

Developing compassion for you and your partner

- Understand your tricky brain and how it can get in the way of a satisfying romantic relationship
- Start to practise mindfulness, learning to pause to become aware of what's going on around you in your relationship, and what's happening inside you
- Learn to soften and soothe criticism towards yourself and your partner, for less hostility and a deeper connection
- Let compassion and love flow from you to your partner
- Allow compassion and love to flow in from your partner
- Send compassion inwards, practising self-compassion

5 Awake and aware
Becoming mindful of your inner and outer world

This is where we begin our practical work together. Having learned how hard relationships can be you'll now learn how compassion can flow in three directions: from you to others, from others to you and from yourself to yourself, as self-compassion.

To develop compassion for you and your partner, you need *wisdom*. Wisdom in Compassionate Mind Training means clarity, insight or understanding about the outer world and our own inner world; to understand the pain around you as well as the pain within. The first thing you need to gain this clarity is the ability to pause for long enough to *notice*. This is part of *mindfulness*.

Mindfulness

According to Dr Jon Kabat-Zinn, meditation teacher and founder of Mindfulness Based Stress Reduction (MBSR), mindfulness is awareness that arises through paying attention, on purpose, in the present moment, non-judgementally. Being mindful means choosing to observe what's going on around us, as well as within us, and not judging what we find. Often mindfulness is promoted as something providing us with calm and relaxation, but really it's about *being with what is*. Feeling calmer and at ease is a bonus. Being present in the moment helps us notice the here and now, rather than dwell on past failures or worry about future mistakes.

The mindful couple

A mindful couple can notice what's going on in their relationship, and when they need to make efforts to reconnect. A relationship where the partners practise mindfulness may be less stressful and more deeply connected, as they can savour the here and now and enjoy the good moments, as well as accept the bad. The partners will be less *reactive* to difficulties along the way, and more *proactive* in meeting each other's needs. Physical intimacy can also be positively heightened for couples able to focus on the present moment, instead of getting stuck inside their heads.

If mindfulness is this good, why don't we all practise it? Partly because it's hard to form new habits, and also because many people think that the only way to practise mindfulness is through hours of seated meditation. However, you can begin your journey to a more mindful relationship through different forms of practice.

Formal meditation vs informal mindfulness practice

Formal mindfulness meditation is often where you sit in an upright posture with your feet on the floor and eyes closed, or with a soft gaze onto the floor. This meditation can be guided by someone, in person or in audio, or you can practise on your own. Free audio exercises are available to download at www.thethomasconnection.co.uk/thelasting connection.

Informal mindfulness practice is where you engage with your outer and inner world, day-to-day. You can do it anywhere, unguided; just slow down and really notice things. Watch your kettle boil, taste the toothpaste in your mouth when brushing your teeth or feel the warmth of the water against your skin in the shower. The list is endless.

Noticing both the outer and inner world

If you don't pay attention how will you hear what your partner is saying, or notice subtle changes in their mood, or appreciate the way their face lights up when they laugh, or recognise the smell of their freshly washed hair, or savour the feeling of running your fingers over their soft skin? Being mindfully aware heightens our experience of the outside world.

Mindfulness also helps us notice what we're experiencing in our inner world. Paying attention to thoughts, feelings, urges, fantasies, memories and body sensations is important. Mindfulness can help you notice when you need to communicate your thoughts and feelings to your partner: they're not mind readers, and neither are you. Being mindful of your urges and wishes can also help you choose carefully before you act, holding back before you shout at your partner, or saying something hurtful.

Noticing the outer world Using your five senses (sight, hearing, smell, taste and touch), describe what you experience around you in the here and now.

Noticing the inner world Your thoughts, feelings or emotions, physical sensations, urges, memories, dreams and fantasies. Your body and mind, exclusive to you.

The spotlight of attention

It's not easy for couples to focus their attention on each other in our modern society, often being too busy to pause for long enough to properly connect. Learning to move your attention at will can help you choose what to focus on. How do you think that you could improve your relationship? By choosing to shift your focus onto your partner when they're talking, instead of thinking about your work, you're more likely to make your partner feel seen and heard.

Imagine that your attention and focus can be directed like a spotlight, lighting up a stage. The stage is dark apart from where the spotlight illuminates it, to help the audience see the actors. Then the spotlight moves, shining on another actor. The audience turns, following with focused attention. Although the first part of the stage now lies in darkness, it hasn't disappeared and you're still aware of it; it's just not the focus *right now*.

Your attention is like that spotlight. You can move it at will, to illuminate whatever you want. Try it for a moment in this exercise.

Try this: Spotlight of attention

1 Sit upright, close your eyes if you wish and focus the spotlight of attention on your left foot, perhaps noticing any sensations in that foot. If there's any impediment to you using your foot, then another body part works just as well.

2 Wiggle your toes, observing the feeling inside your sock or shoe, or the contact with the floor. Notice what shows up inside you: any thoughts such as 'It's not working' or 'I'm not doing it right'? Any urges to move, scratch or stop the exercise?

3 Now move your attention to the right foot, leaving the left foot in 'darkness'. Is the right foot different from or similar to the left? What sensations or urges can you feel?

4 Moving up to your left hand, letting go of the focus on your foot, gently rub your index finger and thumb together to create an anchor for your attention. Notice how this feels – any comfort or discomfort?

5 Moving over to your right hand, touch the fingers together. Notice when your attention drifts away from the hand, gently steering it back into focus.

6 Lastly, move your spotlight to your mouth, focusing all your attention here and noticing what that brings up. Any urges to lick your lips, or swallow, from any sensation of dryness? Any thoughts, memories or feelings showing up?

7 Letting your spotlight rest, let go and open your eyes.

Reflection & Connection

How did it feel to pay attention like this? Perhaps you're new to mindfulness and found it tricky. How did it feel for your partner? Perhaps they've practised mindfulness for a while and felt like skipping this part. Make space for both your experiences, especially if they differed. It can still be beneficial for your relationship overall even if only one of you engages with the practical experiences. Pause to remind yourselves of your intention and why you're doing this work *together*. Your relationship will thank you for it.

Turning off autopilot

Have you ever arrived at work not quite remembering how you got there? This is your *autopilot* kicking in – doing things out of habit.

You'd be utterly overwhelmed by information if you couldn't do things without thinking about them. Imagine being acutely aware of every single step, lifting one foot up and placing it down ahead, shifting your balance so you can lift the other foot. It would be impossible to function day-to-day. But you can turn off the type of autopilot which is *unhelpful*, when you find yourself mindlessly scrolling on social media without noticing how much time you've spent there, or saying 'Uh-huh' in response when you didn't take in something your partner said. Turning off autopilot means that you're becoming aware of the world around you. This will help you deepen both the emotional and physical connection with your partner, being more present in the moment with them. It will also help you catch yourself when you've time travelled. Yes, you actually *can* time travel – in your mind.

The mind as a time traveller

We have a fantastic capacity for imagination and visualisation, related to the frontal lobes of the brain. We can conjure up pictures of something not present; we can go back in time to a past memory, or jump to the future. This ability is both helpful and unhelpful. The benefit of this way of processing information means you can learn from past mistakes, can plan ahead and organise the future. There are side effects, though: you can get stuck in *rumination* (rehashing the past over and over again) and also get caught up in *worry* (imagining a catastrophic hypothetical scenario in the future). No wonder it's so hard to focus on the here and now, and easy to drift away.

Drifting

Imagine that your attention is like a helium balloon, which will drift away if you let go of the string. That's what happens to our focus and attention in any given moment – it tends to drift away from us, despite our best efforts. You can criticise yourself for not being able to stay focused, or you can have an insight and realisation around the nature of our minds as being prone to bouncing around. Even Buddhist monks practising meditation every day, for hours, will drift away at times. A common Buddhist saying is simply that 'If your mind drifts away a thousand times, you steer back a thousand times'. Back to the balloon analogy – if you notice that you're drifting off, gently tug on the string to bring back your focus. Let's try that in another exercise.

Mindfully noticing sounds around you

You can play around with the experience of sound to practise your spotlight of attention as well. Sounds can help you drop an anchor into the here and now, to get less stuck inside your own head. Remember that any exercise can be tricky at first and you might struggle. Go easy on yourself and do what you can, repeating the exercise many times in order to build some strength and habit.

Try this: Mindfulness of sound

1 Sit upright, with your shoulders relaxed and dropped. Start noticing how your body feels, sat on the seat with your feet on the floor.

2 Start to broaden your attention outwards, to the sounds around you. Let the sounds come to you, rather than reaching out for them.

3 Notice the nature and quality of the sounds – what frequency and pitch do they have? Are they intermittent, or constant, like a lower-level background noise? Do you notice sounds you didn't notice before the exercise?

4 Notice your reaction to the sounds – are they sounds you like or dislike? What feelings do they bring up?

5 Notice when your mind wanders off, when you become distracted. Try not to judge yourself: it's what minds do. As soon as you're aware of this gently steer your attention back to the sounds.

6 Now choose one sound to tune into in greater detail, for a minute or so. Is it inside or outside? What kind of sound is it? Is it near or far? Really tune in.

7 Move your attention from a specific sound to the broader picture, noticing several sounds. What is it like to zoom in and out like this? Try this for a minute or so.

8 Notice your body on the seat again. When you feel ready, come back into the room and open your eyes. Pause here and reflect on what you have noticed.

> *What was this like? Did you bounce around a lot in your attention? Don't worry, it takes practice. The act of steering back IS mindfulness. Let's try again, in a different way.*

Dropping anchor

As soon as you become aware that you've drifted off in your attention, you can drop an anchor. This is particularly useful if you've time travelled back to the past, dwelling on something which hurt you, or to the future by worrying about something going wrong. We time travel a lot within our relationships, frequently reacting to something our partner has done to us in the past, or even something done by a previous partner. Dropping anchor means that you're coming back to the here and now. Let's try it.

Try this

Dropping anchor in the outer world – using 5–4–3–2–1

Pause for a moment and use your five senses to notice the world around you, breathing calmly as you go through it.

5 Looking around you, spot five things you can see. Let your gaze touch upon them briefly, taking in the objects with your sense of *sight*. Notice and observe shapes, colours and light.

4 Tuning into your sense of *touch*, notice four things you can feel against your body. Feeling your socks against your toes, or putting two fingers together and noticing that anchoring sensation. Feel the ground under your feet or a breeze against your skin.

3 Using your sense of *hearing*, what three sounds can you hear? Pay attention to the quality of sounds both far away, like traffic or birds, and the closer ones, like the sound of your breath. Are the sounds high or low, pleasant or unpleasant?

2 Now notice two scents with your sense of *smell*, drawing in deep breaths through your nose. Observe smells from the environment around you, or even from yourself, your hands or clothes.

1 Lastly, pay attention to flavours in your mouth, with your sense of *taste*. You might notice toothpaste, coffee, or what you've recently eaten. Or pick something up and taste it, paying full attention to it.

> *Having tried three exercises now, how do you feel? If you struggled to do them, don't worry, we're not aiming for any particular result – we're just practising.*

We'll now merge mindfulness with compassion, creating mindful compassion.

Mindful compassion

Much like you can mindfully notice sounds around you, or sensations in your body, you can notice your thoughts, beliefs and memories around what it means to be compassionate, what experiences you've had of it thus far in your life, and what's getting in the way of you becoming more compassionate.

The power of words – 'compassion'

What comes to mind for you and your partner when thinking about the word 'compassion'? Take the time to jot down some words. Notice the *positive* ones, such as 'support', 'understanding', 'empathy', 'caring', 'love', 'kindness'. But you may also have listed some *negative* words, such as 'weak', 'fluffy', 'self-indulgent', 'pity' or 'lazy'. Both sets of words are important as they may reveal fears, blocks and resistances you and your partner might have around compassion.

Let's refresh our minds on the definition of compassion:

> *'a sensitivity to the suffering of self and others,*
> *with a commitment to try to alleviate it and prevent it.'*

Simply put, the two parts of compassion are about first noticing the pain either of you is in, and then caring about making the pain better.

Noticing the pain

The first part of the definition concerns our ability to *understand, approach* and *engage* with the experience of pain and suffering in ourselves and others.

This is where mindfulness is key. How can you do something about the suffering in yourself and others if you don't notice it? Imagine that you come home upset about something, stomping around in the house. You're not quite sure why you're feeling so grumpy (struggling to notice and make sense of *your own* pain) and you can't manage to get your partner's attention to talk about it (them struggling to notice and make sense of *your* pain). You're more likely to end up in a fight that night. Imagine instead that both of you use the same skills of mindfully paying attention – your partner lifts up their gaze from what they're doing to watch you, spotting the tears in your eyes. They can then choose what to *do* about what they notice. If you pause for long enough to drop that anchor and really notice how you feel in your body, what thoughts are whirling around in your head and how that makes you feel emotionally, you might be able to tell your partner that you want to talk about the crappy day you had at work.

All of this is hard; it's easier to continue your life on autopilot and not make space for the emotional experiences in yourself, or your partner, just turn on the TV or change the topic. You then miss out on opportunities to connect more deeply with yourself and your partner, strengthening your connection. Remember, connection comes from both light and dark moments, and turning towards each other in times of need will also help you feel more passionately about each other. Knowing you can make space for the dark times in life means you continue to make your relationship a safe place to be.

> *Being sensitive to your own suffering and that of your partner takes courage and willingness to tolerate distress, as noticing and sitting with pain is uncomfortable. It means making sense of why each of you feel how you feel, given all you know about each other and yourselves.*

Making the pain better

The second part of the compassion definition concerns the willingness and motivation to *alleviate* the suffering in ourselves and others. Simply put, it's asking yourself how you can be helpful and not harmful to yourself and anybody else.

This is where we need to think about using empathy and clarity about who you and your partner are and what makes you tick, then choosing wisely what actions you can take to care for them and for yourself. You might need to take a few breaths to calm down, so you can start to tell your partner about the challenging day you had. They might need to use their experience of what you're like when you're upset, allowing you the space to talk without interruption and then holding you close to show you support. You need to remind yourself of what your partner wants and needs, and not just assume it's the same as what *you* want and need.

> *Moving towards and lifting the pain in yourself and in your partner takes dedication and wisdom, resting on your caring commitment to be helpful, not harmful, and the insight you have about your partner, yourself and the world.*

What compassion is not

Couples sometimes talk about how they cannot be compassionate to their partner as it would mean they are a pushover, a doormat, or that their partner will take advantage. What we're hitting upon here are the fears, blocks and resistances to being compassionate.

Compassion is not a weak choice; it's a *courageous* one. Compassion means to *suffer with*, sitting with someone else's pain or your own; that takes strength. To be able to hear your partner tell you about something difficult they've experienced takes a lot of commitment on your part, as you'll also be affected by what they're telling you. Compassion is not weak, fluffy or soft. Nor is it selfish or self-indulgent. It's also not pity, feeling sorry for someone.

Compassion as flow

It's easy to assume that compassion is just something we do for others, but it's so much more than that. Compassion can flow in three directions:

Self → Others

Others → Self

Self → Self

You can practise expressing these flows with your partner, by also understanding where you tend to get the most stuck. Do you struggle most with showing care, empathy, kindness and love towards your partner? Or do you find it challenging to reach out to your partner for support, and receive their love? Or do you find it hardest to be kind towards yourself, supporting yourself when you need it? You can be blocked in several or all of these flows. The interesting thing is also to understand how your partner may be blocked, as it will create a dynamic between you. This can be influenced by our tricky brains.

Loops in the mind

The trickiest part of how the old and new parts of the brain have evolved is how they affect each other. The newer parts impact the emotional systems of the older parts of the brain, back and forth in loops. The thought experiment of the lion and the zebra demonstrates how this can play out in a relationship.

Imagine a herd of zebras grazing peacefully on the African savannah. Suddenly the zebras spot a prowling lioness and freeze in fear: their *threat* system becomes activated. The lioness wants to eat the zebra, so her *drive* system is activated. Predators register movement and will chase fleeing prey, so the zebra's first response is to stand still. When the lioness comes nearer, the zebra has to run. The chase is on. The motive behind each animal is different – the zebra is running for its life; the lioness is running for her lunch. Let's imagine that the zebra outruns the lioness. What does the zebra do once it has escaped? It calms down, as the threat is gone, and then resumes grazing, resting, looking after young or mating.

Imagine now that you are walking down the street carrying your lunch and spot a furious wild lion – in a city. What would you do? Your threat system would select this for you, but I imagine that you would initially freeze from shock, then run for safety, taking cover inside a building. What do you then do? The threat is over; you escaped the lion. Do you sit down to eat your lunch, chill out and play a game on your phone? Sending your partner a racy text, hoping for sex? Probably not – you're not a zebra. I imagine that you'll be in shock, trying to contact anyone who might have been hurt by the lion, planning how to get home, and imagining the worst happening to others out there. Even when the lion gets captured, your mind might give you flashbacks, thinking 'What if the lion had caught me?' You might beat yourself up for hiding in a building instead of trying to do something 'heroic'. You're doing this because of your capacity to consider what *has* happened and what *might* happen, and that time travelling and self-criticism keeps the threat going for you. You can't relax and resume your normal activities like the zebra, because the newer parts of the tricky human brain won't let you. The new brain keeps the threat going, as illustrated in the graph below.

This often happens in relationships too – we can't go back to normal just because a threat has gone away, as we can ruminate on it afterwards, worry about it happening again, and beat ourselves up for our actions. This is why you need both mindfulness and compassion to bring yourself back to the present moment, where you're safe, but also to act more kindly to yourself and your partner. Otherwise you'll be stuck in this sort of loop for a long time, and drift further away from each other.

Loops in the mind

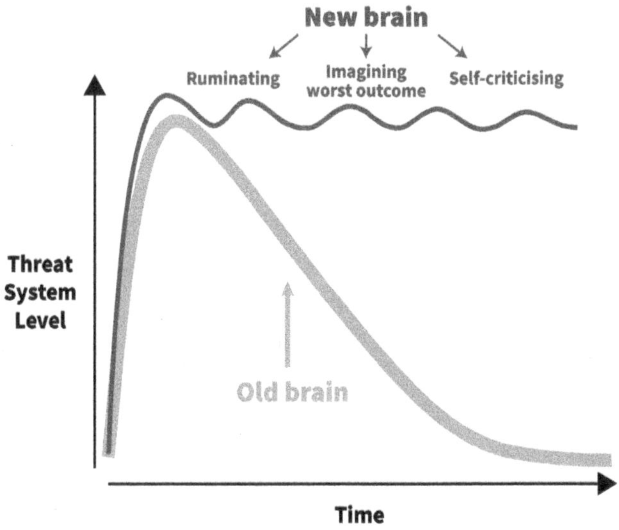

Adapted from Charlie Heriot-Maitland, Compassionate Mind Training *(2016).*

Time to meet our first couple from my therapy sofa, 'Adam' and 'Lisa', illustrating an old brain/new brain loop.

From the sofa

Adam had been married to Lisa for twelve years when they hit a rough patch, as he was made redundant. His old brain (home of our emotions) gave him feelings like anger, guilt, shame, sadness and anxiety, as his basic motives of providing for his family were threatened. Anyone would feel bad being made redundant, but the new brain (our thinking centre) then added insult to injury as he blamed himself for the redundancy and put himself down for being 'useless'. These self-critical thoughts led to more negative feelings, like feeling disgusted with himself and even angry with his wife. When she tried to comfort him, he withdrew or snapped at her. This behaviour activated *her* threat system, as her old brain responded with anxiety and sadness, feeling rejected. Her new brain painted scenarios of things never getting better and being unable to pay the mortgage. This made her feel even more anxious, demanding her husband look for work or ask for help from family. This further fed his thoughts of being useless . . . and so they go back and forth in loop after loop, their stress levels never getting a chance to settle. Even when Adam secured a new job the threat was kept going through his self-criticism and rumination around how disappointed Lisa was with him, and Lisa's threat kept going through remembering all the hostility Adam sent her way and worrying that he might lose this job too. They missed opportunities for supporting each other in their respective suffering and are also not taking accountability for soothing their own distress.

Reflection & Connection

Mindfully exploring the loops of the tricky brain:

- What loops do you get stuck in?
  - Dwelling on past mistakes?
  - Painting worst-case scenarios?
  - Criticising yourself?
- What are the consequences of these loops for your relationship?

Becoming mindful of these loops gives you insight and clarity around what is happening in your relationship and helps you to take action to break your unhelpful cycles of behaving.

My story

You might think, 'Who's this Michaela anyway? Here's this expert telling me what I'm supposed to do and how to live my life.' I want to avoid that trap of you thinking that I'm superhuman and have all the answers, never struggling in my relationship or in life in general. I'll tell you my story as we go along so you'll know I'm only human too.

I really struggled with the concept of mindfulness when I first came across it in my psychologist training around 2004. I was told it had to be an hour of daily practice. Being young and impatient that alienated me, and I gave up on formal practice. Instead my way into mindfulness came informally, through my love for photography. In that moment of capturing a shot, I felt so engrossed and present. I then moved on to being mindfully aware of my surroundings when travelling to new places, taking in the scenes. If I went somewhere with a beach, I would watch the waves of the ocean roll in, listening to the sound of them crashing against the shore, smelling the salty water and feeling the warm sand between my toes. Informal mindfulness practice is what hooked me. I also found mindfulness through yoga, helping me watch my thoughts and sit with my breath, being mindfully aware of both body and mind. It doesn't matter how you find your way into mindfulness. My husband doesn't enjoy formal seated meditations at all. He does mindfulness informally, though, as he likes to fully immerse himself in something, engaging his mind in things like gazing into our fish tank or going on a hike.

Summary

- Your mind is a curious thing; a tricky brain made up of old and new parts. The way they come together can create issues, getting you stuck in loops of thinking.
- To spot these loops you need to practise mindfulness, moving your spotlight to illuminate what's going on around you as well as inside you.
- Mindfulness is the base for compassion, as you can't do anything about your own suffering or your partner's suffering if you don't first notice it.

We'll now move on to understanding your emotions and seeing how your threat, drive and soothing systems play out in your relationship. This is where we start to cultivate your compassionate mind.

6 Understanding your emotions

Balance your emotional systems to balance your relationship

We've evolved to operate on a 'better safe than sorry' principle. We need to look at how the three emotional systems of *threat*, *drive* and *soothing* relate to relationships, so you can see how your own relationship might be out of balance, and how different motives shape our minds and our actions.

How do you make sense of your feelings?

Have you ever said, 'What's WRONG with him?' in exasperation over your partner? Or, 'I don't get why she DOES that?' Most of us have wondered what on earth is going on inside our partner's head at times. There is probably nothing 'wrong' with either of you – it's more likely that your tricky brains have got the better of you. Let's explore why we do the things we do and feel the way we feel, in life and in love.

Our motives

Motives are what drive us to action. Motives evolved from our survival instinct and striving to meet our basic needs (food, shelter and water). This is linked with *caring* (we're built for nurture) but also with *competing* (we're competing with other people over the same limited resources – sometimes even with the person we're in love with!). There are some issues with these motives, though: we can be good at giving care, but not at receiving care when distressed. We can be good at working in a highly competitive environment such as corporate banking, but not so good at shifting into a caring/supportive role at home.

Our emotions

Professor Paul Gilbert has created a *three emotional systems model* to explain how our emotions have evolved, linked to certain motives.

1 Emotions focused on threat and self-protection
2 Emotions focused on doing and achieving
3 Emotions focused on feeling safe and content

Imagine what would improve in your life and relationship if you could better understand your emotions and the choices you make. Imagine if you could move from being reactive to being proactive.

The three emotional systems

The problem in modern society is that we might have too much of one or two of the systems and not enough of the third. We need *threat*, *drive* and *soothing* to thrive, but we need them to be balanced.

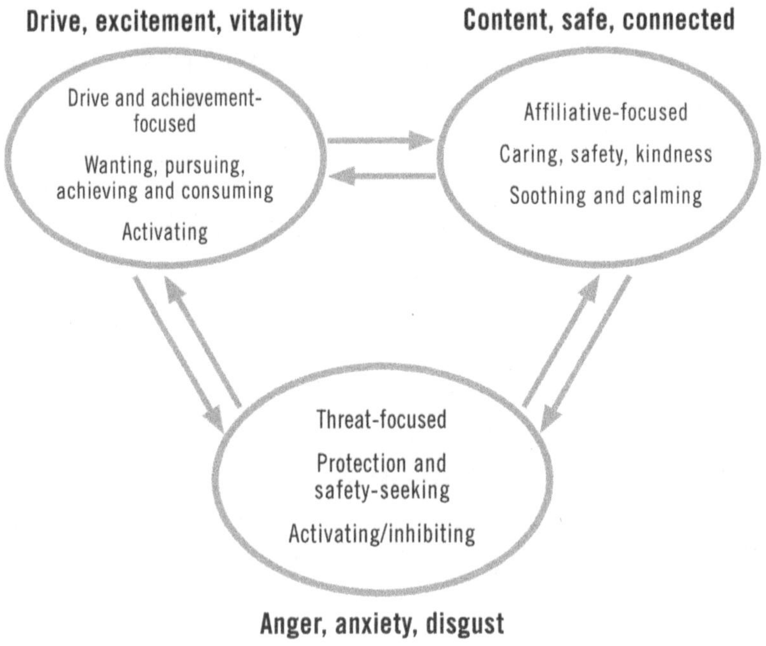

From Irons and Beaumont, The Compassionate Mind Workbook *(2017). Adapted from Gilbert,* The Compassionate Mind *(2009). Reprinted with permission.*

Think about how it is for you – do you spend more time in threat, drive or soothing? Is there anything missing in your life, or in your relationship?

The threat system

This emotional system is particularly relevant to couples seeking help for the negative emotions present in their relationship. Anger, fear, anxiety, disgust and sadness are all associated with the threat system. These may lead to hostility, criticism, arguing, blaming and ignoring, but also to one partner attempting to please the other, to their own detriment.

The threat system is linked to our built-in drive to keep ourselves safe. This also extends to protecting others, as our threat system can come online when someone we care for is threatened (consider a parent protecting a child).

This is both an *activating* system – driving us away from danger through defensive strategies of fight or flight – and an *inhibiting* system, through freeze or appease. We don't consciously choose which way we will react to danger, because this is not a response we can control – it's *not your fault*. However, becoming aware of when we're in our threat system and learning how to calm the threat responses will help us to make better choices.

- **Fight** Physically or verbally protecting yourself through fighting back against your partner.
  Arguing, screaming, throwing things, bullying, criticising, aiming to win
- **Flight** Removing yourself from the situation as fast as you can, to avoid the harmful thing.
  Leaving the room, ending conversations, changing topics, avoiding the call or text, ghosting
- **Freeze** Being unable to take any action, becoming paralysed and going into shutdown.
  Being unable to reply in an argument, stopping talking, being unable to move

- **Appease** Trying to avoid the danger, becoming submissive to make the threat go away.
  Passively agreeing to a decision by self-sacrificing, overcompensating, people-pleasing

The sympathetic nervous system

When we perceive danger or threat, our *sympathetic nervous system* becomes activated. When you get scared you might quickly draw in a breath and then hold it, or take quick, shallow breaths. Your pupils dilate, your digestion slows down, your palms get sweaty and your pulse beats faster – all so you can prepare to spring into action. When you relax following this threat, you release the breath and let go of that activation.

When the old brain spots a threat, hormones such as adrenalin and cortisol are released. This is fine in moderation, as it helps us to prepare for challenges – anything from a job interview to a first date (think of those 'butterflies'!). When something important is at stake, our emotional system responds – but sometimes it's over-activated. Our responses have been shaped by our experiences, which control how and when your threat system is activated. This can have a big impact on how you interact with your partner.

Better safe than sorry

The threat system is highly sensitive and reactive; it impacts our ability to escape danger, like quickly jumping away from a speeding car. When you're under threat you need to process information very quickly. But sometimes we get things wrong because our threat system is a 'blunt tool': it has to operate on a 'better safe than sorry' basis.

This shows up as assuming negative things about your partner and their intentions – sometimes you'll get it wrong, simply because you feel threatened. By exploring and understanding compassionate communication, you'll learn how to pause before you act.

Reflection & Connection

What triggers your threat system in your relationship? What makes either of you fly off the handle? What triggers quiet withdrawal? Which of the four defensive strategies of fight, flight, freeze and appease do you see most often in yourself and your partner? Discuss these patterns in an open, non-judgemental way.

Imagine how different your relationship would be if you could understand how your experiences have shaped you both emotionally and what triggers you to feel threatened.

The drive system

The drive system is also an *activating* emotional system, motivating us towards our goals (like a promotion at work), and is linked with the rewarding 'kick' of the hormone *dopamine*. One part of the drive system is associated with pursuing what we want, and another is linked with the pleasure of consuming it. We can feel alive and happy when we're savouring something tasty or celebrating that promotion. Your wedding day might have been full of drive-related emotions: joy, pride, excitement, achievement and vitality. Going on a date or having a laugh together can also elicit these rewarding feelings.

The dark side of drive

There's a downside to the drive system – when it's infused with threat. When people are motivated to achieve simply to avoid feeling like a failure, or are constantly busy for fear of missing out, they lack balance in their emotional system and run the risk of burnout.

The drive system propels us forward, and without it we would get little done. In depression, the drive system is burning low, as there is a lack of motivation. A flat drive system would mean that one partner lacks initiative and seems unhappy even if doing things together that used to be fun and rewarding. One depressed partner increases the risk of the other also becoming depressed. Depression also puts strain on the relationship overall, increasing the risk of it getting into distress.

Alcohol or drugs, too much caffeine, or even addictive games and social media can feed you an instant kick of reward, an instant gratification. This is why some couples struggle to connect because of their respective preoccupation with their smartphones – imagine if your phone is now giving you the reward you previously got from the social interaction with your partner!

In the early days of a relationship there is a lot of that rewarding drive activation; you go on dates and do lots of fun activities together. When you're in a long-term committed relationship, the rewarding excitement and stimulation of your day-to-day will gradually go down over time, and you may decrease how often you're intimate with each other as desire decreases. If you allow yourselves a deeper connection, your love will be fuelled more by oxytocin than dopamine – as the soothing system lights up.

The soothing system

This emotional system is very important for couples, as it involves both *calm* and *connection*, coming from the nurturing parts of our brain. The 'calm' bit involves relaxing and unwinding – the 'rest and digest' system. The 'connection' part is about giving and receiving care and protection – the 'tend and befriend' system. Whereas the threat and drive systems activate us, moving away from threat or towards what we desire, the soothing system helps us come to stillness and 'just being', thanks to the parasympathetic nervous system in our bodies and the hormone *oxytocin*.

The parasympathetic nervous system

Remember how the zebra calms down and continues to graze once the threat of the lioness is gone? Animals naturally do this – but can only do it once the threat is over. Imagine a dog cowering during a thunderstorm – it only calms down once the storm has passed. We can learn to soothe ourselves during a metaphorical storm in our lives. This is the blessing and the curse of the new brain: we have the capacity to keep a threat going through ruminating and worrying, but also the capacity for mindfulness and self-reflection, telling ourselves that the storm will pass and that it will be OK. That can create an activation of the *parasympathetic nervous system,* breathing out and relaxing into a situation, feeling safe and OK.

The big O – oxytocin

The hormone oxytocin is involved in our connection with our partners, children and other loved ones, but also to ourselves – the oxytocin levels are higher when we feel safe and at ease, even if we're on our own.

Oxytocin is elicited in the prolonged sense of touch – not a quick peck on the cheek, but rather in a longer embrace held for several seconds, or a slow and gentle stroke, or massage. Oxytocin is also released in the climax of an orgasm, increasing the sense of closeness between partners and also making us feel calm and sleepy. Oxytocin is also involved in childbirth and breastfeeding, and if the woman feels under threat can make both of these difficult as the threat system overrides soothing.

The three emotional systems in relationships

The threat system can involve jealousy, anger over betrayal, fear of not being good enough or of losing the person you love, or disgust over something your partner has done towards you. The drive system can be translated as our desire to be close and excited together, in emotional or physical intimacy, of building a meaningful life together full of fun and vitality. The soothing system is linked with the connection and safe space between loving partners, to be accepted as they are and to feel at ease with the world. Balancing your systems will help you to infuse more desire and connection into your life overall, and into your love life specifically.

Reflection & Connection

Looking at the model above, draw your own circles representing how they are in your life at the moment. For ease of remembering make the threat system *red*, the drive system *blue* and the soothing system *green*.

Start by drawing the largest circle, representing the emotions you tend to have the most. If you currently feel a lot of pressure at work, with corresponding conflict at home with your partner, you might have a larger red circle and a large blue circle, with a small green pea for the soothing system. If you worry a lot about a relative being ill, your threat circle might be large to the point of not getting anything done at work, meaning a small blue drive circle. If your partner is supportive in this, you might still have a large green soothing circle. You could even consider doing one set of circles for your work life and one set for your love life. Be curious about what you find – are they balanced differently?

Discuss with your partner how each of you feel about the threat, drive and soothing systems:

Threat *What gets you feeling angry, scared or anxious in your relationship?*

Drive *What gets you feeling excited, motivated and joyful in your relationship?*

Soothing *What gets you feeling calm and relaxed as well as close and connected in your relationship?*

From the sofa

Clara and Delphine were expecting their first baby when they realised they had experiences from the past which hadn't been resolved, and were often arguing. Drawing their three circles, we realised that Clara had a high threat activation from the uncertainty of being pregnant during COVID-19. Her wife, Delphine, was working a lot, worried about not being able to provide financially. Clara had high standards for herself and others and would criticise Delphine for her shortcomings. Delphine would cope with this by withdrawing and becoming more passive, or actively escaping by drinking alcohol.

We established that their anger was driven by a fear of not being safe, with both feeling scared and anxious about becoming mothers when neither had experienced warm and supportive parenting. They lit up when talking about how they'd fallen in love, and the joy of being together. Their drive systems kicked in, showing the reward each took from being in the presence of the other, which had been blocked by fear, anger and anxiety. They both felt soothed and safe when they were being respectful of each other's feelings. They needed to soothe themselves and each other, to balance their emotions and reconnect at this important time in their lives.

Soothing your threat system through the breath

One major way you can calm down your threat reactions is through your breath, stimulating the parasympathetic nervous system. Developing a soothing rhythm of breathing will calm your mind as well as your body, making you less reactive and helping you act like the person you want to be within your relationship. Use the audio downloads on the website to help (see Resources).

Try this

Soothing rhythm breathing

1 Get into a comfortable position with eyes closed. Try to release any tension in your jaw or shoulders.

2 Take a deep breath, then breathe in and out through your nose. The key is to find a rhythm which is a little bit deeper, a little bit slower than your usual breath, but still comfortable. Draw the breath down into the abdomen, letting your belly inflate like a balloon then slowly deflate when breathing out. Watch it rising and falling – perhaps put one hand on your chest and one on your stomach, to see if you're drawing the breath down past the diaphragm.

3 Be aware that your mind will wander. If you get caught up in thoughts, feelings or memories, gently bring back the focus on your breath.

4 Play around with your facial expression. Try a gentle half smile to help yourself feel calm, soothed and at ease. Slow your breathing and ease any tension in your face, shoulders and body. Sometimes it can be helpful to try a counting rhythm to practise slowing down.

Breathing in for 1, 2, 3 . . . Breathing out for 1, 2, 3 (and repeat).

Focus your attention especially on the outbreath, making it slower and longer.

Let's slow it down a bit further now.

Breathing in for 1, 2, 3, 4 . . . Breathing out for 1, 2, 3, 4 (and repeat).

Don't hold your breath, or make it choppy – keep your air flowing in a smooth, even pace. Now settle on a rhythm which feels soothing to you.

5 Settling into this rhythm and keep it going for as long as you need to. When you feel ready, start to pay attention to the sounds around you. Wiggle your toes and fingers so you gradually become more alert, then open your eyes.

6 Notice how this exercise makes you feel. Does it give you space to think more clearly?

Practice will help you improve over time. Sometimes it just doesn't hit the spot, and that's OK; some people find it very threatening to slow down like this.

Soothing your threat system through visualisation

Another way to stimulate your soothing system is by engaging in the new brain skill of *visualisation*. If you imagine a picture of your favourite dessert, your mouth might begin to water. If you imagine someone you think is attractive, the fantasy might make you feel turned on. You can put this to the test using the *safe place imagery* to stimulate your soothing system. This will help you experience a sense of feeling safe within yourself, so you're more likely to open up to connecting more deeply with your partner.

Try this

Safe place imagery

1 Find somewhere you won't be disturbed. Try sitting instead of lying down, as you may fall asleep otherwise. If this happens, go easy on yourself – you probably needed the rest.

2 Settle into your seat, keeping your chin up, feet planted on the floor and eyes closed.

3 Start by finding the soothing breathing rhythm. Allow your breath and your body to slow down, letting go of whatever you're concerned about, and focus on your outbreath. Release whatever tension the day has brought you and notice your body relaxing.

4 Try a gentle smile to soften your facial muscles. Keep breathing in this calming rhythm throughout the exercise.

5 When you feel ready, create an image in your mind of a place that is safe, soothing and calming. It might be a memory of somewhere you've been or something you make up from your imagination.

6 Don't worry if an image doesn't come to mind for a while – just notice what thoughts come up. If you struggle to find a place to visualise or get caught choosing between places, just let it go. Bring your attention back to your soothing breathing rhythm and then try to imagine your safe place again.

7 When an image has come to mind, spend a few moments paying attention to what you can see. What colours, shapes or objects surround you? Focus on what you're visualising to make you feel calm, content and at ease.

8 Notice if there are any sounds present in this image. Notice the different qualities of these sounds. Are they near or far away? Are they loud or soft? Focus on how these sounds make you feel calm and relaxed.

9 Now notice if there are any comforting smells present in this image, like the smell of the ocean, freshly baked bread or the familiar scent

of a comfortable blanket. Take a deep breath and focus on how the scents leave you feeling calm, comfortable and relaxed.

10 Now become aware of any tastes in your mouth. Anything you associate with being calm or relaxed, maybe a sip of fresh cold water or the taste of a fresh berry from your garden. Focus on the sensation of having it in your mouth and notice how you feel.

11 Moving on, use your sense of touch to notice any sensations against your skin. How does your body feel where you're seated or moving around in this image? Maybe you can feel the warmth of the sun on your face, grass tickling your toes or a warm breeze ruffling your hair. Focus on this for a few more moments, with slow breathing and a gentle smile.

12 Let's see if there is anyone else there with you. How does it feel? How would it feel if you were alone?

13 Now, imagine that this place has an awareness and that it has your wellbeing at heart. It wants you to be here and is happy to see you. To be safe and calm, to feel supported and at ease. It wants you to be well, to be happy, to be able to face your difficulties.

14 When you feel ready to leave this place, become more aware of the sounds in the room around you. Letting go of this image, letting it fade. Knowing you can return to this place whenever you want, gently open your eyes.

You can use this exercise before a tricky conversation with your partner, allowing your soothing system to come online. This will make you more able to listen and express yourself.

Reflection & Connection

How was it for you to try to slow down your breath and your body, turning inwards for a visualisation? How was it for your partner? If you found this calming and soothing, great. Some partners find this can create more space to think and feel. Some find themselves provoked by these exercises, often if they have had a lack of soothing and calming in their lives. Just be curious rather than furious about your respective reactions to the exercises.

My story

The breath is the tool I use most from my compassion training. It's simple and easy to remember, and it's always with you. When I have been in moments of darkness, and my mind hasn't wanted me to practise compassion for myself, the breath has been the one effort I could make. I teach it to my son, as even three-year-olds can learn to take a breath. Throughout my motherhood journey, where life has stretched me in more ways than I could ever imagine, taking two minutes to myself has helped me keep in touch with why it's so important to take a moment to pause and just breathe.

Summary

- As humans, we have a built-in capacity for aggression, hostility and territorialism, through our threat system trying to protect us and keep us safe.
- We also have our drive system, helping us pursue things we want and take pleasure from those things.
- Our soothing system helps us feel safe and connected with others, driven by our built-in capacity for being compassionate to others.
- It's not your fault that you get caught up in your threat system and focus on 'better safe than sorry' strategies.
- To have a lasting connection in your relationship, you need balance in the three emotional systems in your mind, to respond to the dangers your mind warns you about and also to create a sense of desire, joy, calm and connection.

We will now move on to developing the compassionate part of you and remembering what it feels like to be compassionate towards someone.

7 The compassionate part of you

Cultivating who you are at your compassionate best

What is a compassionate person? What qualities do they have? What posture, facial expression and tone of voice? Here we explore the qualities of your compassionate self and how these can affect your relationship with your partner.

Practice makes progress

Using self-help books can be hard, as we cannot consume the knowledge through osmosis and strengthen our relationship just by owning or reading the book. We have to use the exercises too. Taking out a subscription to a golf magazine or watching videos on YouTube won't make you a better golf player by default – you also need to put in some practice on the driving range. You'll likely miss a lot of balls at first and that can feel discouraging. But don't give up – you'll move towards hitting more than you miss, and your movements will become smoother. Stay with it.

The first step to improving your relationship is becoming curious as to what is getting in the way of doing the work. Common blocks to practising are:

- Time
- Opportunity
- Lack of support
- Resistance or fear
- Challenging ('This is hard')
- Self-doubt ('No good at it')

Do what you can

This work doesn't have to be 'perfect' to make a difference. Becoming more compassionate towards your partner cannot be another chore on your to-do list, especially if you do so at your own expense. Compassion isn't about self-sacrifice, always putting your partner first. Do what you can, especially when trying out new ways of acting. You'll establish healthy habits for a lifetime. Your relationship is a marathon, not a sprint.

Reflection & Connection

How is your practice with the audios going? Any parts you've found difficult? Really listen to each other, and approach this together – what can *we* do to help each other practise? Do you need to negotiate how other responsibilities are handled in the home, to free up time and energy to practise?

Identify the following:

- My/our most common blocks to practising (*noticing the pain*)
- What I/we can do to improve this (*making the pain better)*

The many different parts of you

You have been shaped by how you have grown up and who has been part of that journey. Get a pen and paper out and start making notes, reflecting on the shaping of you and how it could all be different with a different start in life. Make space to do the same with your partner.

How your culture and upbringing has shaped you

Essentially, we're not just one 'self' – 'This is me, this is who I am, myself'. We have many different selves, many different versions. Some researchers think there might be hundreds or thousands of 'selves'. These parts get different amounts of 'airtime', so to speak, in different contexts.

Some versions of us have been suppressed, perhaps because it wasn't safe to let them out when we were growing up because of expectations around behaviour. 'Boys don't cry' is an expressed norm in many cultures, making some males suppress a softer side of themselves to avoid being seen as 'weak'. This has a strong impact on intimate relationships; if male partners react with anger rather than sadness when something upsets them their partner is pushed away, and they lose the support and care they need. The angry self is in the driving seat, pushing the sad self out.

In many cultures across the globe girls are told they have to be 'good girls' and 'do what you're told'. This can lead to the angrier or assertive part of women being suppressed in romantic relationships, and those in heterosexual relationships might find themselves putting up with unacceptable behaviours from a male partner. Even in a safe and loving relationship, a woman having been fed a rule of 'you need a man to look after you' might be anxious about being abandoned; and as a result her anxious self might silence her wishes and she may do things to appease the man to avoid being left. The anxious self is in the driving seat, telling the angry self it isn't safe to stand up for oneself.

These are statistical averages, of course. There are more differences *within* a group of women or men than there are *between* a group of women and men. But although we may be more similar in terms of our biology than we think, the way in which our gender is construed by social shaping has an impact on how we also behave in our intimate relationships (in both same sex or opposite sex couples).

How you have been shaped by your upbringing

It's important to understand the version of you currently present in your loving relationship. Who could you have been if shaped by a different journey?

Try this

Growing up in a different family

1 Imagine that instead of growing up in your own home, with your parent/s or other caregiver, you were raised by your neighbours. The people living next door – what were they like? What were their children like? What were their interests and what did you see their family doing?

Who would you be today had you been raised by them instead of being in your own family? What would your values and interests be? How would you behave?

2 Imagine now that you have been raised in your partner's family instead of your own. Perhaps your partner had a strong relationship with one parent and another parent was absent? Perhaps the parents made it clear that emotions were not to be expressed? Perhaps they put pressure on your partner to perform? Perhaps they were kind, loving and accepting?

Who would you be today, had you been shaped by your partner's circumstances instead of your own? How does that make you feel towards your partner, on their journey in life?

Which part of you is running the show?

Which part of you might be in the driving seat within your relationship?

Try this

Who is in the driving seat?

Imagine you're having an argument with your partner. Different versions of you might react in different ways – which of the following do you recognise?

Angry self The angry part of you might think it's unfair, that it's your partner's fault, that you don't deserve this. This self thinks that the other person should apologise and make it up to you.

Anxious self The part of you which is more fearful might worry about this not being possible to overcome, that the argument will end badly, and your partner will leave you.

Sad self This version of you might feel hopeless and think that there is no point in trying, things will never change anyway – this part might want to roll into a ball and cry.

Self-critical self This part of you might be pointing the blame in a harsh, hostile way, telling you that it's all your fault, that you're a failure as a person. Sometimes this voice is called the *inner critic*.

1 In arguments with your partner, which version of you shows up the most?

2 Which one is in the driving seat as you argue?

3 How does that part of you act?

4 What facial expression and posture does it have?

5 What kind of tone of voice does it use?

Remember that whichever version you commonly spend time in is not your fault – but you can become accountable for how you show up in your interactions with others.

The compassionate part of you

Just as you have an anxious or angry part, you also have a compassionate part. Think of this as 'you on a really good day'. The intention isn't to always be 'your best self'; it's neither realistic nor possible to never get overcome by anger or competitiveness with your partner or other people, but your brain and body can be trained to step into the compassionate part of yourself *on purpose*. Cultivating our compassionate part helps us be like the partner we want to be.

We have the capacity to be guided by both compassionate motivation and competitive motivation, so let's turn to your memories of when you were nurturing rather than trying to win over your partner. We're going to use *visualisation* again. Merely imagining something has a physiological response in the body – intensely thinking about food stimulates the production of saliva and gastric acid, to prepare for digestion, for example. Unfortunately, it also means we can visualise bad fights with our partner long after the threat of the argument has settled. Let's use this power of visualisation for something helpful.

Memory of being compassionate

Bring to mind a memory of when you have acted as your compassionate self and been kind to your loved one, and see how that fantasy kick-starts your body.

Try this

Memory of being compassionate to your partner

1 Get into a comfortable, upright position with feet on the floor, shoulders down, chin up and a gentle smile on your face. Close your eyes and then tune into your soothing breathing rhythm, to calm down and focus on a memory of kindness.

2 Don't worry about getting it right or not seeing a crystal-clear image. That's not how imagery works – it can be fleeting and hazy. It's all practice. Just do what you can, in this moment.

3 Bring to mind a memory of a time you looked after your partner, being caring and kind towards them, either a long time ago or more recently. Don't pick the most distressing time for your partner, as that might also get you into your threat system, feeling their pain. It can also be a happy time when you felt you loved and cared for your partner. You can change this image next time you try the exercise.

4 Think back to this time, and imagine that you're looking in through the window of your home, seeing yourself being warm and caring to your partner.

5 Focus on your facial expression and body posture in that moment. How can they see that love on your face? In your eyes and in your smile? How can they see your love for them in the way you hold and carry your body? Are you being near them, touching them, putting your hand on them?

6 Doing this can be hard, as you might have a range of different emotions about your partner. You might be sad, or angry or resentful for their shortcomings, as well as feel love and affection. Your mind might recall times when they haven't supported you, thoughts that your partner is never kind to you – just notice and acknowledge those thoughts, then try to let them go. Spend a bit more time thinking back to this time when you were kind and loving.

7 In that moment when you're doing something kind for your partner, what are you doing? Maybe you're doing something practical – bringing them a cup of tea when they're ill, or talking through something upsetting, like a stressful event at work.

8 What does your tone of voice sound like? What little words do you use to show your partner you love them, and how do you say them?

9 Sit with this image and the feeling of loving and caring for your partner for a little while longer. Keep breathing in that smooth rhythm and remember that gentle smile on your face. When you feel ready, let the memory fade and open your eyes.

How does it feel for you in this moment, when you're remembering caring for your partner?

What thoughts do you get about your own actions towards your partner day-to-day – do you make enough effort with this?

What does a compassionate person look like?

Considering the memory of how you were when you cared for your partner, what *physical attributes* were you showing? What attributes or qualities make up a compassionate person?

Facial expression

What kind of facial expression does a compassionate person have? Bring to mind the gentle smile you practised in the soothing breathing rhythm.

Posture

How would a compassionate person stand? How would they carry themselves? Would they stand upright or hunched over? How would they move their body? How would they walk? Imagine a way to stand, move and walk which expresses these compassionate qualities of caring commitment, clarity and courage.

Tone of voice

How would someone compassionate speak? It matters not just *what* they say, but also *how* they say it. A compassionate tone of voice might be warm, gentle, soft and smooth, but it can also be strong, grounded and clear. Compassion has many faces, and we can express our caring commitment, wisdom and strength in different ways (think of the physical differences between Mother Teresa and Barack Obama, for example – yet both can be seen as compassionate and caring).

Try this

The qualities and attributes of a compassionate person

Brainstorm words (kind, caring, patient) you think describe the qualities of a compassionate person. When you remember yourself as being compassionate, what *qualities* or *attributes* did you show towards your partner? Within Compassion Focused Therapy we think of the compassionate self as consisting of three broad categories of qualities.

1 Caring commitment – CARE

In order to be compassionate to yourself and others you first have to care about their wellbeing, wanting both of you to be well. This involves being kind, supportive, empathetic and patient, and is linked to our built-in capacity for nurture. This is our compassionate motivation – 'May I be helpful, not harmful'.

2 Wisdom – CLARITY

Compassionate action requires insight and clarity. You need to understand how we all exist in this tricky life, so full of pain and suffering. You're not to blame for what you have gone through, but you're accountable for what choices you make. We can see our minds as a garden: we might not like all the trees and flowers we find there, but we can choose what we want to cultivate and help grow stronger, and what we want to gently let go – 'It's not your fault, but it is your responsibility how you handle it'.

3 Strength – COURAGE

You need to be able to reliably show up for yourself and others, and that takes strength and resilience. The visual image we use is standing tall like a mountain, or a tree with deep roots. It means having the courage to do something which might scare you, stepping out of your comfort zone. Being compassionate is not an easy choice; it takes courage and strength – 'I can do hard things'.

Your compassionate self

There is scientific evidence that imagining and practising your compassionate self helps to shape your mind. Research has shown that this is associated with an increase in the three flows of compassion, an increase in positive emotion, and decrease of self-criticism, depression and stress.[19] Practising our 'best possible self' is associated with an increased optimism and ability to cope with difficulties.[20] When you step into your compassionate self your motivation to engage in difficulties increases, so you're more able to face your challenges.[21] Research has noticed that this willingness to engage in difficult issues has resulted in physiological benefits too.[22] In fact, having compassionate goals of focusing on the wellbeing of yourself and others, rather than self-focused goals of beating others and being better than them, have been linked to an increased feeling of closeness, trust and social support as it results in the creation of a 'supportive environment'.[23]

Self-improvement means couples improvement

Couples communicate better when they can approach a dispute as their compassionate selves, making space for all the other versions of themselves and preventing the angry or critical self from staying in the driving seat.

Try this: Your compassionate self

1 Get into an upright posture with feet on the floor, engaging your soothing breathing rhythm to slow down your body. Relax your facial muscles, bringing on a gentle smile. As soon as you notice your mind drifting just bring it back to the exercise.

2 Imagine being an actor creating a character description for the role of 'your compassionate best', with the qualities you would like to have as a truly compassionate person. It doesn't matter if you don't feel you have these qualities, or don't believe that you're a compassionate person. *Imagine* having them, like an actor stepping into a role.

3 Focus on the specific compassion qualities here. The first quality is a caring commitment and desire to be helpful and contribute to others' wellbeing, holding your friendly facial expression and speaking in a compassionate tone of voice.

4 The second quality of compassion is clarity – the insight and wisdom around knowing that human life can be difficult. Although it's not your fault, you can take responsibility for doing something about your struggles.

5 The third quality of compassion is strength and courage – the stability and grounding from having clarity about the world and

cultivating a calm mind and an inner stability. The ability to keep showing up for yourselves and others, and the courage to act as the person you want to be.

6 Imagine yourself having this caring commitment, to act with clarity and courage, to be thoughtful, helpful, kind and wise. Notice how that feels, seeing yourself as a strong, confident, calm and compassionate person. Consider how you would speak and move in a compassionate way, with a friendly facial expression and warm voice tone. Imagine other people relating to you as a compassionate person, see yourself relating to them in this ideal compassionate way – like you on a really good day. Who do you want to run the show of your life? The more you imagine this person, the more easily you can find these qualities and can express them in the world.

7 Hold in mind the image of this version of you, taking a snapshot which you can keep, then become more aware of the sounds around you, open your eyes and come back to the room.

Summary

- If you're going to master new skills, you need to practise. Yes, it's hard, but do what you can.
- Work with your partner as a team so you can figure out what gets in the way.
- By focusing more on negotiation and compromise rather than winning or sacrifice, you can move towards compassionate goals of caring, clarity and courage to face your difficulties.
- You can develop the compassionate part of you through your imagination and see how it feels in your body.
- Remember that when you're in a good place and learn how to improve yourself, your relationship is more likely to improve as well.

We're now going to practise letting the compassionate part of you flow out to others, including your partner.

8 Compassion flowing out

Letting love and compassion flow to your partner

Here we continue to develop the compassionate part of you, learning to step into the shoes of your compassionate self. What are the fears, blocks and resistances getting in the way of you showing your partner compassion – how have your past experiences influenced you?

The flow of compassion

Remember the three directions compassion can flow in – self to others, others to self, and self to self? In this chapter we're practising the first level, from you to your partner. Set aside any thoughts along the lines of 'but they aren't compassionate to me'. We're not working on a 'tit for tat' principle. Working on changing *you* may be the start to creating a more compassionate climate in your relationship, and helping your partner change as a result.

Go where it feels safe

Hopefully you're in a place where you want to strengthen your relationship with your partner. If it gets challenging, you can ground yourself with your soothing breathing rhythm. If, however, you're feeling angry, resentful and upset with things your partner does or doesn't do turn to Chapter 10 and work your way back to this point, starting with self-compassion and then working towards being able to express compassion for your partner.

Creating a compassionate climate

Most couples say they want a loving, supportive and caring relationship together. This means creating an environment which helps you thrive

– a garden where you can both grow into the best versions of yourselves. 'You on a really good day' means having the caring commitment to look at yourself with kindness, understanding your own struggles and having the wisdom to know that your struggle isn't your fault. It also means having the strength to hold yourself accountable for the things you can influence.

Get some perspective

When you're hurting, it can be really easy to get caught up in anger about what your partner has said or done. It can be hard to let go of the story we tell ourselves: 'He doesn't love me', 'She doesn't care', 'This relationship is doomed'. It's understandable that we withdraw kindness and compassion from someone who has hurt us: 'Why should I be compassionate to her, when all she does is criticise me?'

It's easier to be compassionate with someone we know, like and trust. So, what happens when you don't find yourself filled with warm, tender feelings towards your significant other? Do we give up on loving them when we're angry? Give up on showing them empathy and understanding when they upset us?

As hard as it can be, try to get a little perspective by stepping into your partner's shoes. Once you discover that their manager yelled at them and called them incompetent, it's not surprising they forgot to call you. If their mum is ill in hospital, perhaps it explains why they got the wrong items from the shop for dinner.

Letting go of blaming your partner doesn't mean you can't hold them accountable for mistakes or hurtful words, but it does mean that you do so gently and with compassion and warmth. When you understand what it feels like to walk a mile in their shoes, you can begin to develop compassion for them – and it might mean your partner starts to do more of the same for you. Compassion is contagious – it creates a climate of warmth, trust and respect.

Embodying the compassionate self

In order for you to be a compassionate person, you first have to behave like one – not just in theory or in your imagination. You can bring the compassionate self to life through *method acting* – acting as if in character.

Take a few steps around the room as your compassionate self, noticing how you would stand, hold your body and walk. Where do you look? How fast do you walk? What happens when you speed up? Do you still feel you can be kind, caring and considerate when you're rushing? Experiment with your walk and gaze and see how it feels.

If this is hard for you, go to the website and download the audio track 'Stepping into the shoes of the compassionate self'.

How 'stupid' compassion leaves us empty

You might feel some resistance here. If you're a parent, you might think, 'My compassionate best? Are you kidding? Me on a really good day? I don't HAVE good days – I'm stressed, the baby doesn't sleep, my pre-schooler is hitting and my job is driving me up the wall! How am I supposed to focus on my partner with all that going on? I've got nothing left to give!'

If you have a busy life, working long hours and battling a commute, or have a caring responsibility, you might feel like the container of care is empty, as you have already poured out all the contents in your day-to-day life. Although we *can* care for others without caring for ourselves, we can only do so for a limited time before we burn out. We sometimes refer to this as 'stupid compassion'. That's why any care, kindness and compassion that flows out needs to be *wise* and balanced to be sustainable.

What gets in the way of being compassionate?

Although you might be struggling because you're stretched too thin, there could be other factors stopping you from stepping into your compassionate self. A questionnaire – the 'Fears of Compassion Scale'

– illustrates the beliefs we hold which get in the way of our being compassionate, of accepting compassion and of giving compassion to ourselves.[24]

Try this

Fears of Compassion Scale
Go to the Resources section and complete the first section – *Compassion for others* – and write down any reflections or memories which come up.

Common blocks preventing us from being compassionate to others are based around thinking that others may take advantage of us or that we will be perceived as weak, as well as thoughts that people need to help themselves, or that perhaps they don't 'deserve' compassion. You might feel, for example, that your partner doesn't deserve to receive your kindness and understanding, after the way they have behaved. Developing your compassionate mind doesn't just benefit your relationship; it benefits you, your partner and everybody else around you. We all need compassionate connection in this world of joy and sorrow.

The pieces of the puzzle

What thoughts and emotions came up for you from the Fears of Compassion Scale? If it's difficult to feel compassion for others, remember it's not your fault; the foundations for any negative beliefs were probably laid at an early age and cemented by what you have experienced throughout life.

This is why it's helpful to understand yourself more deeply, laying the pieces of your jigsaw puzzle so you can see why you react the way you do. By making sense of where your emotions have come from in the past, you can find a better path for the future. It's important to lay your partner's puzzle as well, as you can only feel empathy when you see a situation from someone else's perspective. This will bring you both closer together and make compassion flow more naturally in your relationship.

Let's look at the jigsaw puzzle to see how it could help you understand how patterns have arisen in your relationship.

Our past shapes our present and our future

What you've gone through in the past has shaped who you are in the here and now, what you believe in and how you behave.

The way your parents behaved towards each other will have given you a model of what love looks like – or perhaps what it *shouldn't* look like. Even though you might want to do things very differently, you may still find yourself acting out some of their patterns and habits.

Your relationships with schoolfriends, your first dates and early experiences of relationships and love will also have shaped who you are with your partner today – although you might not know how or why. You don't have to be at the mercy of your past; you have the capacity to change the way you deal with your ghosts to build a better future.

Our experiences have shaped the beliefs we have about the world, other people and ourselves. A past partner cheated on you? You may believe that you can't really trust someone not to hurt you, and have developed a fear of being left for someone 'better'. Your parent criticised you? You might fear that you're not good enough, that others will judge or criticise you, which makes the world feel very unsafe. When we feel unsafe, we do everything we can to protect ourselves from further harm – like putting on a suit of armour.

The suit of armour – our best efforts to keep safe

Imagine you're a medieval knight wearing a suit of armour. It's there to keep you safe from arrows and swords; nobody can hurt you. You might have built your own 'suit of armour' over the course of several experiences where you have been hurt.

But when you're not on the battlefield, the suit of armour has many disadvantages. It's hot and uncomfortable. It's clunky and makes moving around difficult, and even worse, nobody can get close to you. Your armour keeps you safe but it also leaves you feeling isolated, lonely and disconnected; the visor may impair your vision and the weight may bear down on you physically and emotionally.

The drawbacks of 'better safe than sorry'

You developed your suit of armour because your mind is very aware of threat and danger to your survival and seeks to protect you from harm: hence the mantra 'better safe than sorry'.

Since our cave-dwelling days we have kept ourselves safe by being on the look-out for danger. Avoiding danger – and therefore death – meant we could survive long enough to reproduce. The better able we were to survive, the stronger we became through the generations, helping us to thrive as a species.

Although this tendency to protect ourselves works well in terms of avoiding threat and harm, it has some drawbacks for our relationships or in our lives. Firstly, we aren't cave dwellers defending ourselves from predators any more. Maybe our threat system is a bit too sensitively wired for the modern world, responding to threats from our memories. We can't help that these fears and doubts show up in our minds, but the threat system often takes us further away from the rich, meaningful life we want to have – and from being the person we want to be.

This is where the concept of 'workability' comes in – how workable it is for us to keep acting in a particular way. Perhaps you keep people at arm's length so you don't get hurt, but the result is that you find it hard to connect more deeply with a partner, and you may miss out on meaningful love and feel isolated. Your partner may even end up leaving you if you're not able to let them in and form that close bond, so your fear of being left ends up being confirmed and your mind tells you 'I told you so, we should have kept our armour on!'.

Has that happened to you in your relationships – that the very thing you were trying to prevent ended up happening? Let's look at how this might work in practice with a couple we'll call 'Susan' and 'Graham'.

Graham's puzzle

Past experiences	Key fears/beliefs	Best efforts to keep safe	Drawbacks
Growing up with an alcoholic mother and an absent father. Received praise when looked after siblings but not much affection when felt pain, fear or sadness. Didn't do well in school, got bullied and dropped out. Dated early, lots of short relation-ships.	I can't rely on others. I have to take care of them. I'm worthless. I'm unlovable. If I show negative feelings, people will reject me. People will leave me.	Only have short relationships – sabotaging relationships when they get serious, leave someone before they leave me (to avoid rejection). Drink alcohol to cope with feelings. Take care of others, even to own detriment.	Don't get to find out that people might find me lovable. Never form a meaningful relationship, feeling lonely. Alcohol dependency, further pushing partners away. Still feel unlovable.

Susan's puzzle

Past experiences	Key fears/ beliefs	Best efforts to keep safe	Drawbacks
Growing up with two loving parents and an older brother. Parents worked hard, but supported with homework and school plays. Praised for excelling academically. Went to Oxford and got a 1st. Late into dating, as focused on school, but found relationships after university. Took a while to get a job after uni.	There is love, but it's conditional upon me doing well. I have to achieve to be worth something. Other people are better than I am. If I criticise myself, other people won't. If I make a mistake, I'll be judged. Fear of failure.	Always trying to be the best at everything. Work long hours to prove worth at work. Not taking time to relax. Prioritising achievement over enjoyment/ pleasure. Criticising self to make sure to not make a mistake. Judgemental of self and others, to keep in check.	No pleasure or fun. Rigidity in relationships, relationships ending. Stressed, burnt out. Feeling worthless. Productivity suffers as energy levels drop. Making mistakes as concentration drops. Confirms belief that I'm 'no good' and has to 'try harder'.

Try this

Your jigsaw puzzle

Fill in as many of the pieces of the puzzle as you can. If possible, ask your partner to help when you think you've finished. Ask your partner to express with kindness what they have observed about your behaviour and your strategies to keep yourself safe. This will help show you how your fears and beliefs play out in the way you behave in your relationship. Ask yourself questions, such as:

- 'What am I doing too much of in my relationship?' (e.g. criticising, avoiding conversations, silent treatment, slamming doors, etc)
- 'What am I not doing enough of in my relationship?' (e.g. sharing my feelings, praising my partner, initiating intimacy, apologising, etc)

Those behaviours would go into the 'best efforts' column. Then consider:

- 'What do I fear would happen if I did more/less of that? What is it protecting me from?' (e.g. being hurt, making mistakes, being left, others seeing that I'm not good enough)

The answers would go into the 'fears' column. It can be hard to do this on your own, as you might not be fully aware of what you're trying to keep yourself safe from. Do what you can.

Past experiences	Key fears/ beliefs	Best efforts to keep safe	Drawbacks

Try this

Your partner's jigsaw puzzle

Can you fill in the pieces of your partner's puzzle? See what you already know and discuss this with your partner to avoid jumping to conclusions.

Past experiences	Key fears/ beliefs	Best efforts to keep safe	Drawbacks

From the sofa

When Greg and Laura got together, it was stormy. Greg would be really into Laura for a while and then withdraw, leaving her guessing whether he wanted to be with her or not. As a result, Laura often felt that Greg wasn't fully committed to the relationship. A number of months in, she told him he had to be either fully dedicated to the partnership or she would end it.

This ultimatum triggered Greg's threat system, fearing that Laura would leave, so he made more promises to her, as he did love her deeply. He feared being found out as not good enough, not lovable, through experiences of rejection in his teens and also feeling unhappy with his body; he had developed a safety strategy of never letting himself get close, never fully committing and keeping his 'options open'. This meant lying to women about his intentions and cheating in every relationship. No wonder Laura was hesitant about whether he was fully committed to their relationship.

When Laura fell pregnant unexpectedly, Greg panicked and had an infidelity. Laura found out and gave him another ultimatum of either working this through or she would leave, with the baby. His behaviour, which on one level had kept him 'safe', confirmed the story he was telling himself about not being good enough, being 'a shit'.

It's hard to be compassionate with someone who has a history of infidelity, and who hurt you when you're vulnerable (pregnancy), but Laura wanted to understand his actions and see if the pattern could be broken. Her curiosity and compassion towards Greg enabled him to hold himself accountable and repair his mistakes, to change the way he would act going forward. He pursued individual therapy to work on his commitment issues, to be the father he wanted to be – present, reliable and trustworthy – and for the couple to work through the fallout from the infidelity.

Being compassionate to Greg didn't excuse his behaviour or tolerate it in future, but it helped Laura let go of safety strategies of checking his phone or asking where he had been. This wasn't the person she wanted to be, but her threat system made her check to feel safe. Laura had experienced Greg's infidelity once before, and it confirmed what her mind had told her as a story 'men can't be trusted, they will just cheat'. Greg working on committing to Laura and getting close helped them both peel off that suit of armour and they connected in a way they never had before. They had their baby and stayed together.

Letting compassion flow out

Choosing to act compassionately towards someone who has hurt you is not easy, so we start where it's easier and less threatening: by directing your compassionate self towards people you love or care for, where there isn't a presence of anger, hurt, disappointment at the same time. Have a go.

Try this: Directing the compassionate self

1 Sitting in a comfortable, upright position with eyes closed, try to slow down your body and mind using the soothing breathing rhythm.

2 Bringing that gentle smile to your face, imagine your compassionate self standing in front of you. Picture what it looks like, how it stands, what it's wearing. Slowly step into this wise, caring and strong version of you and see how it feels.

3 Imagine that you're walking around in your house as your compassionate self. You have that gentle smile, radiating a calm but courageous presence. Visualise now that you're coming up to your partner, standing in front of them. You become aware that something is troubling them, either physically or mentally. Perhaps they're coming down with the flu, or they've had a stressful meeting at work.

4 Being your compassionate self, try directing that flow of compassion towards your partner. What would you say? Listen compassionately without trying to fix their problems; just make space for them. What would you do? Sit down next to them, give them a cuddle or hold their hand? Speak to them in a soothing voice?

5 Sit with this image for a while, just seeing yourself engage with your partner in this way, noticing how it feels to let your love and compassion flow out to them.

How did this practice feel for you – what was it like to send your warmth and compassion towards your partner? How often do you currently make an effort to do this?

Test driving your compassionate self

Go through the coming week and find some opportunities where you can be 'you on a really good day'. Walk down the street as your compassionate self and engage with your partner as your compassionate self. Not 'weak', 'fluffy', 'pitying', but strong and brave, kind and caring, wise and insightful.

- What kind of questions would your compassionate self ask your partner?
- What kind of facial expression would you have if you were on top form?
- What would you do for your partner during the week if you showed up as your compassionate self?

Summary

- By practising being kind, caring and compassionate towards your partner, you're creating a compassionate climate to breathe, grow and thrive in.
- Understanding yourself and your partner is crucial, so use the jigsaw puzzle to gain clarity around what has shaped you to become the people you are today.
- Although strategies to keep you safe work well in the short term, there are drawbacks with unintended consequences for your relationship.

What you have gone through isn't your fault – but it isn't your partner's fault either. Only you are accountable for changing yourself, so practise what you've learned about letting compassion flow out. Next, we will look at practising letting compassion flow in.

9 Compassion flowing in
Noticing, accepting and requesting compassion from others

Time to practise receiving compassion from others. We use a memory of someone being kind to us and explore the fears and barriers around receiving compassion from our partner. We use imagery to develop an inner guide who can show us compassion – our Ideal Compassionate Mentor. They can be there for you even if your partner can't.

Resisting help

'Would you like a cup of tea?' is one of the most commonly used phrases for expressing concern and care for someone: a sign that they're offering you support and kindness.

But consider this scenario: you're sat at your desk in the office and feeling stressed about a deadline or a difficult task. Your colleague comes over and offers to get you a cup of tea or coffee.

> *What would you do if someone offered you an act of kindness like this?*

You may feel uncomfortable about accepting your colleague's offer as you're concerned that they are also behind with their work and so shouldn't be spending their time making you tea. So, you turn it down, saying 'No thank you, I'm fine; I'll get myself one later.'

At times we don't even *notice* when compassion is being shown to us, and at other times we feel too uncomfortable to *accept* it – and it's even rarer for us to *ask* for it. In many ways, we're blocked from receiving the compassion that flows towards us. There are a number of different reasons why this might be happening, either with you or your partner, but it has a big impact on how you behave within your relationship.

Reflection & Connection

Return to the Fears of Compassion Scale in the Resources section and complete *Compassion from others* to gain more clarity around what is blocking you. If you wish, share your answers with your partner and listen mindfully to how they respond to the same questions.

> *How did you feel when you answered those questions?*
>
> *Were you surprised by your answers?*

Some people worry that when they really need their partner's support they won't be there for them. The root of this may be that previous partners have let them down or said something hurtful when they were feeling vulnerable, or that they haven't had their emotional needs met earlier in life.

If you have developed a potential fear of closeness when someone is caring towards you, you might put your guard up. If you're blocked from receiving the flow of compassion it might not just happen with your partner – it could happen with anyone. Your partner may also be blocked in receiving care and kindness from you. Even though you might be trying your hardest to show them compassion, they may not seem to notice – and certainly never thank you for it. What's that all about?

Go back to the jigsaw puzzle and imagine that you had grown up in your partner's home instead of your own – what kind of resistances around noticing, accepting and requesting compassion might you have as a result?

Let's take another look at an example.

From the sofa

Jamie and Luke were at the start of their relationship. Their relationship was open (meaning they could both be with other men if they wished). In their late twenties and openly gay, they had both experienced criticism and rejection as part of coming out to friends and family earlier in their lives. Gay shame was something which weighed heavily on them both.

Jamie often worried that others wouldn't be there for him, or like and love him, if he expressed who he really was, so he held himself back in the relationship and found himself occasionally lying instead of being honest. After an earlier bad relationship the idea that someone could treat him well and offer him kindness felt alien. Luke had also experienced a similar learning history with a previous partner and struggled to let his guard down.

They were both blocked from receiving compassion from each other. When they started to express what they wanted and needed from each other, daring to let the love in, their connection deepened in both an emotional and sexual way.

As time went on, it became clear to both Jamie and Luke that they felt deep love for each other and the need for the open relationship faded away. Both had felt scared to ask for the relationship to be exclusive, out of fear of being rejected. They promised to keep an open mind and listen compassionately if one of them ever wanted to open up the relationship again and see other people.

Aware, Acknowledge, Accept, Appreciate, Ask

In order for us to be able to appreciate and express gratitude for each other, we need to use the mindfulness skills of *noticing*. If you don't notice that your partner has done something kind for you, it's difficult to acknowledge and then appreciate it. If you don't notice your reluctance in letting the love in, it's very difficult to ultimately ask for it.

Just acknowledging ('I saw that you had paid that bill I forgot to deal with') isn't quite enough to elicit emotion for most couples. To make it more powerful, try connecting the gratitude to how it makes you feel, for example, 'I really appreciated that, thank you for picking up the ball when I drop it, it makes me feel really supported.' Remember it as the Five As – *Awareness*, *Acknowledgement*, *Acceptance*, *Appreciation* and *Asking*.

Awareness of compassion flowing in

Awareness isn't just about noticing what your partner does for you, it's also about becoming aware of your own blocks and resistances. Some partners simply don't notice when kindness or compassion is being offered or they refuse to take it in, which then means they don't necessarily feel very grateful. By being sensitive to the experiences that have shaped your partner and the fears that may have generated, we can practise taking in appreciation. Use that spotlight of attention and shine it on what your partner says to you.

Acknowledging compassion flowing in

This incorporates a mindfulness skill called 'labelling': you simply need to try to label what you see. First, you need to be aware of when your partner has done something nice, then acknowledge that you have seen it. Your partner isn't a mind reader; they don't know that you have spotted their act of kindness. 'I saw that you folded the laundry, that's helpful, thank you', or 'Thank you for trying to cheer me up last night, it was so nice to get my mind off work.'

Accepting compassion flowing in

How did you react the last time your partner paid you a compliment – what was the first thing which popped into your mind? That they're just trying to be nice and don't really mean it, that they want something, or that they have done something bad and are trying to make up for it? These are common thoughts which block kindness coming in. Let's take it deeper. Say that your partner offered you genuine support with something you're struggling with, such as preparing a pitch for work. Would you turn them down, feeling embarrassed about needing the help? If you have beliefs around self-reliance – 'I need to manage on my own at all times', or negative beliefs around your self-worth, 'I don't deserve it' – then you might be blocked in accepting the help and love. What do you think the impact will be on your relationship if you strive to always manage on your own and don't accept the compassion flowing in?

Appreciating compassion flowing in

Taking the time to appreciate what you have noticed and labelled is the next step. Pointing out three things about each other which you appreciate can help the mind to be collaborative and caring rather than competitive, and some really tender moments can follow. The connection which comes from gratitude and appreciation is really important, especially between couples.

Ask for compassion to flow in

This is the hardest step, and is shaped by societal norms. Men have pressure to not appear 'weak' and often don't ask for help when needing it, and women can assume that asking for help means 'failure', not being good enough. Reaching out to your partner for help can trigger these beliefs as well, as can the age-old 'They should just know what I need without me having to ask'.

Soothing your threat system

The flow of compassion which goes unnoticed the most tends to be the flow coming in. If we were able to be more aware as to how our partner feels about us, to really get the warmth and empathy, to see ourselves like our partners often see us, it would soothe our threat system. Validation from others is very powerful, making us feel accepted and allowing us to feel what we feel.

If it's too threatening to experience compassion from others at this point, remember to soothe yourself using the breathing rhythm you've practised. Start small, perhaps accepting that cup of tea from a colleague, or asking for directions from a stranger in the street, then work your way up to people who you might find it harder to dare to rely on. Remember that we're built for nurture and we want to belong with others. Letting that guard down will help you get a closer and longer-lasting connection with others.

My story

Deep down, I know my husband is my biggest fan, but sometimes I get caught up in my threat system and forget that he respects me and wants me to do well and be happy. My husband knows it can be hard for me to take on board certain kinds of praise or affection, so he lets me just sit with it until I'm ready.

The classic example for us is the non-hugging hug. This is essentially my husband coming up to me, putting his arms around me, holding me until I eventually lift my arms to hug him back. There's no pressure for me to hug back. By doing this, he shows me he loves me even when I'm not my best self or when I have made mistakes or when I'm struggling in some way. It's very powerful. I have to practise receiving his compassion without questioning why he's giving it. If you struggle with that too, you're in good company.

Once I was at home with a sickness bug, and my husband called from work to ask if I needed him to get our child from childcare and do bedtime, instead of going out in the evening. I noticed the stories I was telling myself; that it would be selfish to ask him to come home and that I needed to be really, really sick to ask for help. I decided to practise being compassionate towards myself and allow my husband's compassion to flow in.

Remember that compassion is the sensitivity to the suffering of others, with a commitment to alleviate it, or 'what we do when shit gets real'. My husband knows it's hard to manage a young child when you're sick (sensitivity). He was moved by my distress and decided to do something about it (commitment). I accepted his offer to come home early and help with bedtime and noticed the thoughts and the feelings of guilt but decided not to listen to them. We don't have to make those guilty thoughts 'go away' or suppress them – we can notice and drop an anchor, so we can sit with them.

Holding in mind when our partners have been compassionate towards us is really important, as it can soothe our threat systems even when our partners are nowhere near us – through the power of visualisation and memory.

Try this

Memory of your partner being compassionate and kind to you

Part 1 You might argue about little things, shout, or disagree about how to parent your children, or when to see the in-laws. It can be helpful to stop to consider what you do like about your partner, and not just what you don't like.

1 Start tuning into the soothing breathing rhythm with eyes closed and a gentle smile on your face, to help you calm down and focus on kindness. Scan down through the body and let go of any tension. Soften and release.

2 Bring to mind a memory of a time your partner looked after you, doing something caring and kind. It can be a long time ago; it can be recent. Try to pick something that wasn't too upsetting, but when you know that they were there for you. It can also be a happy time when you felt loved and cared for by your partner.

3 Try to think back to that time, and really 'see' your partner. They're being warm and caring towards you. Try to focus on their facial expression in that moment. How can you see that love on their face?

4 Doing this can be hard, because you might have a range of emotions about your partner. You might be really sad, or angry or resentful

about the things they do or don't do, thinking of times where they haven't supported you – just notice and acknowledge those thoughts, then try to let them go and focus on the time when they were kind and loving. We're not trying to replace those difficult feelings with the feeling of gratitude – we're just trying to allow both sides in. You can be mad at your partner *and* love them at the same time.

5 In that memory, what are they doing to show their care for you? Maybe they're giving you a hug after a stressful time at work or telling you to get some rest if you're ill. If you're a parent, maybe this memory is from before you had children, of how kind you used to be to each other when you were dating and didn't have the stress of managing a family together.

6 Pay attention to their tone of voice, if they're saying something kind or caring. What does that tone of voice sound like? What little words do they use to show you they love you, and *how* do they say them?

See if you can sit with this image and the feeling of being loved and cared for a little while longer. Keep breathing in that smooth, calming rhythm and try to remember that gentle smile on your face.

Part 2 Letting this memory fade, now think of any acts of care or kindness your partner has done towards you in the past week. Anything they did that you appreciated, that you would maybe like to see more of. Whatever it was that your partner did, or didn't, do, see if you can feel a sense of appreciation about that time.

It can be helpful to continue to reflect on this even beyond this exercise, to give you that sense of balance and help you show appreciation for the things you *do* like about your partner. It will make them more likely to do those things in the future – like you, your partner probably also wants to feel appreciated, heard and understood.

This is tricky to practise, especially when our relationship is strained, so do what you can. If you're going through a rocky patch this may feel hard, but when we focus on the positive emotions we can often find some healing in those struggles and help in moving towards the kind of partner we want to be and the kind of relationship we want to have.

If you don't feel able or ready to accept compassion from your partner visualisation can help you create a place where you can feel validated, supported and held – your inner team of support.

Your inner compassionate team

Your partner cannot be everything you need them to be, at all times. They can try to be compassionate, caring and supportive, but they're not responsible for your happiness. They're not always there. Your partner might not be able to tolerate everything you have to say without judgement; they're human and flawed, just like you. At a time when you have shared something difficult, they may say the wrong thing. They may feel overwhelmed by your sadness, or your fear, or your anger. It may trigger their threat system when you're in yours; you may then feel let down, disappointed, alone, and it may not be anyone's 'fault'. It's just the reality of relationships – they will get it wrong at times, as will you.

Therefore, we create an inner support team to turn to at times where our outer support may not be able to meet our needs. Practising this, you can soothe and comfort yourself in your pain, and might even be able to come back to your partner again in a way which deepens your connection with them and helps them help you. It will take the pressure off your partner to be perfect – they're not your saviour and cannot heal all your wounds. We have to create something else which can act as such an ideal compassionate nurturer – an inner mentor.

Your ideal compassionate mentor

Imagine a teacher you had in school, who was supportive and cared about you doing well. One who understood how to motivate you, cheer you on when you succeeded and help you get unstuck when you struggled, without judgement for your mistakes. Imagine if you had a teacher like that for yourself, but on the *inside*? That is your ideal compassionate mentor – a guide or coach who will be there for you in times of need.

Together with your compassionate self, this inner mentor forms a nice compassionate team for you to rely on.

Choosing who is on your inner team

When developing your inner mentor be careful who you choose to model this guide on. Some people choose their partner, as they may be supportive in real life. Unfortunately your partner isn't perfect and cannot be compassionate to you at all times; they will make mistakes and mess it up. So, what happens if you choose to have one of your outer team members on your inner team as well, if on that day you happen to have an argument with your partner? Feeling threatened, angry and upset, you're looking to soothe yourself and bring to mind your ideal compassionate inner mentor . . . and there's your partner! That's not going to work.

That's why we try not to choose *actual* people from your outer world. We can, however, choose traits or qualities from people we know. You can draw upon the wise advice you used to get from your grandmother for an inspiration; but if you actually pick your grandmother, and she has sadly passed away, your visualisation might trigger not only a comforting soothing, but also a sadness or grief from the loss.

Care, clarity and courage all rolled into one

We need to endow the inner mentor with the same caring commitment, wisdom and strength of the compassionate self, simply because those are the three legs of the stool on which compassion sits.

Try this: Your inner mentor

Use the audio to help you really get into this exercise.

1 Start by connecting with your soothing breathing rhythm and the safe place imagery, using your five senses. What you can see, hear, smell, taste and touch when you imagine being in a place which makes you feel calm, safe and relaxed.

2 Imagine an inner nurturing being who shows care, commitment, clarity and courage. This being is being genuinely caring towards you, is wise and has clarity into how the world and our brains work, and the courage and strength to keep showing up for you. It's reliable, dependable and able to stay with you whatever you bring up.

3 The inner mentor can have a human or animal form, or be a natural phenomenon like a mist, a cloud or a tree. If you pick an animal, it may be that it's able to take on some characteristics such as a human voice – anything goes. Pay attention to how your inner mentor speaks to you, the tone of voice it uses, its posture, the way it moves and finally, its facial expression (if it has a face). All to show you how compassionate it is towards you.

4 How does it feel to be in the presence of your inner mentor? To be guided by them in life when you're struggling? Remember that the inner *mentor* is not an inner *tormentor*; it will not criticise you for your mistakes, but gently hold you accountable for how you treat yourself and your partner.

How was this exercise for you? If you struggle to receive compassion in real life, it can be helpful to practise this with your inner mentor. Imagining them being kind to you, and tolerating how that feels, can help you also to accept love from your partner.

Summary

- Some of the time we don't even notice when compassion is given; some of the time we feel too uncomfortable to accept it; a lot of the time we struggle to ask for it.
- Your partner cannot be your everything, at all times. They're human and will make mistakes, just like you.
- Instead of putting a lot of pressure on your partner to perfectly meet all your needs, you can create an inner nurturing guide, or mentor, to help you in times of need.

Next we dive deeper into helping you both become more compassionate with yourselves: *self-compassion.*

10 Compassion for yourself

Being kinder to yourself helps you also be there for others

Being kinder to yourself isn't good just for *you*, it's also good for your *relationship* – it helps you be your compassionate best with your partner. In this chapter we learn how to bring the compassionate self together with the compassionate inner mentor, find out what's stopping you from being kinder to yourself and what you would stand to 'lose' if you let go of self-criticism.

Permission to be kind to yourself

This is where the work gets harder – where the temperature rises – so be kind to yourself and allow yourself the permission to *do what you can*. Stay with it, even if it's hard; if it feels overwhelming ease off and use your grounding skills of mindfully noticing sounds or sensations, the soothing breathing rhythm and safe place imagery. You can then choose to return for a bit more when you're ready.

My job is to gently challenge you to try new things and move towards the relationship connection you want, even when it involves things which aren't so comfortable. We can step out of our comfort zones and challenge ourselves, but we do so with compassion. Turn to your partner here and dare to lean on each other if it feels upsetting – don't let this introduction scare you off!

Let's begin by teasing out what self-compassion actually is.

What is self-compassion (and what is self-care)?

Self-compassion involves connecting to your caring, nurturing capacity and directing that flow of compassion towards yourself; treating yourself with the same kindness and care as you would a friend or family member you love.

It involves the two aspects of compassion mentioned previously: *a sensitivity to the suffering* and a *commitment to alleviate it*. Self-compassion means noticing and making sense of your pain and suffering. Instead of engaging in self-blame and self-pity, you want to do something to help yourself. Self-pity keeps you stuck in wallowing, feeling sorry for yourself. At best you might be avoiding taking action to care for yourself; at worst be engaging in action to be destructive to yourself. Self-compassion includes compassionate acts for your own wellbeing, asking yourself 'How can I be helpful, not harmful, to myself?'

Self-care, on the other hand, is often described as a set of things you're *doing* to look after yourself. This connects to the caring *motivation* of self-compassion, so it can be said that self-care sits under the broader umbrella of self-compassion. However, if we think of self-compassion as the same as self-care, we're missing out on the richness of self-compassion. Turning towards yourself with kindness, empathy and compassion isn't just about actions you take, it's about the motivation of wanting yourself to be well, wanting to be able to face your own difficulties and overcome them. If you engage in self-care activities with a competitive or critical motivation, it's not self-compassionate.

Self-care fuelled by threat or vitality?

Have you ever thought 'I should make myself eat [insert healthy food item], it's good for me'? Yes? Even though you really don't like the taste of it? There is a risk that self-care becomes prescriptive and rule-governed if you just do it because 'it's good for you', rather than tuning into your care-giving system and choosing to do it as a way to nourish yourself. Eating kale or fibre or chia seeds may well be good for you (I'm not telling you not to follow a healthy diet – quite the opposite). Rather, consider what the driving force is behind your healthy food choices or exercise regimes. Are you trying to shame yourself into shape? Are you trying to force yourself into being healthy?

Consider the three circles model again, of threat, drive and soothing. Choosing to do things which are self-compassionate, acts of real self-care, means activating your drive system as well as your soothing system. Without the drive system, you wouldn't get anything done. You wouldn't decide to cook a healthy meal, to move your body or get to bed on time for a good rest. But we need to look at the motivation *behind* the action. Is it about genuine care for yourself, or is it fuelled by the threat system? 'If I don't exercise, I'll get really fat and disgusting' is not the same as 'I would like to go to that dance class, I really love moving to great music, it makes me feel alive.' Body shaming yourself as a way to get going with exercise is not based on self-compassionate motivation, it's done with an intention of being punitive, coming from a self-critical space. The first is about fear and anxiety, the second is about vitality and joy. 'I need to go to bed on time or I'll be useless and fail tomorrow' is not the same as 'I'm going to put my phone down earlier tonight, so my body can get some quality rest.'

A compassionate motivation is focused on us flourishing and thriving, a combination of the drive and soothing system. A competitive or critical motivation is about a threat-infused drive, generating stress and a lack of vitality and purpose. So, before you dive into self-care practices be really curious about your motivation and intention.

How do these different statements resonate with you? Are your self-care actions driven by vitality or by threat? If they're driven purely by threat, is your self-care then a truly self-compassionate act?

Why self-compassion is good for your relationship

If you aren't well, your relationship is less likely to be well, as you cannot give what you haven't got. If you're feeling run down and depleted, it's hard to act in line with your values as a partner. It's hard to be your compassionate best with your partner if you're unkind to yourself – and you're more likely to be snappy, irritable and unfair as a result. If you're physically or mentally unwell it may even have a negative impact on your relationship. If you can practise being compassionate with yourself and replenish yourself through self-care, it will benefit your relationship connection too. Self-care is couples care.

Try this: Using the compassionate self to give yourself compassion

1 Get into the usual upright posture with the gentle smile and your feet on the floor. Engage with the soothing breathing rhythm and perhaps visualise your safe place. Let go of tension and relax into it. Don't skip this bit – we need to warm up body and mind before practising new skills.

2 Once your breathing has slowed to a comfortable rhythm, imagine your compassionate self in front of you. Stepping into the compassionate self, you now embody this version of you who has clarity about the world and about you, who cares deeply about you and others, and who is courageous and strong enough to face your difficulties.

3 Take your compassionate self for a walk in your mind, using the friendly facial expression and eye contact, the upright and strong posture, the soothing breathing and the calm walk, embodying you at your compassionate best.

4 Visualise a picture of yourself when you're having a hard time. Not the worst struggle you have ever been in, but a problematic issue you're currently facing. You're looking in on yourself, through the eyes of your compassionate self. What do you see? How does it make you feel to see yourself in distress?

5 Try directing compassion towards the version of you who is in pain, facing a difficulty. What would you say to yourself, as your compassionate self? The compassionate self doesn't blame and shame, but helps you to hold yourself gently accountable.

6 In this moment of time, given all that you know about yourself and the world, doesn't it make sense that you feel the way you do right now?

7 In this moment of time, given all the strength and courage you have as your compassionate self, what would be helpful to do towards yourself right now, to help you face your difficulties?

8 Perhaps imagine yourself sitting next to the version of you who is in pain, holding an arm around yourself and giving yourself warmth and support? Perhaps there are reassuring words to offer yourself, to take the blame and pressure off? Perhaps there are no words, just a peaceful acceptance of you in this moment, with all your feelings being OK as they are. Anything goes here, as long as your compassionate self approaches the struggling you without judgement or criticism.

9 Sit with this image in your mind's eye as long as you wish, breathing calmly. When you feel ready, draw the exercise to a close.

How did this feel, to be kind and caring towards yourself? Did this bring up any blocks or fears, thoughts like 'you don't deserve this kindness'?

Did you find your mind keep wandering off? Let's take a look at that – sometimes tuning out of an experience is a common strategy for keeping ourselves safe if we feel threatened or overwhelmed. So, make sure to use all your compassionate skills to soothe yourself.

The oxygen mask gives sustainable compassion

Professor Paul Gilbert talks about how being compassionate to others without caring for yourself is like jumping into the water to save someone from drowning, and realising mid-jump that you cannot swim. Yes, it takes a lot of courage and strength to jump in, and it definitely takes a caring commitment, as you care about saving this other person's life. But is it *wise* to jump in despite not being able to swim? No – you both might drown. At that point, jumping in is not *sustainable compassion.*

A common piece of advice around self-care is to 'Put on your own oxygen mask first', which comes from the safety demonstration before a flight. Parents are instructed to pull down their mask and place it over their own face before helping their child. Why do you think that is? Surely our children are most important, and we should help them first? In fact, it's the opposite, because if you pass out, who will help your child? This is a useful mantra to remember when you need permission to look after yourself in a self-compassionate way.

You could even say 'Put on your own *oxytocin mask* first, before you put it on your partner', because if *you a*ren't feeling safe and soothed, how can you connect with your partner in a safe and soothing way?

A lot of people are very kind and caring towards others, but forget about themselves. Parents, teachers, health professionals, carers, emergency service staff . . . the list goes on. These people may be susceptible to burnout, depression, stress, anxiety and fatigue: not putting on their own oxygen mask first before they help to put the mask on others.

It's important to note that you're not just looking after yourself *in order* to look after others – you need to be kind to yourself because you deserve to be well. Being able to be kind to others is an important effect stemming from you being well, but that is a worthy goal in itself.

You might logically agree, 'Of course I should look after myself' – but what's stopping you? Why aren't you doing it? Often it's because fear gets in the way of you filling up your own cup.

Fears, blocks and resistances to self-compassion

Coming back to the Fears of Compassion Scale from the Resources section, complete the third section on compassion from self to self, to get some more clarity of what is blocking you. If you wish, share your answers with your partner and listen mindfully to how they filled in theirs.

You might fear that something bad will happen if you're compassionate to yourself, like 'I'll lose my motivation if I'm no longer beating myself up to get stuff done', or 'I'll be lazy and complacent if I take the pressure off myself', or 'If I forgive myself for the mistakes I make in my relationship, I'll make the same mistakes again.' Or it might be about struggling to tolerate the feeling of being kind to yourself. It might bring up a sense of sadness, of how you haven't been treating yourself with kindness before, or grief over how others have treated you badly in the past. One client once told me 'I've never been kind to myself, I don't know how to do it, and if I start now, I'll open the floodgates and fall apart.' Another client told me they had been cultivating a 'passionate unkindness' towards themselves for so long it was almost impossible to unhook from this mantra of having to be cruel to themselves. A third client has said 'I don't deserve being kind to myself, not after how I have acted.'

I have collected so many stories over the years of supporting high-striving, ambitious people with elements of perfectionism, who all have had a harsh inner critical voice saying that they can't allow themselves the 'luxury of compassion'. That it would be a sign of weakness to look after oneself, it would be fluffy and soft – a signal that you're failing. Daring to prioritise yourself and setting boundaries around how you're treating yourself or allowing others to treat you takes courage and strength. So, stay with me, even if this is hard; it just means we're exactly where we need to be.

Coming back to your jigsaw puzzle, how can you make sense of your own fears, blocks and resistances to giving yourself compassion? How can you make sense of your partner's blocks?

You can show yourself empathy and validate these blocks, understanding why it makes complete sense that you're struggling with this. Self-compassion, much like compassion, sits in the middle of threat, drive and soothing. Starting to figure out why you might not have been kind to yourself might activate your threat system. You'll need to engage your drive system in order to take compassionate action for yourself, and reconnect with your soothing system through the aspects of rest, recovery and reconnection.

Strengthening self-compassion

Building on the idea of treating yourself with kindness when you're struggling, we will now learn how to use another skill, a loving kindness meditation.

Try this: Self-compassionate break

Bring to mind a challenging difficulty you're going through. Sitting upright, start your soothing breathing rhythm and channel your inner authority, your compassionate self. Then place your hand over your heart and try to deepen and slow down the breath.

See if you can say to yourself:

> *This is really hard for me right now, the pain I'm going through.*
>
> *It's really hard to be human – I'm not alone in struggling at times.*
>
> *May I be helpful, not harmful, to myself.*
>
> *I can do hard things if I'm kind to myself.*

Repeat this exercise a few times and see what themes are showing up for you, what stories in the mind you're getting caught up in.

Compassionate letter-writing

Using various ways of directing the flow of compassion you're cultivating a different way of relating to yourself, in a caring and supportive way. Journalling is becoming more popular, for personal growth, for reflection, to slow down your thinking, and to get some distance between you and your thoughts (simply because you can't *write* as quickly as you can *think*).

This is not just writing down positive affirmations to yourself such as 'I'm awesome'. Research has shown that positive affirmations don't work for the people who need them the most. Even if they buy into it logically ('I know I have years of experience, so I'm qualified enough'), they might not *feel* any different ('I still feel like an imposter'). This is known as the *head and heart lag*, where you can understand something logically, but it won't sink down to the emotional level. Professor Paul Gilbert established this 'lag' between the way you *think* about yourself and the way you *feel* about yourself. This is why writing a compassionate letter can be so helpful, because it stimulates emotion, not just logic. There's a big difference between telling yourself 'of course I deserve the kind of compassion I would give to my best friend' and truly believing it on an emotional level.

Writing a compassionate letter to yourself

Remember that compassion is:

> *. . . a sensitivity to the suffering of self and others,*
> *with a commitment to try to alleviate it and prevent its return.*

The letter you're going to write to yourself needs to express both concern and empathy; an understanding of your pain. If you're *sensitive* to what hurts, you can gently consider what would be helpful for you to do to *alleviate* your pain. This isn't about beating yourself with a stick – it's about giving yourself gentle, loving kindness. By doing this, you can start to both face and tolerate your feelings, so they don't linger as long as they would if you kept pushing them down and telling yourself off for having them. Remember, what you resist tends to persist.

The letter is:

- Warm, caring and empathetic
- Supporting you to face your difficulties
- Gently holding you accountable for your actions

The letter is not:

- An opportunity to shame yourself
- Avoiding the challenges in your life
- 'Letting you off the hook' for things you have done

Try this: Your self-compassionate letter

These steps are adapted from Chris Irons and Elaine Beaumont's book *The Compassionate Mind Workbook*.

Step 1 Engaging your compassionate mind
It's important that you 'warm up' first with some soothing breathing, perhaps using an audio clip to guide you into your compassionate self.

Step 2 Motivation – why am I writing this letter?
Remember the mantra 'may I be helpful, not harmful' as your motivation behind the letter. This will help you watch out for interference from your inner critic.

Step 3 Beginning the letter and identifying a difficulty
Direct the letter to yourself, either write it as 'Hello (your name)' or 'Dear me' – see what feels good for you. Then start acknowledging, without judgement and criticism, what problems or difficulties you're facing.

> *Dear Fabienne,*
>
> *I know the last few months have been really tough on you, having had so many arguments with your husband and worrying about your marriage ending.*

Step 4 Validation and empathy for the struggle

Acknowledge how hard things have been for you and how understandable it is that you feel this way.

> *I know you're really struggling right now, and anyone would in your situation. It can feel really unsettling to worry about your marriage, wondering if you'll make it through this rough patch. There's also a lot of pressure on you right now, with the decision about selling the house.*

Step 5 Understanding of your attempts to manage your threat system – not your fault

After validating how you feel, also validate how you've been acting as a response to your feelings, knowing that your brain selects these protective strategies (fight-flight-freeze-appease) for you, based on what has shaped you in life.

> *It's understandable that you're irritable because of the stress you're under at work, so no wonder you have been snapping more at your husband. I know you often think that everyone else has a perfect marriage, and that you're failing. I understand why you're so hard on yourself, and how that makes you even more irritable. That isn't your fault – you've always snapped at others to manage how you're feeling.*

Step 6 Taking responsibility and exploring how to help

You didn't choose the fuel and heat you bring to the fire, but they are your responsibility to handle. Remember what is helpful and not harmful. Here you can commit to more compassionate thoughts and actions.

> *It might be helpful to consider how lots of couples go through hard times – you're not alone. And to remind yourself of the challenging time you went through when your child was little. You got through that, and it made you stronger. Maybe there is something you can do to take the load off at work, to feel more like yourself again. See what your inner mentor would say right now, knowing that you're often hard on yourself. Maybe try to open up to Mike about the strain you're under,*

so he can understand why you sometimes lose your patience. I know you think that this will be the end of your marriage, but it may not be as bad as you think.

Step 7 Working with blocks, fears and resistances

This is where you include a bit of clarity around anticipated obstacles, by being mindful of how you could get stuck with these changes or return to old patterns of behaving.

That's one thing to be extra aware of – you have a tendency to hold on more to the negatives than the positives, through no fault of your own, so keep an eye out for those thoughts around how 'your marriage is over'. That might make you feel hopeless and give up trying, and nothing will change. Also be aware of the inner critic saying that you're not trying hard enough.

Step 8 Compassionate commitment to change

The last point of your letter involves how you support yourself through the process of making these changes, making sure to encourage yourself to carry on.

Start by taking some small steps, perhaps reaching out to your manager at work first. I know it's hard, but I've got your back and we'll do this together. Focus on how you want your marriage to be and I'll help you to have those tough conversations with Mike.

Step 9 Compassionately reading the letter to yourself

When you have finished writing your letter, try reading it out aloud to yourself, from your compassionate self or your compassionate inner mentor. Using the warm tone of voice, read through it slowly to really feel the words and your intention. If it's relevant to you, you can also try reading your letter out to your partner. For some, it's hard to write a compassionate letter to themselves, so they start by expressing how hard it is to write it. That can get the letter started.

From the sofa

Sofia and Michael's different communication styles made it tricky for them in their relationship, making them very flammable. Sofia would use a harsh tone to express something she wanted Michael to change, through no fault of her own. She had experienced lots of negativity and hurt from others in her life and had learned that this is how you address people in order to keep safe. It would get Michael into a defensive position before she had finished talking, simply because of her tone of voice and body language.

Michael, on the other hand, would often roll his eyes, shake his head or laugh while Sofia was talking about something vulnerable, as he felt threatened. That further fuelled Sofia's threat by making her feel invalidated and ashamed, and made her ramp up even more. When they noticed these patterns in couples therapy, they each needed to address their own challenges with self-compassion. After practising soothing themselves, Sofia wrote a compassionate letter to herself to make sense of her learning history, expressing compassion for the pain she tried to navigate in her life and the resulting strong emotional outbursts. Michael wrote a compassionate letter about why it made sense that he would react so strongly to Sofia, given his rather cold upbringing. They could then write letters to each other, turning towards each other with more compassion, having been able to soothe their own threat first. Sofia felt more validated and Michael felt less overwhelmed. It took a lot of emotional regulation skills, of calm breathing, taking breaks and physically moving apart to cool down, but it helped them share tender moments of being more authentic and vulnerable, understanding each other's history and why they would be so flammable together. The deepest insight for this couple was that the most compassionate thing they could do for each other, and themselves, was to go their separate ways. They did so amicably, hopefully with enough insight to not replicate the same patterns in another relationship.

Summary

- Self-compassion is a broader concept than self-care.
- Self-care is the activity you engage in so you can look after yourself, while self-compassion is the caring motivation behind acts of self-nourishment.
- Treating yourself with kindness and compassion helps to strengthen the connection between you and your partner too, because self-care is couples care.
- Writing a compassionate letter to yourself can help you start believing it emotionally as well.

You may still be feeling resistant to the idea of treating yourself with kindness and compassion. Next I'm going to introduce you to your inner critic and help you to stop trying to fight fire with fire. Come on – you can do this.

11 Compassion for the inner critic

Understanding the critical part of you so it no longer runs the show

Your *'inner critic'* is that harsh and hostile inner voice that criticises you for the choices you make and the way you behave. Sometimes it's full of fear and doubt, questioning whether you're good enough and have what it takes to do something challenging – fearing that you'll fail if you try. At other times it's angry, vicious and punitive, berating you for something you've said or done. Sometimes the inner critic is more subtle – you may not even realise that it's there, providing a negative running commentary in the background. No matter how it shows up, your inner critic is difficult to ignore.

Your inner critic

Here are some of the things your inner critic typically comes out with:

- 'You're not good enough'
- 'Others can do this – what's wrong with you?'
- 'You'll fail, you'll mess it up'
- 'You're worthless'
- 'Nobody wants to be with you'
- 'You don't deserve it'
- 'If they really knew who you are, they would leave you'

How does it make you feel to read that? Do you recognise these harsh statements? If not, perhaps it's because your inner critic is sneakier than that, less hostile or extreme, so you may be hearing:

- 'You didn't try hard enough'
- 'You need to finish this before you deserve to take a break'

- 'If only you were as attractive as that person'
- 'You need to earn more money'
- 'You should lose some weight'
- 'Wow, that didn't go well, did it? Well, what did you expect?'

The inner critic is such a common phenomenon that researchers have put together scales that measure the experience of this kind of negative self-talk. Details are listed in the Resources section.

The common humanity behind the Imposter Syndrome

The inner critic is often a feature of what is called the *Imposter Syndrome.* Dr Jessamy Hibberd covers this in her book, *The Imposter Cure*, explaining how this syndrome is related to a fear of failure, a fear of being found out as a 'fraud' and putting any successes due to luck rather than giving credit to skill and hard work.[25] It can be reassuring to know that the imposter syndrome affects up to 70 per cent of us, so 'syndrome' isn't really a helpful way of describing it – maybe it's just part of being human: our *common humanity.*

Our complicated brains have the capacity to be aware of ourselves and how we come across to others, as well as a deep fear of being rejected and outcast. No wonder that those fears would show up if you're about to do something which others could criticise.

The form of your inner criticism

To be able to soften your inner critical voice and the pain it causes, you first need to become aware of how it works for you. Use your spotlight of attention to notice the negative self-talk going on in your head.

- What kind of things do you tend to beat yourself up over?
- When you're being hard on yourself, what words or phrases come up?
- How do you feel after you've given yourself a hard time?
- What tone of voice does the critical part of you use?

What does your self-criticism look like?

Does your inner critic have a go at you after you've made a mistake or does it belittle you before you even try to do something?

Self-criticism as the attacker and the attacked

Within Compassion Focused Therapy, we talk about the double impact of the threat generated from self-criticism. When you criticise yourself, you engage your threat system as you're *being attacked* by your inner critical voice. You're also engaging your threat system because you're the one *doing the attacking*. You're simultaneously *the bully* and *the bullied*, which is incredibly stressful for both your body and mind.

Imagine that you're telling your partner off for being late to a brunch date, calling them 'lazy' and 'useless' because they missed their alarm going off. It's stressful for your partner to be on the receiving end of such mean words, but it's also stressful for your body to be in that attacking state. Now imagine that it's *you* who has made the mistake and you're directing this attack towards yourself: you're both the attacker and the attacked.

You've learned that the activation of the threat system blocks compassion because it orientates your mind towards defensive strategies. If you're attacking yourself, it's stressful to the point where you might do anything to 'get rid' of it. Some people drink, others overeat, some numb out with TV or mindlessly scrolling on their phones. The desire to follow that inner critical voice can even lead to physical self-harm.

In her TEDx talk from 2013, *The Space Between Self-esteem and Self-compassion,* researcher Kristin Neff explores this double whammy of threat. To date, this TEDx talk has been viewed 1.3 million times on YouTube. What does that tell you about how many of us are seeking an answer as to why we do this to ourselves?

Why do we put ourselves down?

If self-criticism didn't serve any *function* whatsoever, you would have let go of it by now. It's giving you something, like a reward, or protecting you from something you want to escape from.

So, what reward does your inner critic get for criticising you? Say that it kept telling you off for taking breaks, kept calling you lazy, and making you stay up late to get a project finished for work – then your inner critic might be rewarded for how it has treated you, through the praise you receive from your boss for meeting the deadline. This means you're not only statistically likely to finish your work on time again, but also to do so through that harsh self-punishing way of motivating yourself to work. The inner critic might conclude 'See, I told you it would impress your boss if you just got off your arse.' The reward was the praise you received, even at the cost of your own exhaustion.

What is the inner critic avoiding by beating you up? Often what lies behind the put-down we give ourselves is *fear* – fear of being rejected, fear of being vulnerable (and getting hurt), fear of being inferior and fear of being alone. Your inner critic is trying to protect you from these fears coming true, but it does so in a harsh and unhelpful way. If I tell myself off for an inappropriate comment I made at a dinner party, I might either not do it again or I might apologise to not risk losing those friends. The criticism is protecting me from being rejected, so what's the problem? The punishment doesn't fit the crime. The inner critic is often giving you a harder time than others would, judging yourself more than others would judge you.

The inner critic is trying to protect you

The function of self-criticism is to protect you from having your fears realised, but this only succeeds in keeping the negative talk going. In their research, Gilbert, Clarke, Hempel, Miles and Irons found two categories of functions of self-criticism; one is to try to improve the self and stop the self from making mistakes, and the other involves expressing anger and wanting to harm the self.[26] For example:

To prevent me getting lazy or complacent
'If I don't push myself really hard, I'll stop trying and won't get anywhere.'

To stop me getting 'too big for my boots'
'If I don't tell myself off, I'll become boastful and arrogant.'

To stop me hurting others
'If I don't tell myself off, I'll act like a selfish idiot to people.'

To stop others hurting me
'If I criticise myself first, others can't say anything about me I don't already know.'

To stop me making mistakes
'If I keep pointing out my flaws, I'll be really on it.'

To make me achieve and be successful
'If I kick myself into shape, I'll get more done.'

To stop me being a failure
'If I constantly second-guess myself, I'll spot mistakes before they happen.'

Reflection & Connection

Sit down with your partner and discuss what you've learned so far: try to find the courage to share. Odds are that each of you has an inner critical voice, but it might show up in different ways. Once you've discussed how negative self-talk affects each of you, reflect on this:

What would happen if you didn't have your inner critical voice any more?

What do you fear will happen if you no longer tell yourself off?

Try this: The shape of your inner critic

Because this critical voice is inside our heads, it's hard to see it as self-critical and unhelpful; you might hear it in a way which makes it sound like gospel. If we can imagine the inner critical as an external being, it's easier to relate to it differently. Imagine what your inner critic might look like.

- What size is it, big or small?
- Is it a human, an animal, an entity?
- Is it you, or someone you know?
- What facial expression does it have?
- If it has a voice, what does that sound like?
- What emotions is it directing at you, like fear, anger, shame?
- How do you feel in the presence of your inner critic?
- Does it have your wellbeing in mind, taking joy in you being happy and doing well?

Could you pause here and *draw* the inner critic? Just to capture the essence of it – perhaps a dark, black cloud or the angry facial expression it gives you when you make a mistake. Or look around for an avatar representing this image, searching online to see if any characters from films or cartoons would fit. Could you also give it a name? Once it has taken shape, you can engage with your inner critic in a different way – still being able to utilise its protection, but through self-correction rather than self-criticism.

What happened to your threat system while imagining your inner critic?

Was the voice more hostile than you were expecting? Or more subtle and sneaky than you thought? Does it remind you of anyone you have known in your life?

Is this an image you would want to help someone who is struggling?

Do you and your partner have different experiences here? If you don't have a particularly active inner critical voice, can you step into your partner's shoes for a bit, and imagine what life might be like with this sort of running commentary of criticism?

Self-correction as an act of self-compassion

Carol Dweck has written about so-called *growth mindsets,* where we can learn from our mistakes in a flexible, adaptive way; from correcting what we have got wrong. You might conclude 'I can't do this *yet*' and decide to work on improving. This is different from a *fixed mindset,* where you tell yourself that you can't do something and give up trying, and berate yourself for not being able to do it.[27]

We try to correct our wrongs using self-correction instead of self-criticism.

Self-correction serves as an act of self-compassion, as you can help yourself to grow and develop in an area where you might struggle. This is different from what the inner critic is doing. Although it tries to correct you and prevent you from making a mistake, it's not done in a helpful way. Self-correction is done gently, supporting yourself with kindness through the mistake or challenge. *Self-criticism,* on the other hand, is harsh and activates your threat system and fight or flight, causing you to avoid the task or area where you need to grow and develop. It simply gets too painful to approach your mistakes.

Remember the paradox of not wanting to lose our self-critic because of how it protects us? The thought of not having the inner critical voice to 'keep you on your toes' might make you fear failure or rejection. *Not* having it is hard, but *having* it is hard too. If you can approach yourself, and the inner critic, with compassion, you can soothe that threat by understanding how it's trying to keep you safe (but unfortunately leaving you feeling worse in the process).

From the sofa

Annie and Catherine had been together for many years, but still Annie couldn't trust that Catherine truly loved her, thinking that she wasn't good enough to deserve that kind of love.

Annie was a high-striving individual with a successful career, but worried that others would judge her if they got to know her. She was exhausted by the harsh critical inner monologue running almost non-stop. It dictated how she lived her life, her career path and her spare time – which was very little, as most of her time was spent at work, driven by a fear of failure.

When Catherine got pregnant with their first baby, Annie doubted her own ability to be a mother, the inner critic telling her that she wouldn't be any good at it and that Catherine should have married someone else. Not only did Annie's self-criticism affect her wellbeing, it also impacted her relationship with Catherine. Annie withdrew from her wife whenever she felt a sense of inadequacy, but furthermore, it drove her to attack Catherine for insignificant mistakes.

Catherine felt frustrated with Annie's long working hours, and that despite frequently reassuring her of how loved she was, it never seemed to quieten her negative self-talk. At times, Catherine would get angry and walk away, because she got fed up with Annie's self-defeating talk that lowered the mood between them. This further fuelled the fire within Annie, reinforcing her fear that Catherine would leave and take the baby with her.

Annie worked on soothing her inner critical voice, to reconnect with Catherine and express how afraid she was of losing her and the baby.

Catherine also better understood why Annie would be outwardly critical after having just attacked herself.

Self-criticism turned outwards

The example above shows how our inner critic can turn into outward criticism too, simply by putting us in our threat system.

Correcting, not criticising, your partner

Your partner is less likely to change something if you criticise them than if you can gently help them correct the mistake in a supportive way. If you lay into them they get into their threat zone and so will be less likely to hear you with empathy, and the problem doesn't get resolved. If you lower your criticism, you're not 'letting them off the hook', as the inner critic might tell you. You can still hold yourself and your partner accountable, but go about doing it in a compassionate and corrective, rather than a shaming and critical, way.

Why do you put your partner down?

The outward criticism, directed at your partner, is as corrosive to connection as when it's directed inwards. So why do we do this? They feel bad, you feel bad, and nothing particularly nice comes out of those conversations. Again, you wouldn't do it if it hadn't served a *function* at some point. Looking at your jigsaw puzzle, can you bring clarity to this? Have you or your partner been in a relationship with someone who was disrespectful, or treated you badly? Are your past experiences influencing your behaviour now?

If you were blamed or shamed for your shortcomings as a child, rather than having been shown warmth, understanding and forgiveness for when you got it wrong, it might be hard to offer that to a partner. 'I don't know how to be compassionate with my partner's mistakes – nobody has ever shown me how to do that.'

Reflection & Connection

Let's see what your inner critic has to say about your partner as well. If you can, sit down together to discuss this.

- What kind of things do you tend to have a go at your partner for?
- When you're being hard on your partner, what words or phrases tend to show up?
- How does this leave you feeling, when you have given your partner a hard time?
- How does it leave your partner feeling?

Criticism erodes connection

Our partners can truly infuriate us, and have plenty of opportunities to mess up in the relationship. You need to be able to express when you're not happy about something. I'm not telling you to not speak your mind if you have been hurt, but you need to be clear on the difference between *expressing a concern* and *directing criticism outwards* about something your partner has done or not done. If you can point out mistakes or flaws in a compassionate way you can help your partner to correct and repair what they've done wrong. You can also help them better understand your needs, to lower the risk of mutual resentment.

Criticism erodes connection as it activates the threat system in both the sender and the receiver of that harsh message – so neither of you are actually thinking straight! It's less likely that you can use any of your problem-solving skills to address the issue. This is even more pertinent if you criticise your partner in front of others. Neither of you will be able to show up as the version of you who is kind, caring and compassionate, a version you fell in love with.

Criticism is not the most helpful teacher

Think back to when you were at school, and maybe struggled with a subject. For me it was the physical activities as I had asthma. I remember a teacher who clearly didn't understand and would shame me for 'not trying harder' to run. Saying these things in front of my peers made me feel small and humiliated, the polar opposite of motivated (research on motivation and productivity suggests that we simply respond better to a carrot than a stick). On sports days, I sometimes feigned illness so as not to have to suffer the shame of finishing last. As an adult, I enjoy physical exercise and have done various forms of cardio-based exercise like badminton, aerobics, swimming and dancing. I have even proudly finished two 5k races! No thanks to that teacher from junior school, but rather thanks to my own understanding of how warming up slowly is key to exercising with asthma, using a growth mindset.

Which teacher would you want for your own child struggling with a challenging task? One who puts them down, points out all the mistakes and expresses frustration with them; or one who patiently and kindly helps them correct their mistakes and helps them learn from the experience?

It's not rocket science which one we would choose.

> *So if a compassionate voice is the most helpful teacher, how come that's not the way you speak to yourself? Or the way you speak to your partner? Or they to you?*

My story

I've worked very hard on reducing the criticism I direct both towards myself and to others. My husband has been in the line of fire many times, as my inward criticism makes me stressed and irritable. His loving acceptance of my journey so far in life has made it possible for me to lay down my weapons, knowing that I *didn't choose* to receive criticism in my upbringing. As a child, I received praise when I did well, and developed a pressure to keep doing well, for fear of not being good enough otherwise. This has landed me achievements and life-long dreams, but it came at a cost. Until more recent years, those achievements were more propelled by threat than by vitality, meaning and purpose – leading to me feeling exhausted and even burnt out. Writing this book is a major exercise in noticing my self-criticism, tolerating being in the presence of my inner critic and still choosing courageously to move forward, but I'm scared of what my professional peers will think of this level of self-disclosure. I can notice that fear and how the inner critic is trying to protect me from public humiliation, and still move forward, not letting my fear hold me back from living a meaningful life. This is why I now specialise in helping overachievers let go of that pressure of perfection, softening the negative self-talk to not let it hold them back from utilising their potential. We do that by developing compassion for the inner critic, odd as that may sound. Try this with me – it will help.

Compassion for the critical part of you

It's not a pleasant experience to be on the receiving end of criticism, and that goes for self-criticism too. So why don't we just get rid of the inner critic? Sadly, it doesn't work like that – you can't fight fire with fire. Much like a dragon cannot be hurt by its own fiery breath, your inner critical voice will not go away because you tell it to. Remember the double whammy of adrenalin when we attack ourselves? The inner critic is still a *part* of you, and if you attack it you're still experiencing that release of stress hormones because of the fight mode, because of experiencing aggression.

What's the answer? Coming back to the principles of cultivating the *compassionate mind* you can draw upon your compassionate self and the compassionate inner mentor here. Use the clarity you've gained from your jigsaw puzzle, and from figuring out *why* you put yourself down. Knowing this can help you soothe yourself when the critical voice is having a field day about something. Let's see if we can show some compassion for your inner critic instead of trying to get rid of it.

Try this: Compassion for the inner critic

You might find it helpful to start by drawing a picture of your inner critic. Use the audio download to make it easier to visualise this interaction, and don't worry if it's difficult at first – it can get easier with practice.

1 In the usual upright posture, using your soothing breathing rhythm and the gentle smile on your face, start by imagining yourself stepping into the shoes of your compassionate self and embody those qualities of care, clarity and courage.

2 Visualise yourself walking down the street as your compassionate self, with its strong and grounded posture. Imagine that you're coming to face your inner critic. Pay attention to what it feels like to stand in the presence of this critical version. How do you feel emotionally when it's being harsh towards you? How does the inner critic look, stand and sound?

3 Using your sense of clarity, what do you know about your inner critic? What drives it – why does it behave the way it does? What is it trying to do *for* you? What is it trying to protect you from, and how is that working out? What journey has it travelled to get to this point? Can you reflect on your past experiences to make sense of why the inner critic is so hard on you?

4 Call upon the courage of compassion to choose how you want to live your life even when the inner critic tells you off for the choices you make. If this stuff starts to show up, it means you're moving towards something important, outside your comfort zone. Stay grounded and breathe calmly, standing tall like a mountain, to tolerate what the inner critic is sending your way.

5 Lastly, bring the caring commitment of the compassionate self, being like the teacher you would want for your child. Try to send that flow of compassion towards the critical part of you, telling it that you understand the fears and what it's trying to protect you from, but the way it does it isn't so helpful.

6 If at any point it's too strong, climb down the ladder by going to your safe place. Bring in your inner mentor to support you in relating to your inner critic in a different way. Your inner mentor is there to back you up – not to fight the inner critic or criticise it, but to help soothe it.

How did this leave you, and your partner, feeling? It's hard for a lot of people, so go easy on yourself. It can be helpful to pause here and see how the inner critical parts of both you and your partner may get in the way of you connecting more deeply with each other.

You might also find it helpful to write it out in a compassionate letter to the critic, understanding what it's doing and how it leaves you feeling, and what can be more helpful for both of you going forward. Like Charlie Heriot-Maitland phrases it in his great animation *Compassion for Voices*, available on YouTube, the inner critic is 'still part of the family, but no longer running the show'.[28]

Summary

- The inner critic, an often harsh and punitive inner voice, tries to protect you from making mistakes and facing failure and humiliation, but it does so in a way which keeps you stuck in your threat zone through frequent self-attacking.
- Criticism doesn't help you change a behaviour, nor does it help your partner change theirs. Instead, compassionately correcting what has gone wrong will help facilitate growth and connection.
- If you can understand the function of your inner critic you can start to talk to it differently, developing compassion for it.
- You can't fight fire with fire, but you can soothe the critic so that it's no longer calling all the shots in your life.

You have many parts to you, some of them unpleasant to the point of being your *dark side*. Next, we're moving into learning more about the dark side of you and of your partner, showing compassion for all the parts of both of you.

12 Compassion for every part of you

Accepting even the parts you don't like

You might have heard people say 'it's important to love yourself' – well, *which* self? So far we have focused on you as 'the compassionate best version of you' or 'you on a really good day'. Is that your 'self'? In this chapter you'll discover that there are many different parts of you, and look at how they can turn up in arguments with your partner – and learn how to have the compassionate part of yourself in the driving seat.

All the versions of you

Within Compassion Focused Therapy we essentially think of the self as having *multiple parts*, or versions. The version of you reading this right now is not the same as you when you argue with your partner, or the same as you running out of a burning building. This also goes for your partner – different versions of them come out at different times. It's tricky to find one true authentic self – it's more helpful to think of yourself as having *many selves*.

Let's revisit the three versions that commonly show up in our everyday lives.

1 *The angry part* focuses on directing the blame outwards, feeling like it has been wronged by others and that an injustice has been committed. Things are unfair and others should pay for their mistakes by apologising and making up for it. It's a place of physical tension.

2 *The anxious part* is on the lookout for threat and danger, preparing for something bad happening, and is often fearful for the future. It scans the situation with your partner and jumps to worst-case scenario conclusions, and might want to run away, or please the partner to make the threat go away.

3 *The sad part* experiences a flatter, more demotivated feeling. It's the version of you who feels that something important has been lost or is missing. This part feels a deep need for connection, wanting to cry and be comforted.

And then we can bring in *the compassionate self*: the version of you that can balance your needs with those of your partner, but also has the courage to say no and set boundaries rather than accepting bad behaviour. This version of you is empathetic enough to see that behaviour in context and wants to take into account your partner's perspective as well as your own. Your compassionate self uses wisdom, knowing that all relationships struggle and need to weather a storm from time to time. We will now widen that wisdom to include understanding when the different parts of you are in conflict.

Conflicting parts of you

It's normal to have conflicting wishes coming from different versions of you. After all, if you always allowed the angry part of you to be in the driving seat, you might do things that are illegal or destructive. So just notice those impulses and urges, understanding why you have them and knowing that thinking about something is not the same as doing it.

A word of caution here: if you have a history of physically hurting others because of your anger, you need help. Read Russell Kolts' book *The Compassionate Mind Approach to Managing Your Anger* and seek out an individual therapist. Couples therapy isn't advised if there is active domestic violence between partners.

Let's explore how different parts of you show up in your life and relationship.

Try this: Your multiple selves

Do this together with your partner, choosing a fairly recent argument or disagreement. Read through these common thoughts and actions, as well as what each version of you would consider the ideal outcome to the argument.

Angry part	**Anxious part**
Thoughts: This is so unfair, it's all your fault, how dare you treat me like this? Physical feelings: Tense, wound up, tightness in the jaw, racing heartbeat, tight fists. Memories: Other times my partner has wronged me or made a mistake. Action urges: Slamming doors, shouting, throwing things. Ideal outcome: Partner realises it was all their fault, apologises profusely and makes it up to me, and never does this again.	Thoughts: What if you'll leave me? Maybe we can't repair this, and it will never be the same between us? Physical feelings: Tense, wound up, jittery, racing heartbeat, churning stomach. Memories: Other times when people have been upset with me or left me. Action urges: Running away, avoiding talking about it, apologising profusely to appease. Ideal outcome: The argument stops, calms down and we make up, partner reassures me they're staying.
Sad part	**Compassionate part**
Thoughts: This always happens, we just can't do this any more, the love is lost and won't ever come back. Physical feelings: Flat, empty, exhausted, tearfulness. Memories: Times I've been alone, or things haven't worked out in relationships. Action urges: Cry, hide, get comforted, give up on the relationship, dwell on mistakes. Ideal outcome: The argument stops and never happens again; the partner comforts me.	Thoughts: This is so hard; we have got so stuck in this pattern of fighting. No wonder we're both fed up and scared about what will happen between us. This is a rough patch which we need to work on together. Physical feelings: Calmer, grounded. Memories: Times where we as a couple have worked together as a team to resolve things. Action urges: Listening, empathising, apologising, forgiving, resolving. Ideal outcome: Being able to really understand each other, empathising with the other person, letting go and moving forward with a compromise both partners can live with.

1 Draw four squares on a piece of paper. Close your eyes for a moment and explore how the angry part of you felt about this argument – what really irritated you? Write down the thoughts, physical feelings, action, memories and urges and ideal outcome.

2 Do the same for the anxious part, and then the sad part, each time taking a moment to pause with eyes closed so you can bring to mind that part of you before you put pen to paper.

3 When you come to the last square remember that you need to warm up your body and mind in order to step into the compassionate part of you. Use your soothing breathing rhythm, your safe place imagery or any of the relevant audios. Then consider this argument again and fill in the square with your compassionate self in the driving seat.

4 Discuss this with your partner – how does this exercise change how you view this argument? Do you reach any new understanding of what happened? Did you act as a version of you which isn't who you want to be, in a way that wasn't in line with your values? That might be the dark side of your personality showing up.

The dark side of the moon

Couples often feel bad about themselves for having picked a fight or for having hurt their partner. This comes from our in-built capacity to reflect on our own actions, and can help us repair, forgive and move forward. Sometimes, however, couples get stuck, one or both partners feeling really bad about who they are rather than about how they *act*. They sometimes say that they don't like themselves, or they don't like their partner – who they have become.

It is difficult to cultivate compassion for the parts of yourself you don't like. Naturally, it's then also difficult to do that for your partner's flaws or shortcomings. Professor Paul Gilbert talks about developing compassion for the 'dark side' of ourselves. This stems from Jungian psychology and involves understanding our least desired traits as being part of our '*shadow self*'. Sometimes we think of it as the *dark side of the moon*, facing away from the sun and not illuminated. For instance, if you see yourself as a kind and funny person, your shadow self might be mean and boring. You wouldn't want to acknowledge this part of you, as you don't want these characteristics to be the 'real' or 'true' you.

Imagine that you would also do the same for your partner. When you first get to know them, you might think of your partner as generous with their time and money. After a while, you might see the shadow part of that – for instance, that they spend your household money on others and don't spend enough time with the family due to taking on too many other commitments for others. Within more recent personality theory, these shadow parts are seen as qualities which get *overextended*, almost too much of a good thing.

Compassion for your dark side

You'll occasionally say and do things which drive your partner insane, not acting in line with the values you hold in life and then regretting it. This is natural. Rather than beating yourself up for it let's try to develop more compassion for your shortcomings. The first step is understanding why you act like you do – understanding the different parts of you better.

For instance, the angry part of you might come from inheriting a 'hot' temperament from one of your parents, or your anxious side from having been left by previous partner 'out of the blue'. Perhaps your sad self gets a lot of airtime at the moment, because your work situation feels stuck and you've been made redundant. Although *it's not your fault* that these different qualities or sides of you show up at times, it's your *responsibility* to do something about them, without shaming and blaming yourself.

Think back to that two-part definition of compassion – the sensitivity and the commitment. Given what you've gone through, doesn't it make sense that you have these parts to you? Given your values around how you want to be, what could be helpful? Lean on your inner mentor here, guiding you in the self-discovery about your dark sides without putting yourself down. You can also write a compassionate letter to yourself about your dark side.

My story

My husband frequently asks me where things are, before he looks himself. After years together he knows this drives me up the wall, as it adds to the maternal mental load of having to keep track of everything in the household. Considering that we both want to be equal partners, he tries to catch himself before finishing the sentence starting 'Where is . . . ?', which I highly appreciate.

It shows he has listened to my frustration; it shows he cares about not annoying me unnecessarily. But when he's stressed and in a rush that question still comes out. When he isn't the best version of himself, his darker sides come out, like they do for all of us. Although it irritates me, I try to breathe through it and either calmly ask him to look for it himself or help him look if he's running late. His dark sides can trigger mine (which are about having a reactive temperament and strong emotions), so it's important that I soothe myself so as not to make a stressful situation worse.

Sometimes we don't get it 'right' and we end up snapping and shouting at each other, displaying our worst versions of ourselves. That will not end our marriage – we know that our dark sides are not our only sides, and we're so much more than that. If we make space for discussing those sides, and what happened, we can repair a rupture to forgive and let go.

Compassion for your partner's dark side

Odds are that your partner will also say and do things which drive you insane, things they may regret. Often, we focus much more on our partner's bad traits and qualities than we do on our own – but remember that you can't make your partner change. Accepting their dark sides isn't the same as liking them; acceptance means stopping the struggle against something outside of your control. You can't control your partner, as much as you may have tried through being critical of them. You're still able to raise a complaint about the things you don't like, however.

Let's look at the dark sides of you and your partner.

Reflection & Connection

1 *Write down five qualities you value about yourself, like 'kind' or 'funny'.* Lots of us find this difficult, so notice the inner critic preventing you from saying nice things about yourself.

2 *Do the same for your partner– five qualities you like about them.* The qualities don't have to be present and true all of the time.

3 *What is the polar-opposite word to each one of those ten words?* For instance, the opposite of 'kind' could be 'selfish' or 'unkind' or 'uncaring'. That is the so-called dark side, or shadow self. Can you see any patterns emerging? Are the opposites of what you like about yourself also what you tend to berate yourself for? Is it the same for the list you made for your partner? Close your eyes for a few moments and think about how those harsh words make you feel, and how they would make your partner feel.

4 *What happens when you come across your own dark side?* Notice what happens when you act in a way that is the opposite of your desired qualities. What happens when your partner shows the qualities opposite to what you most admire in them? Are there any overlaps between what you dislike in yourself and what you dislike in your partner?

You on a really bad day – the goblin

Think of a time when you were really horrible to your partner (we've all been there), and about which version of you was acting that way. Certainly not your compassionate best: you on a really good day. No, it was probably more like you on a really *bad* day. When things weren't going well at work, you'd had a bad night's sleep, the kids pushed your buttons, your mother-in-law nitpicked your cooking and the car's MOT resulted in a huge repair bill.

Your compassionate self feels a million miles away. Imagine that your partner comes home from work, tired and a bit moany, and you're in this worst version of yourself. An impatient, selfish, arrogant version of you, sitting on the sofa like some sort of argumentative goblin, waiting for your opportunity to strike. To pick a fight. The goblin is only happy when getting to WIN, motivated by competitive rather than compassionate goals. Do you recognise that goblin state of being?

What can you do when you're in your worst self, your goblin self, to still walk in line with your values and act like the partner you want to be?

Discussing this together with your partner, what happens when your partner is having a goblin moment? How can you work on allowing your partner's worst self to come out occasionally without taking it personally, without letting it define your love and connection with each other? How can you let go of criticism and start holding yourself and your partner gently accountable when they're letting the goblin sit in the driving seat?

Criticism is an army of termites eating your house

When you tell your partner off for something in a harsh way, you may feel more in control and may think that it's effective. You might think that they're alright with how you're speaking to them, as you get rewarded with their compliance; they do as you tell them. But how does it feel for *them*? Is your control and coercion met with submission and avoidance? Maybe they feel less inclined to come to you with their problems, to show you their vulnerabilities. So, your connection weakens, and you drift further apart. Or maybe they try even harder to please you, to be perfect in your eyes, to avoid criticism.

This is where *self-silencing* can come in, of not expressing their own needs to you for fear of judgement or criticism. Alternatively, your criticism triggers anger in them, 'How dare you talk to me this way?' and they may respond with retaliation, defensiveness and hostility. Or they eventually have enough of you and end the relationship.

Criticism is like termites. One little bug here and there is probably OK (you're not perfect and will lose your temper and go into your worst self occasionally). Each little act of unkindness to your partner might seem insignificant as it's possible to repair, but don't let it build up to an infestation. A big group of termites can cause damage to the foundation of your relationship, bringing the whole house down.

If you're criticising your partner, how will that feel *for you*? Do you feel good, like you're 'winning'? Even if your mind tells you that you're entitled to deliver this harsh message, your body might disagree: it doesn't just stress your body to *receive criticism*, it also stresses the body to *give criticism*. To be harsh, hostile and aggressive is part of our human nature, but it strains us. It's exhausting to spend longer periods of time in the goblin frame of mind, of being competitive rather than collaborative, being critical rather than compassionate.

From the sofa

Benjamin and Joaquin were stuck in a vicious cycle of criticism, frequently being the worst versions of themselves. Benjamin was struggling with work stress, feeling burnt out from the pressure. Joaquin faced his own challenges, worrying about not finding a job once he finished his Masters degree, as a mature student competing with young graduates. Neither of them slept well, tossing and turning all night. They had been together for over a decade and were very comfortable with their day-to-day life, but now both felt that their partner had shown an unpleasant side.

When Joaquin was studying for an exam, he would get irritable and had the tendency to overeat to manage his emotions, resulting in putting on weight and feeling even more irritable. Benjamin started avoiding Joaquin's anger outbursts by staying later at work, feeling even more stressed and becoming very anxious both about failing at work and in his relationship. When he was at work, he kept texting Joaquin to see what he was doing, to make sure he wasn't sleeping with another guy, which further irritated Joaquin as he felt mistrusted when he was just trying to study in the library.

It took an external person to help them notice how they both were struggling and that it wasn't anybody's 'fault', but that they each had responsibility for how they approached the other person even when under pressure. They aimed for small, manageable actions along the mantra of 'Do what you can when the shit hits the fan'; each little smile or gentle stroke, or 'Do you want to talk?' question created a ripple effect of more emotional connection. They each tried to understand this new side to their partner, the angry and irritable version of Joaquin and the stressed and anxious version of Benjamin. As part of that, they wrote each other compassionate letters.

Writing a compassionate letter to your partner

Try writing a letter to your partner, directing that flow of compassion towards them. Imagine that you're shining the spotlight of attention on them. Your issues have gone into darkness for the moment, as you're choosing to illuminate your partner's experience and really take that in. You can steer the spotlight back to yourself whenever you choose to.

The letter you write to your partner is about expressing concern and empathy, understanding their pain. If you're *sensitive* to what hurts for your partner, you can also gently consider what would be helpful to *alleviate* that pain. If you soothe and comfort your partner, they're more likely to respond to you in a similar way.

Empathy and compassion are a great way to extinguish those fires we talked about earlier. Being seen, heard and validated for feeling what we're feeling makes a huge difference to the strength of those emotions.

If you can truly sit with your partner's pain they're less likely to feel the need to ramp up the intensity, not needing to shout louder to be heard.

Like you did in your own letter, try to send your partner gentle loving kindness, helping them to face and tolerate their feelings, rather than telling them off for having them.

> *Dear Rahul,*
>
> *It really hurts me to see you so upset at the moment, losing your dad. I can't begin to imagine what you're going through, as I haven't lost my parents. I get that this is also frustrating at times, that I can't fully understand what it feels like. I just want you to know I'm here for you and I love you. I'll support you in any way I can. It doesn't matter that we're not going away this summer, I know you're blaming yourself for cancelling the trip. What's most important to me is that we're together, we can go on a trip whenever.*
>
> *I know you're struggling to get out of bed at the moment, and that happens to lots of people who grieve. But that day when you got up to have breakfast with me, you told me it felt like a better morning. Maybe we can try to spend more time together, as I don't think it's helping you to have so much alone time in bed, I have seen how low you feel those days. I know it's really, really hard, and I don't expect anything from you right now. Let me help you – we will get up together and have breakfast together to get the day started. Try to not be so hard on yourself, we will get through this together. It's OK to feel really sad about your dad.*

The essence of this letter is the intention of helping to build on the team that is the couple – 'we will do this together'. That can be incredibly hard to do if you have also been very hurt by your partner – say that if Rahul had been so irritable that he had shouted at his partner and said really horrible things.

Being supportive is not passively accepting bad treatment. It's putting it in context and using validation and empathy to communicate that you need something else from your partner and helping them understand that. Not passively neglecting our needs or aggressively trying to get our needs met at the expense of our partner's, but balancing our own needs with our partner's needs.

Summary

- Your angry self might want to win an argument while your anxious self wants to appease your partner to make the threat go away.
- Your sad self might want to hide away and give up, whereas your compassionate self wants to find a compromise balancing your needs with your partner's.
- It's harder to be compassionate with people you don't like, including parts of yourself which you don't like. We call that the 'dark side' of ourselves, your shadow self, or your 'goblin' – you on a really bad day.
- Being human means we're capable of aggression and hostility, and understanding that makes it easier to accept and tolerate the worst parts of yourself and your partner, while still taking ownership for working on it.

In Part III we apply the compassion skills learned so far to the practical skills from Behavioural Couples Therapy and Acceptance and Commitment Therapy. We'll look at what values you hold for yourself in life, and in love, so you can take action to move towards what matters most to you. Let's go!

PART III

Building a lasting connection with compassion

- Understand the values you hold in life and love, to act like the partner you want to be
- Use compassionate communication to resolve issues and connect more deeply, both emotionally and physically, through good times and bad
- Learn to bridge the gap from your incompatibilities with compassion, instead of aiming for perfect compatibility
- Understand the difference between compromise and sacrifice, to make decisions and solve problems as a team
- Aim for connection and not perfection, by repairing a rupture in your relationship and giving forgiveness to each other and yourselves

13 Doing what matters

Making the choice to act like the partner you want to be

In our busy modern lives it can be difficult to protect our connection with a partner. Moving towards what matters, choosing to act more like the kind of person you want to be in your relationship, gives you the best chance of living a valuable and connected life together.

Finding direction with values

Have you ever thought about what really matters to you in your life? In your relationship?

Most people don't stop for long enough to reflect on how they can create a meaningful life together, where they live and love in line with the guiding principles important to them. Understanding the *values* you hold can help you to move in the direction of what really matters to you.

Living a valued life together

How do we explain 'values'? For me it's 'how you want to *be* and how you would like to *act*, to move in a certain *direction* in your life'. Russ Harris, author of *The Happiness Trap*, explains it as 'your heart's deepest desire for how you want to behave – how you want to treat yourself, others, and the world around you'.[29] You choose these ways of behaving: it's not about following 'shoulds' or 'musts'. Values are not the same as goals, which you can tick off when you have met them. Acting in line with values isn't about *arriving* at a particular destination; it's about the day-to-day *journey*. Goals are things you aim for in the future, but values are what you choose to do in this moment, how you choose to be. 'Getting married' or 'having a baby' are goals to work towards, whereas 'being a kind and loving partner' is values-based.

In your relationships, perhaps you value things to do with being a good team, like *fairness, caring, supportiveness, trust, kindness, equality* or *connection*. How would you act if those things were your guiding principles? You might try to share the housework with your partner in a fair way, you might want to look after them when they're sick, you might make space for both of you to share how your day was. It isn't possible to get to the destination or goal of 'being a fair and caring partner' and stay there. Having done the housework once doesn't mean you can tick that 'fair partner' box and be done with it – it's the guiding principle for how you behave on an ongoing basis. Every time you do something to care for your partner, you travel in that direction of what you hold as important.

Perhaps you prioritise values linked with positive experiences together, such as *fun, sensuality, curiosity, challenge* or *playfulness?* Lots of couples say that they *used to* make space for those things, but over the years they have drifted away from acting in a fun and playful way. Having children, getting sick or losing your job – those stressful life events can hook you away from acting like you used to. You can't prevent stressful things from happening, but you *can* influence how you act towards each other in your relationship. If you value *honesty* and *justice*, you can choose to act in accordance with those values. If you lie, cheat or make major life decisions without discussing them with your partner, you're actively taking steps away from those values. Your actions don't tally up with what you believe in: a values gap has been created.

Try this

Identifying your values

The words in the box below describe values we commonly hold. Do this exercise independently of your partner and compare notes once you've completed your lists.

Values you hold in life

1 Start by considering what you hold important in your life overall, reading through the description of each value.

2 Rate each value from 1 to 10 in terms of how important it is to you, with 10 being the most important.

3 Then choose the ten or so most important ones to you and write those down in a list.

Values you hold in love

Using the same procedure choose what you value in loving relationships.

Common values

These are common things people hold as valuable, being neither 'right' nor 'wrong'. Some values will be important in one domain of your life, but not in others: for example you can find yourself wanting to be orderly and organised at work, but flexible and fun as a parent at home.

Acceptance: To be open to and accepting of myself, others, life, etc.

Adventure: To be adventurous, to creatively explore novel or stimulating experiences

Assertiveness: To respectfully stand up for my rights and request what I want

Authenticity: To be authentic, genuine and real; to be true to myself

Caring: To be caring towards myself, others, the environment, etc.

Compassion: To act kindly towards myself and others in pain and suffering

Conformity: To be respectful and obedient of rules and regulations

Connection: To engage fully in whatever I'm doing and be fully present with others

Contribution/generosity: To contribute, give, help, assist or share; to make a difference

Cooperation: To be cooperative or collaborative with others

Courage: To be courageous or brave; to persist in the face of fear, threat or difficulty

Creativity: To be creative or innovative

Curiosity: To be curious, open-minded, and interested; to explore and discover

Encouragement: To encourage and reward behaviour that I value in myself and others

Engagement: To engage fully in what I'm doing

Fairness/justice: To be fair and just to myself and others, treating others as equal to myself

Fitness: To maintain or improve or look after my physical and mental health

Flexibility: To adjust and adapt readily to changing circumstances

Forgiveness: To be forgiving towards myself and others for mistakes and shortcomings

Freedom: To live freely; to choose how I live and behave, or help others do likewise

Friendliness: To be friendly, companionable, or agreeable towards others

Fun/humour: To be fun-loving; to seek, create and engage in fun-filled activities

Gratitude: To be grateful for and appreciative of myself, others and life

Honesty: To be honest, truthful and sincere with myself and others

Humility: To be humble and modest; to let my achievements speak for themselves

Independence: To be self-supportive, and choose my own way of doing things

Industry: To be industrious, hardworking and dedicated

Intimacy: To open up, reveal and share myself, emotionally or physically

Kindness: To be kind, considerate, nurturing or caring towards myself or others

Love: To act lovingly or affectionately towards myself or others

Open-mindedness: To think things through, to see things from others' points of view

Order: To be orderly and organised

Patience: To wait calmly for what I want; being patient with myself and others

Persistence: To continue resolutely, not giving up despite problems or difficulties

Power: To strongly influence or take charge; leading or organising others

Reciprocity: To build relationships in which there is a fair balance of giving and taking

Respect: To be respectful towards myself and others; to be polite and considerate

Responsibility: To be responsible and accountable for my actions

Romance: To be romantic; to display and express love or strong affection

Safety/protection: To secure, protect and ensure my own safety and that of others

Savouring: To be conscious and mindful, and curious about my here-and-now experiences

Self-awareness: To be aware of my own thoughts, feelings and actions

Self-control: To act in accordance with my own ideals

Self-development: To keep growing, advancing or improving knowledge, skills or character

Sensuality: To create and enjoy pleasurable and sensual experiences

Sexuality: To explore or express my sexuality

Skilfulness: To continually practise and improve my skills and apply myself fully

Spirituality: To connect with things bigger than myself

Supportiveness: To be supportive, helpful and available to myself or others

Trust: To be trustworthy; to be loyal, faithful, sincere and reliable

Other – adding your own values.

From *ACT Made Simple* by Russ Harris (2019)

Are there a lot of differences between the values you chose for how you want to be in your life overall and for how you want to be as a partner?

Are there any overlaps or significant differences between what you and your partner chose, in life or in love?

The values gap in relationships

If you're not acting in accordance with what you believe in, you might start to *feel bad*. It can give rise to strong, negative emotions such as sadness, hopelessness and despair, and lead to depression and anxiety. It's almost like this values gap creates an unpleasant sound, or *dissonance* – a lack of harmony between your actions and your values. You might feel like you lack purpose in life, not being true to yourself.

If you think smoking is really harmful for you and the people around you, but you still smoke, then there is dissonance between your behaviour and your values. They don't line up. This gap commonly occurs in relationships too, where partners might value things like kindness, support and empathy, but frequently shout at their partner instead of listening and validating. They have lost sight of the direction they want to walk in. Don't be hard on yourself here – this is common – but if you don't become aware of it, you can't do anything about it. The good news? There's always *a choice.*

The choice point

Russ Harris talks of how we often come to a 'choice point' in life, where you can choose to either go *towards* or *away* from what truly matters to you. By becoming aware of the effects of your actions, you can move towards a closer relationship with your partner.

Unfortunately, tricky thoughts and feelings might show up and 'hook' you away. For instance, if you value patience, you might benefit from noticing when you're rushing your partner through a story they're telling you and notice what effect that has on your relationship. If you then become aware of self-critical thoughts, such as 'I'm being a terrible partner, I should just LISTEN without interrupting!', you're likely to keep acting away from what is important to you. How do you get back to acting like a patient partner? You might choose to take a deep breath before you speak, to really allow the other person the chance to finish. You might visualise your inner mentor sitting there with you, helping you slow down and practise what is important to you – *being a patient partner.*

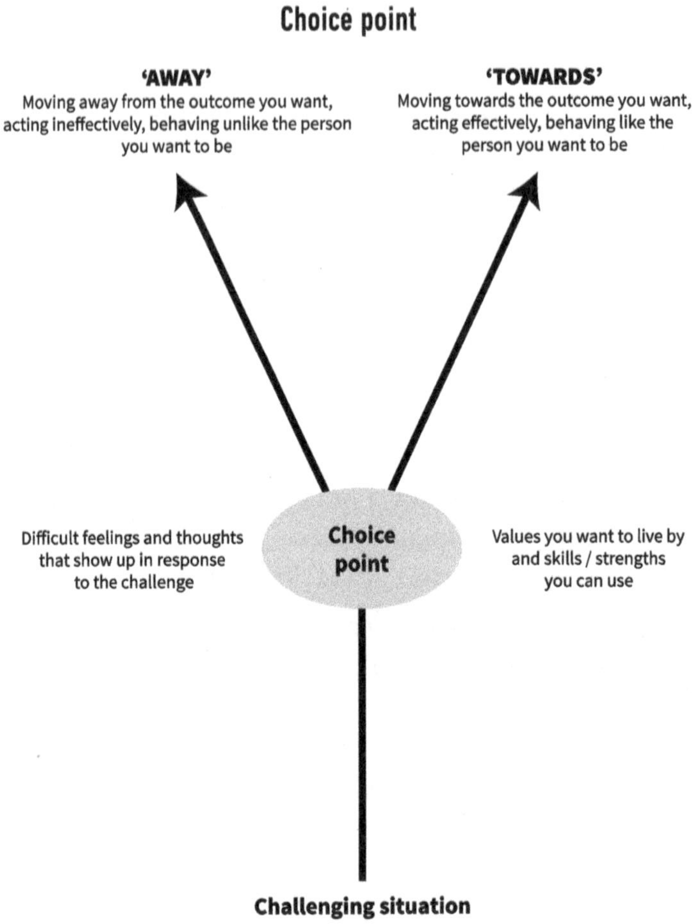

From ACT Made Simple *by Russ Harris (2019)*

Try this

Noticing the values gap

How can you know if there is a values gap in your life or in your relationship? Let's explore some steps you can take to gain clarity on this.

The values gap in your life

1 Start by stepping into your compassionate self. It's important to approach this with curiosity, not blame and shame.

> *What kind of person do you want to be overall in your life?*
> *How do you want to show up in your life?*

2 Go back to the values you have chosen: how much you have been following each one over the past month or so? Rate each value from 1 to 10, where 10 is 'fully acting in line with this value' and 1 is 'not at all acting in line with this value'. If you value something as very important, say 9, and you haven't made much effort to act like that, rating it at 2, there's a large gap between what you hold as important and the steps you currently take.

3 Pause here and start *noticing* your thoughts, feelings and behaviours, using those mindfulness skills of paying purposeful attention.

> *What is pulling you away from acting like the person you want to be?*
>
> *What thoughts, emotions or feelings in your body hook you when you try to take steps towards what matters to you?*
>
> *How does your threat system get activated when you try to act like the person you want to be, in life overall?*

This can be hard, so try to sit with the discomfort for a while.

4 Consider your own behaviour and what you need to change to close the gap. Approach this with self-compassion.

5 The last step is to try to close the gap, by starting to act more in line with your values.

> *What are you doing too much of, or not enough of, to create this gap?*
>
> *What can you say or do today or this week which is more like the person you want to be in your life?*

The values gap in your relationship

Take a deep breath and step into your compassionate self again. Consider what gap you might have between what you value in your *relationship* and how you have been acting towards your partner over the past month, using the same steps as above.

> *What kind of partner do you want to be in your relationship?*
>
> *What are you doing too much of, or not enough of, to create a gap?*
>
> *What can you say or do today or this week which is more like the partner you want to be?*

Sounds simple? Do less of the stuff which takes you away from the person you want to be, and do more of the stuff which is in line with that? Things are never that easy – it's incredibly hard to do. Noticing and addressing your gap takes effort, choosing to take action instead of avoiding: *committed action*. You choose to do something on purpose, even if it's hard and uncomfortable, to lead towards what feels meaningful to you in life and in love. To take committed action, you need *willingness*, building on the *courage* you have already worked on developing.

Willingness to take committed action

What do you do if you have that dissonance, that lack of harmony? You can come clean and admit that you don't really value those things, like kindness or responsibility, which means you don't have to change your behaviour. This may have some unintended results – your relationship may end. Alternatively you can admit to yourself that you haven't been the person you aspired to be, which hurts. We do so with gentle kindness, knowing that you'll get it wrong at times, despite your best intention. It takes *willingness* to be with discomfort if you're to build a truly meaningful life with your partner.

In the next chapter on compassionate communication, you might become aware of some unhelpful habits you have in conversations with your partner, perhaps cutting them off or trying to convince them of your viewpoint. Neither of those actions are in line with the value of *patience* or *caring*. It's easier to cut your partner off than it is to notice your own impatience and take ownership of that. Now use that courage and willingness to find the way together.

Finding direction together

Couples relationships are hard – it's easy to get lost and act ineffectively. If you've got stuck in a bad place, how do you figure out how to find your way again? How do you get unstuck?

Being lost in the woods

Imagine that you and your partner are on a familiar walk in the woods. You start arguing, and after a while you realise you've got lost, as you didn't pay attention to the path. You start to feel uneasy, seeing the last rays of sunshine. You might have a go at your partner for not following the usual path, or you might beat yourself up for being 'so stupid' that you got lost. Your pulse goes up and you walk faster, as the threat system activates. That's what a lot of couples do – when they're lost they walk faster out of sheer panic and end up walking in circles, repeating old patterns and arguments. They desperately want to get out of whatever discomfort they *experience* but lose sight of how they want to *be*.

You come to a halt – you don't know what to do. This is where *creative hopelessness* can come in. When you surrender into this moment, of not knowing where you are or where you're going, you can get creative in your thinking. You take a deep breath and suddenly remember that you have a map and compass (you just forgot you'd packed them).

You didn't think you would need them on this familiar walk – you've done it so many times before. What's on that map? Which direction is the compass needle pointing to? Sometimes it's so overwhelming that you can't see the wood for the trees, and just become *reactive* instead of *proactive*.

The metaphorical forest of your relationship

What does this mean for *your* relationship? This 'stuckness' happens when couples get too busy with everyday life, forgetting to pay attention to where they're going and how they're acting, getting complacent about using a map and compass.

Anything can throw you off track in your relationship if you're not prepared and proactive, and don't routinely check in with where you are. If you then panic and frantically try to escape, you'll be causing more hurt and confusion about which is the right way to go. Anger, fear and sadness set in, together with hopelessness and thoughts that things will never change. The pain is too much, so the defensive systems kick in to get rid of the threat.

'Getting lost in the woods' can be that you start having such frequent arguments that you forget to notice the nice things about your relationship, the 'nature' around you. You lose sight of the connection between you. You stop communicating in a respectful way, the way you might have done earlier on in your relationship or you do with people other than your partner. Walking around in circles could be the blaming and shaming, trying to figure out whose fault something is instead of trying to find the way out together. Let's now try more of a visual overview.

Try this

Values map and compass – the bull's eye

Some find this visual representation far easier to get to grips with than the list of values words, so use what works for you and your partner. This exercise is called 'the bull's eye', helping you to see how close to the target you are. You may have some areas, or domains, of your life where you're acting in line with your values and some where you don't. Take a moment to reflect on this with your partner. Being clear on this will help you in the moments when you get lost in the woods.

The Bull's Eye

Adapted from Living Beyond Your Pain *by J. Dahl and T. Lundgren, by permission of the author.*

From the sofa

Lee worked in a large investment bank in London, working eighty hours a week and often taking calls outside of work hours or even in the middle of the night, when markets closed. He started sleeping in the spare room at home, as the calls disturbed his wife Elizabeth. As a result, they rarely talked, cuddled or had sex. Elizabeth also had all the nightly wake ups with their youngest child. Lee was torn between providing for his family as his wife was on maternity leave, and also getting to have time together with his wife and children.

Lee felt miserable. As a husband, he wanted to be loving, connected and supportive. As an employee, he wanted to be loyal, dependable and driven. In fact, he had a time-management issue between these two domains of his life, with it being difficult to hit the bull's eye on both his work and his family domain.

Here is where he had a choice point, a crossroads of choosing whether to act in line with his values and which values to prioritise. It's important to note that not all steps in the direction of what is important have to be the same size – it isn't about quantity. He may not be able to change his working pattern for now, but he could choose to act more like a caring and supportive husband than he is currently doing, to feel better about who he is as a husband, improve his own wellbeing and his relationship quality.

Lee could use compassion and committed action to move towards his values of *love, connection* and *supportiveness* in his relationship:

Compassion and love flowing out

- Use compassionate communication to express how he feels about being away from the family so much (they may not realise how much he loves them)
- Give his wife a kiss or cuddle when coming in from work, listening compassionately to how her day has been
- Play intently with the children in the pockets of time he does have with them, as being fully attentive for even short periods of time deepens connection
- Check in with his wife during the work day with a brief call or text

Compassion and love flowing in

- Negotiate how he can have a break on the weekend so he can also reset before the next working week, balancing it with looking after his wife's needs, e.g. each getting one morning lie-in
- Seek and accept any external support, e.g. babysitting or food parcels from friends and family, to give the two partners a break and chance to reconnect

Compassion for self

- Express to his wife how exhausted he is from work – that it's not about her and the children
- Practise self-care, to help support himself through nutrition, exercise and relaxation

- Consider expressing to a manager that he wishes to work from home more, reduce his hours or change his shift patterns, to make space for the demands of his home life
- If not getting needs met from his current job, consider looking for a less stressful job

What gets in the way of valued living

A lot of the time doing what matters to you may even feel worse than *not* doing it. This has to do with the timing of reinforcement: when will it *reward* us to act this way? If Lee greeted his wife kindly and offered her a kiss, and she smiled at him and kissed him back, that is an immediate reward – he is more likely to kiss her again the next day. Considering their reality, though, his wife may bat him off in an irritated way, as there is resentment and they're both exhausted. Lee acted as the caring and connected husband he wants to be, but he didn't get immediate reinforcement for his behaviour. In the moment he may even have experienced punishment (feeling rejected by his wife).

How do you then keep going in line with what you believe in and value, in the face of difficult experiences such as rejection or criticism?

- Remind yourself that moving towards what matters is a long-term commitment, which may not feel good immediately. When you change your behaviour to act more in line with your values, people around you need time to adjust too; use your compassionate strength to tolerate that.
- Communicate with your partner how you feel about their reactions to your new way of acting, asking them to respond to how you're acting now and not to how you were acting back then. You can work through past resentment later, when you're more back on track.
- Set a joint commitment to work through this process as a team effort, trusting that you are both working on yourselves.
- Soothe your own threat system if you feel rejected or criticised despite trying hard – this is a marathon and not a sprint.

How to be with each other

It can be alarming for a couple to realise that they don't have the exact same values, or that the things they used to value when first getting together have now changed and there is a wider gap than they thought. How can we be together if we're this different, want different things? It all depends on how you handle your differences, or incompatibilities. Trying to force each other to be a certain way doesn't work – you can't make each other share values.

With loving flexibility comes freedom

Using dog walking as a metaphor can help to explain how we can explore our own needs and values within a loving relationship. If you treat your dog with care and compassion, it will most likely become attached to you. You'll serve as a secure base from which it can go off exploring, but then want to come back home with you. If you hold the dog on a very tight lead, consistently shouting 'No' to it as soon as it wants to sniff at things, it will feel stressed from your walks. It will not get to act in line with its nature, of exploring and playing. A dog which is consistently shouted at, controlled and punished will cower in fear, and although it may still be loyal to its owner, the loyalty is driven by fear and not by loving connection.

If you allow it off the lead, to stretch its legs and run around the park, it will have a joyful experience and turn back towards you again, happily wagging its tail. Regardless of whether the owner shares the value of playfulness with the dog or not, it's allowing the dog to be that way – to follow its heart's desire.

We're humans with complex needs, but what we share with our canine friends is our need for nurture and belonging, as well as our need to feel safe and protected. And – often forgotten – our need for play, curiosity and exploration. You can't scare or shame your partner into loyalty by thwarting their needs or denying what they value and find important. They will turn away from you, pull harder on that lead – and if they get loose it's not certain that they will keep coming back. If you both can make space for the other person's desires, as long as it isn't harmful to either of you, you're on the road towards loving flexibility.

Be curious, not furious

You can't control another person – you can't *make* them love you. Allowing loving flexibility means being curious, not furious, when they explore the world. What does this mean for your relationship? Is there an adventure out there which you would love to explore? Something new you want to learn? How could you support each other in these discoveries, to help each of you feel fulfilled?

Say that you're watching a cooking show on TV one night and feel inspired to look into cookery classes. Your partner could say 'Why on earth would you bother with that, the kids only eat fish fingers anyway?', or they could say 'Wow, you'll be doing lots of new dishes from now on then.' One is said with judgement and lack of support, the other is said with curiosity and a willingness to make space for your journey of exploration.

However, if the cookery course costs £2000 and your family is struggling to make ends meet, then no, that isn't a wise choice *at that moment*, as it would impact your loved ones. You have to keep it realistic – *'dream big and start small'*. You could watch your favourite cooking show on TV and try some dishes from it, or buy a new cook book. Taking committed action towards your purpose is easiest when broken down into smaller, more manageable steps.

If your partner can be flexible and curious enough to allow you to be *you*, all the versions of you, you're more likely to live and love in a connected way. It goes without saying that you also need to do the same with your partner – it's important to give out what you most want to come back. Think about who you might be over time if you can use this curiosity and flexibility, instead of control and anger.

Let's time travel to the future – to your fiftieth anniversary together.

Reflection & Connection

Imagine that you're having a celebration together with your partner to honour your fiftieth anniversary, or whatever significant milestone fits for you as a couple. Given the couple you have been so far in the past, and are today in the present, imagine what the effects will be of that in the future.

Close your eyes and visualise that you and your partner are sitting there together, old and wrinkled after a lifetime together, and see if you can imagine what you might say to each other about the relationship you've had.

Think about how you would look back at your own life at your fiftieth anniversary, with hopefully your partner doing the same:

> *What kind of person do you think you've been with friends and family, at work, in your hobbies and interests? How have you acted? How would your partner see you in your life?*
>
> *What kind of partner have you been to your significant other? How have you acted? How would your partner see you as their partner?*

Discuss how you see each other and yourselves, considering also:

> *What steps can you take today or this week towards being the partner you want to be?*

My story

I like long-term, deep and meaningful connections with people, rather than having many fleeting and superficial interactions. This goes for both my friendships and for my intimate relationships, which is why

I still have friends from when I was six years old and why I was never much one for the casual dating scene. There is no judgement there; I simply love the closeness which comes from really getting to know someone, sharing history together.

That said, I know I can get too comfortable with relationships with friends and family, where I take it for granted that the person knows how much they mean to me. They may sense it, but actions speak louder than words, so I would like to both tell them and make more efforts in prioritising them. I can hear that sound of dissonance between what I value (connection) and how I'm acting at times (forgetting to reply to messages).

This is particularly important in my marital relationship. What suffers in my marriage when I'm not making an effort isn't the *quantity of when* we see each other, as we live together, it's the *quality of how* we see each other. As I value that connection, I choose to sometimes bring out a board game instead of watching TV, or stop to have a chat instead of just doing the normal chores. It's a deliberate *choice*, taking valued action to be more how I want to be as a spouse.

Summary

- We have explored what matters to you in your life and in your relationship, noticing the unpleasant feelings you'll experience if there is a gap between how you act and how you want to be as a person.
- We've looked at finding direction by reminding you of what is important, taking action to walk in line with those values when you're standing at the choice point.

To make space for each other's values in a loving, connected way, you'll need compassionate communication. You're more likely to deepen your connection with your partner if you learn to listen compassionately and share your thoughts and feelings in a way they can hear. Let's get talking, but more importantly, let's get *listening*.

14 Compassionate communication

Speaking and listening with compassion to deepen connection

Here we'll use mindful compassion to have better conversations with your partner, changing your body language, tone of voice and facial expression. Learning to listen and speak to your partner in a compassionate way facilitates problem-solving and effective decision-making as a team, as well as learning from mistakes. Being aware of the present moment and noticing without judgement will enable you to raise a complaint rather than a criticism.

Communicate to connect

Couples who stop talking to each other, or can no longer have a conversation without arguing, are more likely to feel dissatisfied with their relationship. The knock-on effect is that decision-making and problem-solving suffer, and the partners may also feel like they no longer know each other.

You need your partner to *tell you* what's going on in their life – yet even then we often get it wrong and misunderstand one another. The majority of communication is *non-verbal*, so it's important to not just listen to *what* your partner says but also *how* they say it. Learning how to bring your mindful compassionate self into conversations with your partner will help improve your communication patterns. Let's start by entering a tough conversation in a more effective way.

Raising a complaint, not a criticism

It's important to address things your partner does which upset you by raising a *complaint* about it in a way they can take in. What often happens in reality is that the complaint comes out in such a way that it's automatically perceived by the other partner as *criticism*.

Marriage researcher John Gottman spent decades observing what makes a healthy relationship work. He coined the term *'harsh start-up'*, which means starting a conversation in a way the other partner perceives as an attack and struggles to take on board (remember the three circles model and the significance of threat, drive and soothing?).[30]

Often the partner who wants to complain does so while they're in their threat system, so is more likely to come across as hostile and attacking rather than calm and composed. They thus deliver a criticism rather than a complaint. If that's ever happened to you it's not your fault – it's just how the threat system is designed. By practising the skills of mindful compassion, you can gently hold yourself accountable for the way you start a conversation when you want to address an issue.

The partner who is on the receiving end of a criticism will most likely get defensive, having quickly moved into their own threat system. Has your partner ever expressed themselves in a way which made you feel like you were being instantly attacked? Now *both* of you are flooded with stress hormones blocking your soothing systems (feelings of being calm and connected) *and* your drive systems (being able to use problem-solving). End result? Both of you miss an opportunity to express empathy and compassion and to jointly resolve the conflict – that part of your brain is switched off. The connection comes from the ability to deeply understand each other; not just hear what is said, but to really take it in and appreciate the feedback as a way to grow as a couple. Letting our threat systems get the better of us can result in conflict and missed opportunity for connection.

From the sofa

Lucy and Rishi were a married couple who had drifted apart. They frequently argued and hadn't felt connected to each other for some time.

One Friday evening, Lucy decided to surprise Rishi with a nice meal as a way to reconnect with him. An hour after the dinner was ready, Rishi still wasn't home and wasn't answering Lucy's text messages. This sparked a range of threat emotions in Lucy. She was *angry* as the meal was ruined, *sad* because their date didn't happen, and *anxious* as she worried about what had happened to Rishi, as being so late was out of character.

Rishi, on the other hand, had had a very difficult meeting at work, having received criticism from his manager for a mistake. He was feeling upset – anxious about the ramifications of the mistake and angry about how unfairly criticised he felt. He decided to go for a drink with a colleague to let off steam, completely forgetting to check his phone.

By now, both partners were upset and exhausted, with several threat emotions present. As soon as Rishi got in, he saw that Lucy was angry. She launched into Rishi for not letting her know he would be late home and for smelling of alcohol. Rishi retaliated, saying he couldn't deal with this right now and telling Lucy she needed to get off his case. He stormed off into the bedroom, slamming the door.

Neither partner got seen or heard in their pain. Even worse, Lucy's underlying good intentions of trying to reconnect with Rishi went to waste. Rishi missed out on a lovely meal with Lucy and she missed the opportunity to support Rishi after the criticism he received, connecting by being a compassionate partner. Each could only see one of the threat emotions, not the softer and more vulnerable feelings underneath.

Keep this example of Lucy and Rishi in mind as you learn more about the building blocks for holding more compassionate conversations with your partner.

Sharing thoughts and feelings with compassion

In Behavioural Couples Therapy, Professor Donald Baucom has developed guidelines for couples on how to listen and speak effectively to each other. Look at these principles together so you can see what you struggle with in your conversations.

Guidelines for sharing thoughts and feelings

Skills for sharing thoughts and feelings (the speaker)

- Talk about your opinions subjectively. They're *your* feelings and thoughts, not absolute truths.

  'I got upset when you did that, it made me think that I'm not worth much to you.'

- Include your emotions or feelings, how this makes you feel.

  'I felt really rejected and sad when we argued like that.'

- Discuss how you feel about your partner and not just an event.

  'When this happened, I felt really frustrated with you, like you let me down.'

- When you share negative emotions or concerns, include positive feelings you have as well.

  'I felt upset after you didn't come home, I wanted time with you.'

- Make your statement as specific as possible, both in terms of specific emotions and thoughts.

  'When you did X, it made me feel Y and worry about Z.'

- Speak in 'paragraphs'. Give your partner a chance to respond to one idea at a time, keeping to the present moment, instead of covering several other similar situations.

  'I didn't know when you'd be back last night, I'd like you to tell me if you make plans after work' is more helpful than
  'You should have told me you weren't coming home, you're just like your mum, I can't stand how your parents never tell me their plans, just like over Christmas, we're not having them over again if they're going to be like that!'

- Use tact and timing to choose how and when to express your feelings and thoughts, to give your partner the best chance of taking in what you're saying.

  'Is this a good time to talk about something, or do you need to finish what you're doing first?'

Skills for listening to your partner (the listener)

When your partner is speaking . . .

- Show that you understand and accept what your partner has to say. Use your tone of voice, facial expressions and posture to show understanding. Accepting what they say as true to them doesn't mean you have to agree with their opinion.
- Try to put yourself in your partner's place, thinking about the situation from their perspective to know how they feel about the issue.

When your partner finishes speaking . . .

- *Summarise* your partner's most important feelings, desires, conflicts and thoughts. You can then check with them that this is what they meant, to reduce misunderstandings.

When you're the listener, don't . . .

- Ask questions, except for clarification.
- Express your own viewpoint or opinion.
- Interpret or change the meaning of your partner's statements.
- Attempt to solve a problem if one exists.
- Judge what your partner has said.

Adapted from *Enhanced cognitive-behavioral therapy for couples: A contextual approach* by N. Epstein & D. B. Baucom (2002)

Which skills do you think you need to practise most from the speaking and listening guidelines?

You can only change yourself, not your partner, so focus your efforts on taking accountability for how you can approach conversations in a more compassionate way, to be the kind of partner you want to be.

The communication ball game

When you're in a conversation with your partner, it's as if you're throwing a ball back and forth. The way you throw it impacts on how well your partner can receive it, so think about that before releasing the ball. If you throw it hard at your partner, they will either duck to avoid getting hit, and not take on board what you've said, or they will be hit and be hurt. Nothing good comes out of that, as they either get angry and defensive, retaliating with an equally hard throw back, or give up trying to play, feeling too sad or injured to go on. Game over.

If you throw it gently, a throw you think your partner can catch, they can return the ball with a follow-up question or validating comment, and keep the connection going. They also need to try their best to catch and return the ball you're sending their way, to not miss an opportunity to play and connect. How fun is it to play catch with someone who never returns the ball, regardless of how nicely you throw it?

Some partners have had lots of practice playing the communication game, perhaps from previous relationships or from an upbringing where the parents modelled good communication. Others haven't, and need to be patient as they build up skills. If you approach your communication this way, tolerating some dropped balls along the way, you can develop a healthy communication pattern which is about playing on the same team rather than trying to beat each other.

Let's reflect on the example of Lucy and Rishi, to help you think about how you can practise to both throw and catch skilfully.

Reflection & Connection

Sit down and discuss this with your partner.

1 How could Lucy and Rishi have done things differently and got a better outcome?

2 What compassion skills could they have used to manage their own threat emotions?

3 What specific communication skills, such as tact and timing, did they forget to use?

4 If this was you and your partner, how would the situation have played out? What threat emotions would have showed up for each of you, and what actions would you have taken?

5 Take a moment to slow yourself down and step into your compassionate self. How might you have handled things better for your *partner*, if you'd had Rishi's difficult day at work, or Lucy's dinner failure? How could you have been more compassionate to *yourself* if you had been in either Lucy's or Rishi's shoes?

Lucy and Rishi could have prevented the bust-up and repaired the situation quicker if they'd behaved more compassionately towards each other. That would have got them in touch with more connection and less irritability, getting a deeper sense of understanding for each other.

Lucy

- Holding off judgement, waiting to express the anger and disappointment until knowing that Rishi is safe and OK, as this was out of the ordinary for him.
- Reading Rishi's facial expression when he's coming in, asking about what has happened before getting critical.
- Using self-soothing skills while waiting, reminding herself that it's understandable to have mixed feelings of worry and anger if one's partner doesn't show, and a meal is ruined.
- Giving Rishi space to cool down in the bedroom, then gently seeking him out with a curious rather than furious mind, asking what is going on for him.
- Trying to find a way to express the softer feeling underneath the anger, that the disappointment was about wanting to treat Rishi to a nice meal and reconnecting.
- If unable to be calm and compassionate because of her own anger, finding a way to apologise for harsh words spoken once finding out about Rishi's day, repairing the rupture afterwards.
- Raising a complaint about not notifying her of the lateness, making a request for how she wants Rishi to act in the future if this happens again.

Rishi

- Allowing space for Lucy even when upset and overwhelmed himself, by using his compassionate self to understand the surprise Lucy had made for them.
- Balancing his needs with Lucy's, remembering her tendency to worry if he doesn't come home and sending a message that he's going out after work.
- Calming himself down before coming through the door, using the soothing breathing rhythm, to explain to Lucy how he feels.
- Allowing compassion to flow in from Lucy, by expressing the vulnerability and sadness around having made a mistake and been criticised at work.
- Using self-compassion to go gentle on himself for how he acted with Lucy, so he can apologise and repair, stepping into the soothing system.
- Trying to make up for the missed meal by offering something else nice to connect over, like going out for dessert.

With these skills in place, the interaction would have been a very different one. Rishi could have come home on time and received support, closeness and a nice meal to ease his difficult day and they may have moved closer towards each other rather than apart. Or he could have made an agreement with Lucy to come home later, explaining he needed some space to decompress with his colleague. The big fight might still have occurred, but stepping into our caring motivation means we make an effort to repair and forgive when we steer off course.

Compassionate communication empowers you to hold each other in mind with compassion and decide actions to take which would move you closer to who you want to be as partners, rather than further away.

Non-verbal communication

Now it's time to learn how to use the more subtle, but equally important, non-verbal means of communication. We'll rely on the compassionate self and your inner mentor to show your partner that you're listening and caring.

Compassionate posture

How you sit, stand and move can have a real impact on the direction of your conversation. Partly because of how your partner perceives it (it sends out 'clues'), and partly because of how it influences how you feel in your own body. If you're sitting with your arms crossed over your chest and looking away from your partner while they're speaking to you, you're sending them a clue which could be interpreted as 'not interested'. Your brain will jump to conclusions such as 'crossed arms = cross spouse' before you're even aware of it, simply because you need that speed of processing to be able to carry on a conversation.

Try this

The 'Goldilocks' of compassionate body posture

Stand up and walk around the room, playing around with how high you hold your head, how straight you keep your body, and where you direct your eye gaze. Assessing your posture in terms of 'passive', 'aggressive' and 'assertive' will help you find the 'just right' balance in the 'Goldilocks' sense.

1 *Not enough – passive* Stand, but make yourself small, tilting your chin towards your chest and casting your gaze down to the floor. How does it feel? How easy is it to be aware of the world around you when you're staring at your feet? If you don't stand up tall, you're more likely to feel inferior and small. It's harder to breathe as your airways aren't as open, and you create tension in the body. You're more likely to be perceived as insignificant and disinterested, and you might be talked over by your partner and others.

Their needs are more important than your own.

2 *Too much – aggressive* Stand up tall, shoulders pulled back and chest puffed out. Look upwards, to where the wall meets the ceiling, with

your chin up high, and see how you feel. You might feel more powerful, but you're more likely to be perceived as arrogant and haughty. How do you think this would affect a conversation with your partner? They might perceive you as picking a fight or wanting to 'win' rather than caring about their opinion.

Your needs are more important than others' needs.

3 *Just right – compassionately assertive* Stand up tall, but in a relaxed way. Let your shoulders drop down and breathe calmly into your abdomen. Look straight ahead, with your eye gaze on the horizon and keep eye contact without staring. How does this feel? Walk slowly around the room, stepping into your compassionate self. You're now more likely to feel and be perceived as engaged and interested, on equal terms. That gentle smile on your face signals kindness, and lightens your own mood. You have a caring commitment towards your partner, having the courage to say no or set a boundary.

You're balancing your needs with others' needs.

Compassionate tone of voice

It's not just about *what* you say to yourself and others, or your body posture – it also matters *how* you say things, what tone of voice you use. The way you speak to yourself inside your head affects how you feel emotionally, and the same goes for how you speak to your partner.

Try this

'Hello'

1 Sit down and take a few deep breaths. Say the word 'Hello' over and over to yourself in your own mind, in the warm, kind and loving tone of voice you might use to greet a dear friend you haven't seen for a long time. How does that make you feel, emotionally? How does that feel physically in your body? In your face? Which circle are you in – threat, drive or soothing?

2 Now try the 'Hello' again, but in a harsh and hostile tone. Dripping with contempt and sarcasm, the way you might sound if you're really mad at someone and don't think very highly of them. How does that make you feel, emotionally? How does that feel physically in your body? In your face? Which circle are you in – threat, drive or soothing?

3 How do you think your partner might feel if you use the warm, friendly tone of voice as opposed to the hostile, contemptuous one? How might that feel in their body? Which circle are they in – threat, drive or soothing? Which one are *you* in? And how is that working out for you in that moment, in your relationship?

Can you bring this gentle tone of voice into a conversation with your partner? If this is hard, remember that all new things take practice to learn and make habitual, especially if we have been taught rules around how we should or shouldn't be with others.

Tuning in

Next, we'll put the verbal and non-verbal skills into practice by *tuning in* – simply noticing *what is happening as it's happening* in you and your partner. You can become aware of your partner's words, facial expressions, body language and tone of voice, as well as observing your own inner feelings and thoughts, urges and memories, to really tune in to your partner's wavelength.

Try this

Mindful conversation

1 Ask your partner about their day, using the compassionate communication guidelines. Intently focus on what they're saying. Don't interrupt, even if you disagree, or try to 'fix'. Just listen and ask for clarifications if you don't understand, then reflect back to your partner what you've heard. If your mind wanders, don't worry: as soon as you've noticed that you've drifted off (especially if onto what you

want to say next) gently steer your attention back to you focusing on your partner.

2 What do you notice in *your partner*? How is their:
   - *Facial expression?*
   - *Tone of voice?*
   - *Posture?*
   - *Mood?*
   - What's the *topic* of conversation and the *meaning* of it?

3 How do you feel focusing on your partner like this? How easy or hard is it?

4 What do you notice in *yourself*? What inner stuff, like thoughts, feelings, memories and urges, shows up for you, potentially hooking you away from focusing on your partner?

5 What kind of person do you think tries to pay attention to someone they care for (e.g. 'a caring partner' or 'a thoughtful partner')? How does this fit with your values, how you want to be in your relationship? What committed actions did you take?

6 How did this conversation play out, compared to ones where you've been distracted, disengaged or trying to problem-solve? Were there any points of connection in that interaction, from just focusing more on your partner than on your own agenda?

Example

1 Ask your partner about their day.

2 What do you notice in *your partner*?

Facial expression *Looking down, looking tense, shiny eyes*
Tone of voice *Low, mumbling*
Posture *Slumped over, hugging knees to chest*
Mood *Sad, upset*
Topic and meaning of conversation *Worry about a presentation at work – she thinks she isn't good enough to do it; the project will fail, and it will be her fault*

3 How do you feel focusing on your partner in this way?

I'm really there for her, listening and making her feel heard. I feel good focusing on her, but it's hard to stop myself jumping in with solutions. I wish I could make her not feel so bad about it, as I don't think she's going to fail.

4 What inner stuff, like thoughts, feelings, memories and urges, shows up for you?

I worry that it'll take all evening, like it has done before. I'm tired and want to watch TV to 'flake out', but that wouldn't be nice to her or for our relationship. I'm also worried about my own work stuff – maybe I'm selfish?

5 What kind of person do you think tries to pay attention to someone they care for?

I feel like I was the kind of partner I promised to be in our wedding vows – respectful and kind, supportive and caring – being there for the bad times and making her aware that I care about her problems.

6 How did this conversation play out, compared to past ones?

She crawled into my arms at the end of the conversation, instead of storming off angry. That was nice and I think she felt supported. It didn't take up the whole evening or end in a fight, and we moved onto talking about other things, like the work things I was worried about. We felt closer to each other, with some give and take, and I guess that's the connection we've been wanting.

My story

During a stressful time, my husband forgot his backpack on the train home. When he told me, he looked ashamed and expressed that he worried I'd be really mad at him for 'messing up'. This was a huge wake-up call to me in terms of how I approach other people's mistakes.

Which version of me was he expecting to see? The person I am on a really good day would patiently say that it doesn't matter, and try to find a solution to the problem together. Not to shame and criticise, but to reassure and support. So, I tried to show him with my whole being that it was *OK* – open arms, drawing him close and having a gentle facial expression instead of a judgemental look. I tried to tell him, through my tone of voice, that I wasn't angry or upset with him, it was a mistake anyone could have made. This opened up a conversation about what was going on for him right now, with work, and we could connect more deeply. The backpack? He got it back from Lost and Found the next day.

Summary

- How you *start* a conversation determines how it *continues*, with a worse outcome if you throw a hard ball, pushing your partner into their threat system.
- Raise complaints rather than harsh criticisms, throwing a ball your partner can catch.
- Speaking and listening in an effective, mindful and compassionate way, with a kind facial expression, posture and tone of voice, improves connection and reduces conflict.

Now we'll move onto what we do when we mess up – how you can set realistic expectations for your relationship and let go of 'shoulds'. Relationships are about connection, not perfection.

15 Connection, not perfection

Letting go of 'should' to get closer together

It's impossible to have a 'perfect' couples relationship, always getting it just right – you'll inevitably make mistakes. The key to a lasting connection lies in tolerating *imperfection*, being flexible and letting go of 'shoulds'. The important thing is to at least *some* of the time, rather than *all* of the time, be the version of yourself you want to be as a partner.

Imperfection feeds connection

At times, life is hard, and you're unable to be the best version of yourself. When you're under pressure, your shadow self is more likely to get in the driving seat and direct your behaviour, which might hurt your partner. Loving in an imperfect way means accepting that you both are doing your best at living life.

You can't remove disappointment, fear of rejection, pain and vulnerability from your relationship without also removing love and connection. They're like the yin to the yang, or light to dark. You need to hold compassion for the parts of your partner you don't like. If you're able to accept your partner's imperfections and mistakes, you'll become more approachable and tolerant, which will strengthen your connection to your partner, as well as with your friends, family and colleagues.

Being the perfect partner

Perhaps you have high standards for yourself, or for your partner? Perhaps you feel under pressure to be perfect? There is no such thing as a perfect partner – only excessively high expectations around perfection. You can only try your best to be 'good enough'.

Paediatrician and psychoanalyst Donald Winnicott established the term 'the good enough mother' in the 1950s, emphasising how being an imperfect mother was the best way to meet the emotional needs of one's baby. The parent who met their child's needs 'perfectly' every time didn't show the child how the world works – and exhausted themselves in the process.[31] The same goes for being in a loving relationship – it's most helpful to be a 'good enough partner'.

If you strive to *be* the perfect partner you'll exhaust yourself trying to keep up the façade, and your partner won't get to know the real you. That pretence will create a distance between you. Interestingly, someone being imperfect is often rated as more likeable than someone being perfect, because we struggle to relate to perfection. We can't *connect* as well with someone who's always trying to be what they think you want them to be, rather than being themselves.

Finding the perfect partner

If you strive to *find* the perfect partner, you'll probably end up disappointed and alone, as nobody will ever feel good enough. People who have high standards for themselves often put a lot of pressure on their partners, who inevitably will fall short. This pressure drives disconnection, if you can't forgive and let go of slights you have experienced, and instead blame and shame your partner for not being up to scratch. That level of pressure makes it *more* likely that they will make a mistake and disappoint you, not less, as they may spend a lot of time in their threat system.

If you think that your relationship issues are all to do with your partner's shortcomings and nothing to do with you, you've possibly got blind spots. We may think that the grass is greener elsewhere, but remember: '*Wherever you go, there you are*'.[32] If you want to end your relationship because you could 'do better', you may replicate the same patterns in your next relationship. Look out for tendencies to abandon ship too soon instead of figuring out why your relationship isn't working and giving your partner a chance to correct what they're 'doing wrong'. Otherwise you may never find any meaningful and lasting long-term connection.

Dare to share

In order to truly connect with someone, you need to be brave enough to be vulnerable with them – telling them things you're scared to say, for fear of not being liked, or because you worry about them not wanting to be around you if they 'really knew' what you're like.

Imagine that you're under pressure at work and scared of making a mistake, but don't tell your partner as you fear it will make you look weak, or less capable. Your partner then only sees the *symptoms* of the pressure you're under, but not the vulnerable *cause*. They might see you cancel plans because you're exhausted, and assume you're not interested, or see you being irritable and snappy and assume you don't want to be with them any more. They might see you turning down invites for intimacy, and assume you're not attracted any more. Connection starts to fade, to thin out – until it may snap.

If you're brave enough to say what's bothering you and how you feel, you give your partner a *choice* – hopefully to move towards you and support you. They may also return the share (remember the communication ball game?), telling you how they feel, or how they have felt like that before. Suddenly you have empathy and understanding, warmth and closeness – connection grows if you dare to take the risk and let love in.

> *The cave you fear to enter, holds the treasure you seek.*
> *Joseph Campbell*

Find the courage to enter that cave of vulnerability, to lower your guard, to take off a piece of armour. Remember your jigsaw puzzle? Can you make sense of why you might not dare to share and realise what the armour protects you from?

Vulnerability researcher Brené Brown illuminates the importance of taking risks: 'In order for connection to happen, we have to allow ourselves to be seen.'[33] You need courage to take that risk, so channel your compassionate self to dare to share.

From the sofa

Natalie needed help because of stress, anxiety and indecisiveness related to perfectionism, and this impacted on her relationship with her husband Adam. Natalie would suppress her own needs (*self-silencing*) and give up on negotiating any purchases for the home, thinking her choices wouldn't be 'good enough'. Avoiding these decisions meant her confidence eroded even further – she then didn't trust herself to pick even minor details for the home and would berate herself for having 'bad taste'.

Although this couple didn't need help to improve their relationship as such, Natalie's issues were helped by bringing her husband on board to help build confidence and let go of the pressure of perfection. They had to learn how to negotiate in a way which turned into compromises between them, rather than sacrifices of what Natalie wanted, to 'keep Adam happy' and to 'be perfect'.

When he found out what Natalie had been doing, through compassionate communication, Adam wanted to give more power back to Natalie as it wasn't in line with his values as a husband to get to decide everything. He also struggled with self-criticism, berating himself for mistakes, so tolerating imperfections helped strengthen their marriage and prepare them for their next life stage of trying for a baby. By being vulnerable with each other about their struggles, as well as each being accountable for what they needed to work on, they could focus on growing together, with less criticism being directed to one another and to themselves.

Choose growth

If you accept that both of you are flawed and imperfect, you can learn from the mistakes you'll make over the lifespan of your relationship, increasing your chances of having a lasting connection. It's like tending to a garden, cultivating the flowers and plants you want and having the tenacity to also weed out the things getting in the way. Some things are easy to pull out, and change or improve, like how my husband leaves his socks inside out in the laundry basket. It's not the hardest thing to address, as he now makes more of an effort to turn them the right way. Other things growing in your garden might be harder to pull out, like my temperament being hotter than my husband's. Then we have to think about accepting what we cannot control or change, to stop struggling against it.

Bend to not break

Imagine holding a pencil in your hands, applying pressure to it. Press hard enough and it will snap, because the pencil is rigid and not able to bend.

What doesn't bend, will break.

If you have rigid rules and fixed thoughts about your partner and about how relationships should be, it's more likely you'll break under pressure. 'If my partner really cared for me, they should never be late home from work' or 'A loving relationship should mean sex every week' are examples of rigidly held beliefs.

Imagine that instead of holding that rigid pencil (the strict rules and 'shoulds') you're holding a headphone cord. If you apply pressure, it bends and adapts. It will definitely get tangled up at times, and even if there sometimes is a great deal of frustration involved you'll be able to untie the knots.

If you have some *flexibility* instead of *rigidity* around your relationship, to adapt to an ever-changing environment, you might find yourself a bit more content. You might do what works best in any given situation and take the pressure off by bending more, which lowers the likelihood of breakage.

What bends, does not break.

The perfectly imperfect couple

We often get caught up in how we think a relationship 'should' be, based on what we see on TV or read in books, or see on social media feeds. Why can't we be as happy as that couple who just posted a smiling holiday snap? Why do we fight about silly things? Why can't we have more sex in that passionate way we see in films? Why aren't we as cute as that young couple nuzzling up together?

To compare is unfair

If we can become aware of these comparisons (which we all make), and how unfairly they're measuring up our entire relationship against snippets of the best bits of other people's lives, we can settle into the imperfection which makes up any committed relationship. To compare is unfair, as we tend to compare upwards, meaning comparing ourselves with people we perceive to be 'better', rather than comparing downwards, with people who might be worse off. If you only compare your love and relationship with that sweet young couple in the early stages of dating, you might wonder what's wrong with your relationship and why you no longer coo at each other after eighteen years of marriage. Notice mindfully when you get caught up in comparisons, as it may leave you feeling worse, simply by how unfairly weighted the comparison is.

To compare is unfair and can leave you in despair.

Making a mess

'Making a mess' essentially means getting it wrong, having been caught up in your threat system so that you've been reactive and harmful, rather than proactive and helpful. If you want to be a kind person but find yourself saying something really unkind or unhelpful in your relationship, you then have opportunity for a repair, for a *gentle return* to what you believe is right, to who you want to be. In the Disney film *Frozen 2*, the characters talk about doing the 'next right thing' after wrong decisions have been made, after hurt has been caused. Watch the film for some inspiration around the courage to act in line with your values.

Gentle returns

Professor Kelly Wilson, co-founder of Acceptance and Commitment Therapy, talks about 'gentle returns' when we drift off course, acting away from our values. The *return* is important, as it shows our commitment and dedication to doing what matters to us, doing the next thing right. The *gentle* means we do this return in a self-compassionate way, rather than shaming and blaming ourselves when we get it wrong. If you beat yourself up for the mistakes you make, it doesn't make you any less likely to make them again.

A marriage or long-term committed relationship is essentially a lifetime of gentle returns.

Try this

When you make a mistake

1 Notice that you've drifted off course, catching yourself as soon as you can.

2 Acknowledge the mistake, what you've said or done that wasn't in line with who you want to be as a partner.

3 Gently steer back to your values, reconnecting with what is important.

4 Step into that compassionate version of you, finding the courage to hold yourself accountable and be able to take compassionate action in line with your values.

5 Repair the rupture by making it up to your partner, doing the next thing right.

> *When you have made a mess in your relationship, having been hurtful and done something wrong, what is the next thing you can do right?*
>
> *What small thing can you do today or tomorrow to allow a gentle return?*

The 'should' trap

People often use the word 'should', saying things like 'My partner should know when I'm upset and need to talk.' Or they use 'shoulds' about themselves, like 'I should want to have sex more often, what's wrong with me?' Rarely are those conversations accompanied by smiles, joy and laughter – usually they're accompanied by heartache, guilt, blame and shame. If we can soften these 'shoulds' into 'coulds', it would soften the rigid expectations.

Can you soften a should into a could?

'A loving relationship COULD mean regular sex, but my partner and I have both been under stress from work and we're really tired. We can reconnect and be there for each other in other ways for now, we'll get back to the sexual intimacy soon enough.' This – a lengthier phrase than 'I should want more sex' – generally acknowledges the greyscale of life, rather than being a rigid black-and-white statement.

> *'My partner could know when I'm upset and need to talk, but it's probably difficult to know for sure without me telling them.'*
>
> *'I could be wanting to have sex more often, but with the sleep deprivation of having two young kids, it's probably not so realistic right now. I can do other things to show my partner affection.'*

Reflection & Connection: Your 'should' stories

Sit down with your partner and look at this list of 'shoulds'. How do these examples compare to your own?

- I should be thinner and prettier
- I shouldn't be angry
- I should always please others
- I shouldn't make a fuss
- I should always be funny
- I should keep it together
- I shouldn't talk about my feelings
- I should be strong at all times

What story do you tell yourself about how you, your life and your relationship 'should' *be*, and what you should or shouldn't *do*? Does it take you closer towards or further away from having a meaningful, fulfilling relationship?

1 What is your own 'should' story?

2 What is your partner's 'should' story?

My story

In 2018, when I attended a training course in advanced ACT (Acceptance and Commitment Therapy) with Russ Harris, I volunteered to role play with him, to follow my values around connection, love and compassion, feeling lost in terms of how I was parenting my toddler. I was so sleep-deprived that I would often lose my temper. I felt as if I was failing. I was ready to try anything to help.

Russ talked it through with me on stage, in front of one hundred of my peer psychologists and therapists. Then he had me do this exercise, of writing down the *story* of the things I was telling myself, like 'You can't cope', 'Other parents can do this', 'You should know better, you're a psychologist', 'You're failing' and my all-time favourite: 'You're doing damage to your child'. We noticed how the statements made me feel emotionally and where that sat in the body, noticing feelings of guilt and shame and a pressure over the chest, with heavy sighing. I was very much in my threat system, confessing all of this in front of other professionals.

Then Russ flipped the paper over and wrote something. He asked me to read my story – which we had named *The Failure Story* – again, and then turn to the flip side, which read, 'Ah! Here it is again, *The Failure Story*. I know it well.' Those words released me from getting too attached to the thoughts, realising they were stories I was telling myself about a situation which would be hard for anyone who had been sleep-deprived for years.

The most powerful thing Russ said was 'You're probably going to make these mistakes again, you can try not to, but this is imperfect and messy, and the story will show up again.' Then he asked me to carry the story around with me, which I did for months (in my messy handbag) until it fell apart.

By then I had remembered the words and knew what showed up for me when I made a mistake as a parent or as a partner. I was able to hold it a bit more lightly. Not fighting against it, just to say that it's there. I still make mistakes, but I beat myself up less and can learn from what I get wrong. What did my peers think? I can't tell what they all thought, but several people came up to me expressing that they had recognised themselves in my story, telling me that I was brave. Connection was made when I dared to be vulnerable and real.

Let's take you through the same exercise.

Try this

The story your mind tells you

1 On side A of a piece of paper, write down the thoughts which show up for you when you make a mistake in your relationship. Perhaps they are 'shoulds' or 'should nots'; 'musts' or 'must nots'; or 'I am' or 'I am nots'.

2 Name the story based on the theme you see, perhaps 'the Failure story' like mine, or 'the Not Good Enough story', or the 'this is Never Going to Change' story. You might see it as one chapter in a bigger book of stories.

3 Flip over to side B and use your own words to just spot and describe that it's 'the Story', to step back from it and not get fused with it.

4 Read side A and then side B as often as you can over the next few months, carrying the paper with you.

5 Hold it lightly. If you can start to refer to your story as something which your mind just tells you, rather than an absolute truth, you'll become liberated from it.

> *'I'm noticing that my mind is telling me that I'm not good enough because I made a mistake, that's my Failure story coming online' is very different from 'I'm not good enough because I made a mistake.'*

How does this make you feel about your own relationship and the stories you tell yourself about your relationship connection?

Let's now think about how perfection shows up in one aspect of long-lasting connection – the 'perfect wedding day'.

The 'good enough' marriage beyond the 'perfect' wedding day

A lasting connection can exist in any set-up, monogamous or polyamorous, cohabiting or living separately, being married or not. So it's without judgement I'm going to cover what can happen around proposals and wedding planning in our pressured modern society.

If you're *already* married, look back at the time leading up to your wedding and consider the messages you were fed from the media about creating the perfect proposal and having the perfect wedding. We're encouraged to spend money on everything from favours to chair covers – the 'Compare and Despair' story can really hook you here, looking at what other couples have. For some couples, the pressure comes from their families, from who to invite to decisions about the food. Rather than just planning the 'perfect wedding day', did you also reflect on what marriage means to you? Did you reflect on your marital values? It's worth digging them out now, to refresh your mind around what you promised.

If you're considering *getting married*, think wisely about how you approach this. Connect it with your values, to consider *what* you want to promise each other in this commitment, but also *why*. It's easy to get caught up in the whirlwind of wedding planning and lose sight of why you're making this commitment.

The hidden cost of an expensive wedding

An interesting piece of research by Francis-Tan and Mialon, surveying three thousand married couples in the USA, found an inverse relationship between the cost of the engagement ring and wedding day, and marital duration: the bigger the diamond and the bigger the party, the higher the risk of divorce. Less-expensive wedding ceremonies were associated with a better chance for a lasting marriage, perhaps as they were more connected to the values and the reasons *why* the couple were getting married.[34]

The phrase of 'connection, not perfection' makes a lot of sense here. Focus on what matters to you, rather than trying to upkeep a perfect image, to keep connecting to your partner. Many couples are so spent and exhausted after a wedding day of trying to please everyone, and having 'the best day of your life', that they collapse into bed and have no energy for considering the promises they have just made to each other or being intimate on their wedding night.

If you can let go of the pressure of perfection, you can be more in the moment and really enjoy your wedding day for what it is – messy, full of mistakes and mishaps, but often a deep, emotional moment of coming together with loved ones to celebrate the efforts of a long-term, committed relationship between two people choosing to keep following their values and treat each other well.

Many people see marriage as an outdated institution There aren't any 'shoulds' regarding how you live your life with another person, as long as you both are clear on the set-up and respect each other's feelings. For some, getting married or not getting married is a deal-breaker. Others may detest the idea of marriage, perhaps having grown up with divorced parents, or parents who lived in an unhappy marriage and did nothing about it. The way we have been socialised around marriage does affect our choices.

Summary

- In order to connect more deeply, allow yourself to be vulnerable and imperfect with your partner – it's harder to get to know, like and trust someone who is always trying to be perfect.
- To become more content in your relationship, accept what is and become more flexible. Then you can also find the strength and courage to change the things you need to change, not using up all your energy on unnecessary battles.
- The stories in your mind can get you caught up in what you 'should' or 'shouldn't' do, so learn how to notice these stories and hold them lightly.

We will now move on to how to compassionately navigate the decisions in your life as a couple. You'll learn how to make compromises, not sacrifices, around how to live and how to love.

16 Compromise, not sacrifice

Compassionately making decisions as a team

Compromise in a relationship means both partners have at least partially got their needs met, whereas a sacrifice means one partner gives up their needs and resentment may set in. Approaching problems together as a team, using problem-solving and decision-making skills around how to live and how to love, will help you work towards a lasting connection. It's also important to recognise where no compromise can be reached.

Compromise is a 'good enough' solution

When couples talk about 'problems' in their relationship, they often see *the other person* as the problem. Here's where it gets tricky: that person isn't a problem to fix. Instead you need to see yourselves as a team who together solve the problems *between you*.

Small problems left unresolved can be like those little termites of unkindness and hostility – if there are enough unresolved problems festering in your foundation, they can bring your whole house down. This is where *compromise* comes in – a good enough solution where both partners feel their needs are at least partially met. This is very different from *sacrifice*, where one partner just gives in to the other and ends up feeling resentful.

Reflection & Connection

Sit down together and discuss what seems to stop you from resolving problems with compromises. Which of these common scenarios do you recognise?

1 Some couples don't know *how* to resolve their issues.

2 Some couples know how to problem-solve, but just don't *do it.* You may be too busy with everyday life, or get too anxious and overwhelmed by the prospect of another marathon sitting of hot emotions with your partner, or fear that you'll have to part ways over an issue neither of you can compromise on.

The team spirit of 'us'

Being in a romantic relationship isn't always romantic. Once the initial romance settles, the true strength of the relationship shines through; it's no longer just about passion, lust or infatuation, but about a deeper connection and meaningful friendship.

Long-lasting love requires us to form a team with our partner, making choices and decisions from a joint perspective, having *togetherness.* Thinking of 'us' and not just 'me' and 'you'. It's about being a family and working together in a collaborative and compassionate way, being other-focused rather than just self-focused. No person is an island, so forming a team rests on the foundation of *interdependence.* Allowing yourselves to depend on each other for nurture and support is a cornerstone in good teamwork, and enables productive problem-solving.

Producing a solution or going around in circles?

Productive problem-solving is like a productive cough, where you bring up the mucus and might feel a sense of relief (even if just temporarily). *Non-productive problem-solving* is more like a hacking, dry cough, where you just feel really irritated and nothing comes up. You go round and round, worrying about the problem without coming up with a solution, or end up just having a go at each other without any resolution. Most couples engage in this sort of 'head-to-head' occasionally – but you can do something to help.

Try this

Productive problem-solving

1 Start by defining the problem – what *is* the problem you need to discuss?

2 Use compassionate communication skills to listen and talk about your thoughts and feelings around the issue. What is bothering you most? Make space for your partner's feelings as well as your own.

3 Generate possible solutions, brainstorming as many ideas as you can. Have some creative fun and even think of 'silly' solutions, such as 'sending the in-laws to Siberia'. It will keep the discussion light-hearted but doesn't mean you're actually going to pick that solution.

4 It can be helpful to hold this question in mind:

> *If a friend was telling you about going through something like this, what ideas might you have for them? If you can't give yourself the same advice, why might that be?*

5 Discuss the pros and cons of each solution, trying to be fair to each of your suggestions.

6 Work on agreeing on a possible compromise that meets at least some of your respective needs. How do you each feel about the option you picked? Remind yourselves of the togetherness aspect – *how does this affect us as a family?* It will help you to be focused on your partner too, and not *just* on yourself.

7 Implement the solution by taking committed action, checking that it's in line with your values before you start. Break it down into smaller steps to make it manageable, and then *begin*.

8 Evaluate how the solution is working by listening to each other's experience of it.

9 Keep using the same solution if it's working well enough or go back to the drawing board if it isn't, starting from Step 1 again.

If you tried this exercise with your partner, how did it feel? Did you find yourselves more productive and focused on finding an answer? If not, be curious about what got in the way – if you got too heated emotionally engage your compassion skills to calm things down.

From the sofa

Nina and Geoff have been together for eleven years and have two children. They frequently argue about Nina's parents and how they treat Geoff. This is what happened when they tried the productive problem-solving around how to spend the upcoming holidays:

Problem Nina's parents want us to spend a week of the holidays at their house, which in the past has meant lots of arguments between them and Geoff, and we feel stressed out as a couple, but the kids want to see their grandparents.

Compassionate communication about the problem Nina used soothing breathing to calm herself down, to step back from the situation and share how she felt. She then realised that she feels on edge about Christmas because she's anticipating a bust-up where she has to 'take sides', instead of getting to enjoy seeing her parents play with the kids, and reassured Geoff that she wanted to hear how he feels about it too. Geoff could then tune into his story of how he isn't welcome in the family. He lacked love in his own family growing up, so it saddens him when Nina's family seems to not like him. He feels worried about receiving criticism and can't relax over Christmas. He shared with Nina that the in-laws often say things which his inner critic also tells him, so it's hard to not take it on board – his father-in-law's words feed the story Geoff is already telling himself, that he isn't good enough.

Brainstorming solutions

1. Stay at home, with just the kids, making up an excuse or feigning illness.
2. Stay at home, with just the kids, telling the in-laws why we don't want to come.
3. Go to the in-laws and try to keep the peace, to just get through it.
4. Go to the in-laws and talk about how it isn't working, finding resolution.
5. Go to the in-laws and Nina stands up for Geoff if needed.
6. Send the in-laws on a cruise as their holiday gift, so as not to have to see them.
7. Send the in-laws off to Siberia and hope they don't find their way back.

Pros/cons

1. Although nice to have a quiet Christmas, the kids miss out on the grandparents, and the in-laws may see through the excuse.
2. Although nice to have a quiet Christmas, the kids miss out on the grandparents, and there might be bad blood from the confrontation.
3. Having to put up with insults and slights isn't nice, but it's only one week, and the kids get to see their grandparents.
4. Might put a stop to the insults and slights and the kids get to see their grandparents, but it will be uncomfortable, and we might still not get through to them.
5. Middle ground between putting up with it and being confrontational, but Nina might not be in the room when Geoff gets criticised. Kids see their grandparents.
6. A relief to not spend Christmas in their house, but the cruise would be expensive, and the kids miss out on their grandparents.
7. Tempting as it sounds, they would probably die from the cold in Siberia and then the kids would definitely miss out on their grandparents forever. Plus, the trip must cost a fortune.

Compassionate communication about solutions Clearly, we both want the kids to get to see their grandparents, so that rules out 'not going' or 'sending the in-laws away'. Out of the 'going' options, the middle ground is to watch and wait for any altercation, then have a united front as a team. If the in-laws criticise Geoff when Nina isn't around, for Geoff to walk away and calm down, then talk to Nina. This feels less confrontational for Nina, and Geoff feels supported.

Taking valued action, implementing the solution Both of us value a connection between our children and their grandparents, so as much as they're annoying, we need to make ourselves uncomfortable at times for the sake of their bond. We went to their house for the holidays and when Nina's dad gave Geoff a hard time, Nina said that it isn't necessary to speak to Geoff like that. Nina then walked in line with her values of supportiveness towards Geoff.

Compassionate communication about how the solution worked out Standing up to Nina's dad put him in a sulk and he avoided talking much to Geoff, which Geoff felt more relief than sadness about, as he escaped the criticism. The peace was kept reasonably well, and the kids got to play lots with their grandparents. Overall, most of our needs were met, even though it was exhausting.

Plan going forward We will do this for some of the big family get-togethers, not letting Geoff's father-in-law's mood create a rift between us as a couple. Together we can get through it, for the sake of the kids, and for the sake of giving Geoff an OK-ish experience of a family holiday. As a compromise, we can have some Easters just the four of us, staying at home.

Deciding, not sliding

One common problem for couples is that they don't make wise decisions together. Many find themselves going down a particular life path and can't remember making a conscious choice regarding how they got there. 'It just sort of happened' they say, explaining how they came to start living together, married or had children. It's as if they are sliding, not deciding.

For example, a couple *slides* into living together because it saves money on rent, rather than *decides* to move on to this next stage of the relationship. That couple might fail to consider the impact of sharing a space and everyday life together and end up arguing because of not having negotiated boundaries.

A couple who have been living together for years might end up getting married because it feels like 'the next step' or because it's expected. They *slide* past discussing whether they believe in the institution of marriage or whether they're ready for it at this point in their relationship.

Another couple starts a family and one partner ends up taking more responsibility for the management of the children than the other – was that a conscious decision? Did they negotiate this when they fell pregnant, and understand the impact it would have on each partner? The answer in a lot of cases is *no*.

Most couples don't consciously decide how they will live their lives together in a way that feels fair and meaningful. They don't consider the consequences of the choices they make, whether those choices take them closer towards or further away from the way they want to live, with the values they have.

Decisions, big and small

Couples can struggle with decision-making for very different reasons. Some feel empowered to make major, life-altering decisions, such as whether to have a baby or not, whereas others feel they don't even have the power to make small, everyday decisions.

Try this

Compassionately making an everyday decision as a team

Use your mindful and compassionate listening skills, as well as the productive problem-solving skills introduced above.

1 Sit down to discuss an everyday decision requiring you to negotiate. Consider something non-life changing, like buying a new sofa.

2 Don't give up your power by avoiding expressing what you want and need, but also don't argue over things that don't matter to you.

If you don't care about the colour of the sofa, don't dig your heels in. If it's important to you to have lots of space for guests don't agree to the small three-seater sofa your partner likes.

3 What would be a compromise for you, where you get some of your wishes or needs met? What would be a sacrifice, where you don't get your wishes or needs met at all? Would two separate three-seater sofas seat as many people as one large corner sofa? If your partner really cares about it being a particular design, can you afford to compromise and let go of one seat to get the style your partner likes?

How did it feel to do this together? Being able to discuss decisions and choices flexibly is a difficult skill to learn, but if you practise you'll get better at it.

How to live and how to love

Couples face many difficult decisions which they have to negotiate, which I broadly categorise under two headings: *How to live* and *How to love*. Look at the possible values which may come up in different choices.

How to live

Location, in which country, in a city vs in the countryside?

(excitement or *calm)*

Live close to family or as far away as possible?

(connection or *freedom)*

Living close to where we grew up, or somewhere new to both of us?

(safety or *novelty)*

Put down roots, or move around?

(comfort or *adventure)*

Move in together or have two places?

(togetherness or *independence)*

In a house or a flat, to rent or to buy?

(freedom or *responsibility)*

How to spend our weekends/evenings/time off from work?

(fun or *rest)*

How to raise our children, choosing parenting styles?

(routine or *flexibility)*

How to spend our money?

(organisation or *spontaneity)*

How to work, in what profession/job?

(security or *ambition)*

How to love

How to show gratitude and appreciation for each other?

(appreciation)

How to make efforts for each other?

(caring)

How to communicate and decide to meet needs?

(collaboration)

How to give and receive love and physical affection?

(love)

How to repair a rupture, forgive and reconcile?

(compassion)

How to show and receive support in the hard times?

(supportiveness)

How to celebrate wins and good times together?

(enjoyment)

How to initiate sexual intimacy and maintain physical closeness?

(intimacy)

What is the 'right' way to live and love?

As long as neither partner is getting hurt and boundaries have been clearly set, pretty much anything goes in terms of how to live and love. Regardless of how the relationship is structured – exclusive couples, polyamorous relationships with three partners together, open relationships, or on/off relationships where partners consciously take breaks from each other – the key is whether the decisions about how to live and how to love have been made with compassion and consideration of each other's needs.

Try this

Compassionately making a major decision as a team

Choose one area together from the list of decisions around how to live and how to love.

1 Start by 'warming up' separately, using something from your compassionate tool kit in order to get yourselves in the frame of mind where you can hear each other. Five minutes of soothing breathing rhythm or safe place imagery can calm down your body and mind for the tricky discussions to come.

2 Step into your compassionate self before you start the conversation, to balance your needs with your partner's.

3 Take turns speaking and listening using the compassionate communication guidelines, to really hear and understand each other's viewpoint.

4 Find where your middle ground is, where the compromise lies between your wishes. If there's no compromise to be had, can you acknowledge how hard it is to not find a fair compromise? Can you be flexible? Or do you need to agree to disagree over something?

The deal-breakers where no compromise can be made

Sometimes it's not possible to find a compromise in a particular decision, either because there isn't one or because one or both partners aren't willing to make it. If it fundamentally goes against what you believe in, or against your values to the point where you couldn't live like that, you're looking at a sacrifice you're not willing to make – it becomes a *deal-breaker*.

From the sofa

Yee and Christopher needed help with a big decision. They loved each other very much, describing themselves as best friends, and scored highly on the Couples Satisfaction Index. They had been married for a number of years and, now being in their thirties, felt they needed to decide on whether or not they would start a family.

Yee felt that she wanted to have a baby, Christopher didn't. Christopher sought out personal therapy, feeling guilty for having had a change of heart, having previously thought it would be on the cards. The couple were faced with the decision of either ending their marriage or one of them going against their wishes. They also struggled to decide where they wanted to live, as they had travelled around and lived in a number of countries during their time together.

Focusing on values, and understanding what they each see as a meaningful life, would help them make a wise decision about starting a family, or whether to end the marriage over this deal-breaker. Another option was to allow each other more flexibility to pursue the things which were important to them *before* entering into parenthood.

Christopher wanted more freedom to find out who he was, to explore the world on his own instead of just defining himself by his relationship. He wanted to take off his wedding ring while spending some time apart, travelling. Yee couldn't agree to an open relationship – a sacrifice she wasn't willing to make – so that became the second deal-breaker.

Yee and Christopher were so respectful of each other's feelings, from deep love and care for each other, that they didn't dare to go fully into the more emotional parts of their decisions – *'experiential avoidance'* (avoiding the experience of the emotions or thoughts related to a topic). They needed help in really getting in touch with their thoughts and feelings around their decision. Yee needed clarity on whether she *wanted* to be a parent or thought she *ought* to. They decided that if they couldn't become parents for fertility reasons, that would be OK, so they saw a fertility specialist. As they both were able to conceive, and Yee had more time 'on the clock' than she had worried about, Christopher dared to say he wanted to leave, letting Yee go so she would still have time to meet someone else who would want a family.

The couple separated, as the two deal-breakers couldn't be resolved and there was no compromise around the wish for freedom and the wish for a family. Christopher explored the freedom he valued through dating other women. He gained clarity of where he wanted to live and how he wanted to work, in a different country which had more fun, culture and warmth than his current location. He realised he wanted to share those experiences with Yee, who also wanted to reunite, albeit with strong feelings of anger towards Christopher for the hurt caused. In their attempts to reunite the couple moved towards the clarity that although they still loved each other, reconciliation would still mean a sacrifice neither of them could make, as it had become clearer than ever that Yee wanted a child and Christopher didn't. The most compassionate thing was to let Yee go and heal the hurt, rather than stringing her along in the hope of Christopher changing his mind.

Fair or flexible?

Couples often struggle with the concept of *fairness*. When we have a sense of injustice, it's normal to feel angry; no wonder couples argue when they feel things aren't fair. This potential for a sense of unfairness needs to inform decisions about who does what in the home and in the relationship – *defining the roles*. Enter these discussions with the mantra of *'fair or flexible?'* – can I be flexible? Who determines what is fair in our family? Am I likely to be like a dog with a bone until I get my way? This sort of inflexible behaviour can get you into trouble – you need to 'give an inch to gain a mile', as the expression goes. Or as couples therapist Esther Perel says on her relationship podcast *Where do we begin?* – 'You can be right – or you can be married.'

My story

I do more of the nursery pick-ups than my husband, as his working hours don't get him home in time. His work doesn't allow him flexible working hours and, up until COVID-19, he didn't work from home. That isn't fair, as doing all the pick-ups impact on my work as well as my socialising opportunities. It's also draining for me, with the emotional impact of managing a tired child on top of working. So it's not fair, but it's flexible as I'm self-employed and have decided to work from home a couple of days a week, to facilitate our family life. So the flexible, not fair, option is that I do most of the pick-ups and my husband does most of the drop-offs. The way to navigate this is to keep having conversations about balance, making space for feelings of unfairness and discussing options of making it fairer. My husband is now getting to work from home more and we are sharing the emotional labour of the childcare more fairly.

Summary

- Relationships can suffer from sliding instead of deciding how to live and love.
- Compromise needs to be a good enough solution which balances your needs with your partner's; you also need to find the courage to express what is important to you.
- Problem-solving and decision-making are practical skills required in order to progress with important life decisions, to reduce the risk of resentment and bitterness by deciding things together as a team.

Now we will look at the differences between you two, helping you focus on the areas in which you overlap as well as where you differ. You need to learn how to accept what you can't change, change what you can, and find the wisdom to know the difference.

17 Bridging the gap

Being different adds strength to your partnership

'Great minds think alike' or 'Opposites attract'. . . Do you need to agree on everything to feel satisfied in your relationship? Connection and compassion are more important than chemistry and compatibility – it's important to know when to agree to disagree instead of trying to win. Your respective strengths bring added value to your partnership team, and help you in working out what to accept and what to change.

Chemistry, compatibility, connection and compassion

'I think I've met THE ONE!' a client once exclaimed after meeting someone on an Internet dating site. She felt that they were drawn to each other like moths to light, having great *chemistry*. She was thrilled that they appeared to share the same likes and interests – that they were so *compatible*. She had met her perfect match. A year down the line, they broke up. Why? What went wrong?

Firstly, she had unrealistic expectations around relationships, buying into the myth of the 'perfect partner'. When he wasn't living up to her every expectation, disappointment set in. Secondly, she'd only focused on the ways they were similar, ignoring the ways they differed. When they started to disagree and argue she concluded that she'd been wrong and they weren't compatible after all. Thirdly, she didn't make enough efforts for their relationship connection, and got furious rather than curious when her partner's opinion differed from hers. Her expectations put pressure on the partner, with her criticism of his opinions straining their connection. The relationship ended after the honeymoon phase, when the electric feelings of that initial 'click' had faded. She'd managed two out of the four Cs – *chemistry* and *compatibility* – but she failed to keep the *connection* going through a lack of *compassion* for her partner.

Being a good fit is not enough for longevity

Shared interests make for positive experiences and memories, but chemistry and compatibility aren't the 'be all and end all' to creating *longevity* in a relationship. Good couples relationships aren't based on partners needing to have the same temperament and liking the exact same things. It may be that what you're initially attracted to in each other isn't able to stand the test of time – one of you loses interest in whatever initially bound you together. You then have to discover new things you can do together to keep the positive feelings going.

It's also important to be aware of how we tend to want to mould around others, wanting to create a *good fit*. Sometimes we play up interests to impress the other person, to 'click' with them. Unfortunately some people do this in a malicious way, playing a *game* of trying to pursue and catch you, but most of us are just looking for ways in which we are the same as someone. Sameness, however, isn't enough for a lasting connection.

Coping compassionately with incompatibility

It's more important to have togetherness and a way of compassionately coping with your *incompatibilities* than being compatible on every point. If you create a compassionate climate where you can respectfully dare to disagree at times the disagreements won't rupture your relationship completely. Using your skills in finding compromise will help when learning how to cope with differences between you and your partner.

What you bring to the table

If you can utilise one partner's strengths to accommodate for the other's weaknesses, you've bridged some of your differences. For instance, if one of you is less structured and frequently books the wrong flights, make the most of the other person's organisational skills and get them to take that on. If that organised person sometimes plans too much and struggles to relax, the more spontaneous partner can slow them down and help them let go. The fact that you'll be passionate about different things can provide a richness and a meaningful exchange.

Asking yourself 'How can I start to see the world a bit more like my partner does?' will result in less heartache than if you always ask yourself 'Why doesn't my partner see the world like I do?' That willingness to take their perspective will help your relationship grow, your connection to deepen and you to function more as a partnership team with different roles to play.

Imagine what life would be like if you were in a relationship with someone exactly like yourself, sharing every fault and flaw, every strength and skill. What things would you struggle with in your relationship? What things would you just never do, as neither of you would have the skill set to manage it?

Same, but different too?

Some couples only notice their differences. You might feel that you're on the same wavelength about how you want to treat each other as partners but might differ in how you want to act as parents raising your children; alternatively you might feel united in your parental values but can't reconcile the difference between you as romantic partners. We can be totally different as people, but still want and value the same things in life.

What things in life do you and your partner tend to agree on?

What values do you both hold as important?

What interests do you have in common?

What skills and qualities have you got in common?

Now think about how many of your differences result from *being different people,* and how much of that is about *having different values.*

Your partial overlap

The partners in a relationship can be seen as two individual yet overlapping circles. Each partner leans on the other through the process of *interdependence,* but each also has their own agency and free will.

The overlap is only ever partial – you don't need everything in common. If you can harness that overlap as a strength, you're more likely to have a lasting connection with your partner. This will help you accept and tolerate all the ways in which you don't overlap.

Your incompatibility, however, still needs to be workable.

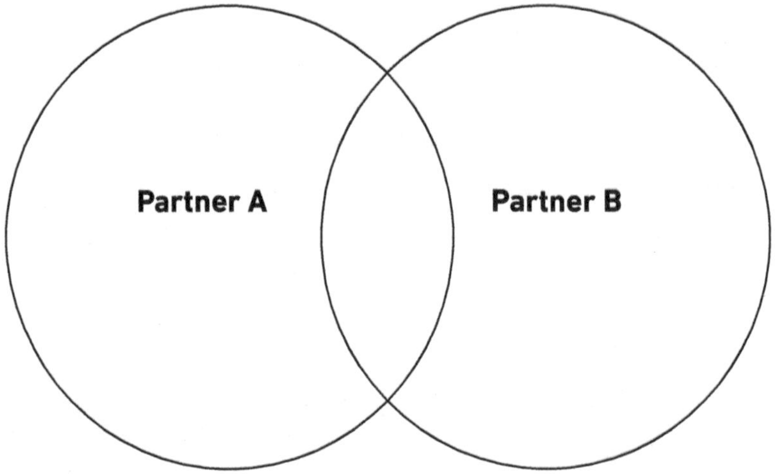

A workable relationship

Workability means *doing what works,* so a workable relationship is one where you can come up with flexible solutions to your 'stuckness'. If one partner's strength is numbers and the other one is better with feelings, then divide up your roles to play to your strengths. One partner might be designated to keep on top of the financial planning or helping the kids pass their maths test, and the other may be the go-to for when the teenage child has a painful break-up. This makes your everyday life more *workable.* Being different doesn't make one of you superior, it just makes you *different*. Doing what works means helping each other out when you feel out of your depth with something which is outside your comfort zone or skill set. It also means encouraging each other to grow confident in areas which aren't your forte, but where one of you has an aptitude.

Accepting or changing?

How do you know if you can bridge the differences between you with compassion? Perhaps there are things neither of you can change, and it's more about accepting that 'It is what it is'. The change aspect is less about changing what you like or dislike, as you can't really make anyone change their preference. It's more about changing how you approach your partner around whatever you disagree on. Think of the *Serenity Prayer*, which is very apt for any kind of self-reflection:

> *'Grant me the serenity to accept the things I cannot change,*
> *change the things which are under my influence,*
> *and the wisdom to know the difference.'*

Using a compassionate lens, ask yourself what you can do something about and what you choose to live with in your relationship.

- *Serenity* comes from stimulating your soothing system, calming down and reducing threat so you're able to get some perspective and clarity on your relationship.
- *Acceptance* is being able to see the world as it is, not as how you want it to be. Accepting with compassion means that you try to understand the journey you and your partner have been on, and what has shaped each of you. Accepting is not liking; you can accept your partner's flaws without liking them.
- *Change* is what happens when you become accountable for yourself, finding the courage and strength to take committed action to change your behaviour, and have that positive change ripple out of your relationship.

- *Influence* is what is within your control, what you can actually resolve. Often couples attempt to solve unsolvable problems, such as having different personalities or preferences instead of accepting that it is what it is.
- *Wisdom* is the 'doing what works' part, understanding how the world works and how you two in your relationship work, and then doing what gets you the best consequences – knowing when to address an issue to promote change, or when just to live with it.

My story

My husband and I are different in a lot of ways. We have a slight age gap, we're from different countries, we have grown up speaking different languages, and we have very different aptitudes. The insight into each other's strengths and weaknesses has helped us to compassionately support each other when we struggle. I failed orienteering in school and just WILL get lost when I go somewhere new, whereas my husband is excellent at reading maps. *Different skills, different thrills* – together we make an excellent pub quiz team. My husband, on the other hand, doesn't want to inconvenience others, and will not ask for help if we're lost. I can knock on someone's door to ask for directions, tolerating the embarrassment. Yes, this has led to friction many times, but a lasting connection is not about *not* having friction – it's about understanding the friction and working through it. We can complement each other if we work as a team, with our unique blend, and sometimes we just need to agree to disagree.

During the coronavirus pandemic it turned out that our different skill sets helped us work well together to survive in a crisis. We took on different roles and responsibilities tailoring to our strengths, and even though we often felt strained through juggling work and childcare, we grew closer than ever. Everything doesn't have to be perfect and shiny to strengthen your connection.

Agree to disagree

There are things within your partnership upon which you'll not be able to see eye-to-eye. John Gottman calls these '*perpetual problems*': no matter how much you discuss, negotiate and try to compromise, you'll not be fully satisfied with the solution and the problems will keep coming back. It's key to learn to accept these moments, as you otherwise run the risk of bailing and breaking the connection with your partner. Sometimes it just isn't workable to try to get an answer or a compromise to a dispute, and you know you'll have to find the most workable solution. They pick some, you pick some.

> *When is it most helpful and flexible to agree to disagree in your relationship?*

Deal or no deal

What are you willing to live with, agreeing to disagree, and what is a deal-breaker?

> *What are your deal-breakers? What couldn't you possibly put up with?*

- **Values-related** Racist/sexist views, use of physical discipline in child rearing, work/life balance differences.
- **Behaviour-related** Infidelity, making demeaning comments, harmful use of pornography, putting one's career ahead of family commitments, demanding sex, refusing to see partner's family.
- **Decision-related** Anything from how to live and how to love.

From the sofa

It's sometimes hard to find a 'right' or 'wrong' answer to disagreements, and this can cause arguments. This is what happens with James and Paula when it comes to the temperature in their bedroom at night.

Paula likes it cool and refreshing, James likes it warm and cosy. They're just *different*. Neither partner can dictate what is the 'right' temperature to sleep in – it's a subjective matter. What options do they have? They can identify the problem and why it matters to each of them, then brainstorm possible solutions with their compassionate self in the driving seat, then choose and implement one solution. James feels the topic has got inflamed, that Paula gets to 'dictate everything' in the household, so he digs his heels in. Paula feels James is 'ridiculous' wanting a duvet in the middle of summer and mocks him for his 'disgusting cold feet'.

Suddenly it isn't just about the temperature in the room. It's about their wider communication patterns and lack of perspective-taking for the other. When they approach it with more compassionate communication, sharing thoughts and feelings, Paula understands how James has felt left out of their decision-making ever since they had their bathroom renovation and he's now fighting the temperature issue as a way to 'rebel'. James understands that Paula is fighting the temperature issue as the menopause transition has left her feeling anxious at night if it's too hot, something which she has felt ashamed about. This makes it easier for both of them to give a little (compromise) to gain a lot (connection).

The compassionate couple bridges the gap

Couples who are compassionate and accepting of their individual differences can manage the strain of everyday romantic life better. That compassion can be strengthened by gaining clarity and wisdom around how different we all are.

Your personality portrait

Nikita Mikhailov, a psychometrician specialising in personality, defines personality as 'What you like, what you do, what you tend to overdo' – a more palatable explanation than the American Psychological Association definition of 'the unique psychological qualities of an individual that influence a variety of characteristic behaviour patterns (both overt and covert) across different situations over time'.[35]

Seeing how your personalities overlap and diverge helps us understand that there are different versions of you showing up in different contexts, rather than thinking that you're *either/or*. For instance, rather than thinking that you're either extrovert *or* introvert, there are some contexts in which you feel outgoing, confident and talkative, and some where you feel more shy, withdrawn and quiet. Each of you has the capacity for both extroversion and introversion. Personality portraits can show couples how the same quality can be a helpful addition to the team at times and at other times be a right nuisance.

From the sofa

Jasper and Kerry were very different people, Jasper being a focused and ambitious corporate manager and Kerry an expressive and intuitive full-time parent. Jasper built his career on being solutions-focused, taking this approach also to his marriage. The upside to this strategy was a calm and clear focus, but the downside was it made Kerry feel met with a 'cold business agenda' instead of validation and empathy. Kerry's strength was being people-focused, which also made her feel overwhelmed and unfocused when faced with a problem that stretched her emotionally. In their *everyday* personas, these qualities were helpful to their relationship as they complemented each other well in parenting their children. When either of them was under pressure, however, these qualities became *overextended*; they engaged in them too much. A stressed-out Jasper became cold, controlling and invalidating; a stressed-out Kerry became overwhelmed and couldn't take action.

Time to look at their respective values and explore the strengths and weaknesses they each brought to the partnership. Jasper worked on noticing his need for control and structure. That helped him pause and slow down his breathing to stop his solution-focused mind racing into fixes, and soften it with more flexibility, taking a leaf out of Kerry's book. He then made efforts to act in line with his values of being a 'caring, respectful and supportive husband'. Kerry worked on calming down her frazzled mind so she was more receptive to Jasper's ideas without getting angry. She could also calmly ask him just to listen if he fell into old habits of finding solutions. She was then able to use the strength of her personality to have deeper and more meaningful conversations with Jasper, and act in line with her values of being a 'kind, warm and attentive' wife. This had a positive ripple effect in Jasper's management style and he became more liked and respected amongst his staff. Although neither of them changed their personality completely they made tweaks to how they were acting and improved their interactions.

Reflection & Connection

Map out your skill sets, your strengths and weaknesses, naming things you can soar high in the sky on, or perhaps fly lower to the ground on, rather than being 'good' and 'bad' at.

YOU	YOUR PARTNER
Soar high	Soar high
Fly low	Fly low

You can tie this in with showing appreciation and gratitude for all your partner does for your relationship or family. They might be very self-critical of their own shortcomings, and so might you, so noticing the low points with kindness is key. If you find it difficult to elicit qualities in yourself or your partner, try this playful little game:

Try this

Who brings what?
Sit down with your partner, taking two pairs of your shoes and swap so that you each have one shoe from each pair. When you think your partner best fits the answer, you hold up their shoe. When you think you best fit, hold up your own shoe.

- Who brings spontaneity and fun to the relationship?
- Who brings structure and order?
- Who is good at planning an event?

- Who is the diplomat, navigating conflicts well?
- Who is the better cook?
- Who will easily get lost?
- Who won't ask for directions?
- Who says sorry first after a fight?
- Who is the better entertainer at a party?
- Who needs the most downtime after a party?
- Who gets more nervous about giving a speech?
- Who remembers birthday presents?
- Who would quit their job first if it was unfulfilling?

Through discussion you may find some of the qualities you bring to the table: being responsible, fun-loving, organised, spontaneous, open to new ideas, focused, and so on. This list is not exhaustive – you can come up with other questions yourselves! Then fill in the soar high/fly low list again.

Compassion for your differences

Let's bring to mind the three aspects of compassion in relationships: clarity, caring commitment and courage.

The *clarity* is that you're different people, with different temperaments and personalities, so you'll hold different opinions at times. With compassion and acceptance you can find a better *process* for dealing with the *content* showing up in your disagreements.

The *care* is around valuing what your partner wants and needs, respecting what they think as important even if you don't believe in or value the same thing. If your needs never get met and your opinion is never listened to, you will start to feel unwell, and it's important that you *care* about this not happening to either of you.

The *courage* is daring to express your opinion, even if you'll differ; to brave a difficult conversation even if it might get vulnerable and heated. It takes a lot of courage to recognise a need in yourself and ask for it to be met in your relationship. Use your compassionate self and inner mentor to help you if something is a deal-breaker to you.

My story

My husband and I just like different things when it comes to interior design and this is an unsolvable problem as we can't change each other's preferences. This popped up when we were planning our wedding, buying our first home together, renovating our kitchen and decorating our son's nursery. We will most likely always disagree on style choices, meaning that this theme may always stay with us and cause friction; but the process of how we go about these discussions is crucial for our relationship wellbeing, trying to not make it worse by adding insult to injury.

The process of adding insult to injury

Partners who approach their argument with compassion (clarity, care and courage) will behave very differently from partners who approach the fight with competitiveness, with the intention to beat the other person. The compassionate couple can make space for the differences, with a willingness to give an inch to gain a mile. If you're at an impasse where it's tricky to resolve the issue around your different needs, say that you want to socialise more and your partner wants to unwind at home, then the process of approaching that difference can be either competitive or compassionate.

If you're hurling abuse at your partner about being 'a boring house plant', and they have a go at you for being 'a manic social butterfly', you will also *add insult to injury* through approaching your difficulties with hostility and criticism. It's like you have created *problems around your problems*, which couples researchers refer to as *'primary distress'* and *'secondary distress'*.[36]

Your primary distress is about your fundamental needs not being met in this relationship – the more outgoing person doesn't get their social connection needs met, and the quieter person doesn't get their need met for alone time to recharge. The way they go about resolving that can cause secondary distress. If you attack, belittle or blame your partner because of differences in social need you add insult to injury.

You can also decide to choose your battles wisely and not disagree over things which mean less to you and focus your efforts where it really counts.

Can we change from 'who we are'?

It's common to hear a frustrated partner express 'but this is just who I am!' upon their partner requesting that they change.

Unfortunately saying this does not excuse you from not taking ownership of how you act in your relationship. Personality traits are fairly stable, but also a lot less set than previously thought; therapy can be effective in creating change in behaviour even with personality disorders.

The *good news* is that *you can change,* and *your partner can change.* You just can't *make* each other change.

The *bad news* is that change isn't easy; it takes hard work and dedication. If you want to change the things which irritate your partner, it may well be within your capacity to do so. Remember our multiple selves, the different parts of you? You can choose which version of you to allow into the driving seat and as a result your partner may feel that you 'have changed for the better', if you're willing to set foot into the other person's perspective. You can both change how you express your opinions, laying down your weapons to let go of the battle.

Compassionate communication is key

Compassionate communication is key in helping understand the themes in what you disagree about, and how you approach these differences. For a lot of partners, it's less bothersome to shift their viewpoint than to be subject to hurtful words *about* their viewpoint. If Paula and James had been able to communicate better about the temperature situation, they might have acknowledged that this theme of *decision-making* often shows up in their disagreements, and that they would engage in name calling and attacking instead of listening empathically to each other's perspective. In the end, they agreed to lower the heating in winter and have a window open in summer to make Paula comfortable, and to have separate duvets to make James comfortable. Understanding each other's feelings about the topic helped them to act in a more caring, rather than competitive, way.

Summary

- It's more important to be curious about each other's differences than it is to be exactly the same.
- With empathy and compassion, you can step into the shoes of your partner and care about what is important to them, even if you have to agree to disagree.
- Accepting is not liking – it means that 'it is what it is'.
- Understanding your personality portraits, with strengths and weaknesses, will make it easier to accept with compassion, using clarity, care and courage – to change the things you can and accept the things you can't.

Now we're going to see what happens when your relationship is under pressure, helping you to turn down the heat on conflict and arguments.

18 Turning down the heat

Decrease the negatives to strengthen connection

If you constantly argue and criticise each other, it doesn't matter how many date nights you go on; the threat will block the opportunity to feel close. Identifying the things you're doing too much of or not enough of in your relationship, and making a commitment to try to act more with love, will help you resolve your conflicts better.

Noticing and reducing the negatives

Couples wanting to improve their relationship need to focus on *increasing positives* and *decreasing negatives*. Positives are things like affection, compassion, fun, trust, team spirit and closeness; negatives can be hostility, criticism, mistrust, conflict, blaming and shaming. Before you can dial up your positives, you need to focus on decreasing the negatives. What do you think would happen in a hostile relationship if you attempt to breathe some warm positivity into it without first addressing the negatives?

Imagine this scenario: you've been fighting a lot and decide that it might be helpful to go on a date night, something you used to enjoy together in the past. You go to the cinema, but instead of having a nice moment of reconnection you argue about the film choice. You criticise your partner for choosing a 'mind-numbingly stupid action film' and your partner calls you 'bloody boring' for choosing an independent film about child labour in Pakistan. You can't compromise, as you get into the negatives which have been overshadowing your relationship. One of you storms out of the cinema to go home. Date night over.

The presence of negatives (name calling, criticism, personal attacks and lack of compromise) got in the way of the positives, the *intention* of reconnecting and having a good time. The actual film is secondary to the togetherness, of having shared time together. If you approach a potentially rewarding situation with a competitive rather than compassionate motivation you're headed for trouble.

Choose your battles

There are some fights you can't 'win' in your relationship, often relating to personal preference or standards. For example, how tidy your home should be or how you're going to spend your holidays. The challenging thing about these battles is that there is no 'right' or 'wrong'; both partners are 'right' at the same time, as they're entitled to a preference. This can create negative 'heat' in a relationship, especially if you're fairly reactive in your personality styles.

It's easy to get bogged down in these everyday battles, but being in a committed, loving relationship is about *living a life, not winning a war*. It's not about keeping a score card. Let go of some of your battles and come to a compromise faster to turn down the negative heat in your relationship, helping you get on better day-to-day. Spend your time and effort on things which matter to you as a loving couple – perhaps being close, showing each other affection, caring for each other.

The window of tolerance

When you and your partner have conflict, you both enter your threat system and get a stress response. How you react to this relationship stress depends on a lot of factors, including earlier life experiences. Some partners get more triggered than others and might very quickly leave their *window of tolerance*. This term, coined by Dr Dan Siegel, refers to the space where you're able to tolerate your own emotional experience and function properly.

It's as if the volume control on your emotional stereo is turned up too high and it's hard to think over all the noise. You might scream and shout, storm off, threaten, say things you don't mean and burn bridges, because of strong feelings of anxiety, anger or shame. You've become *hyper-aroused* – the rational thinking part of your brain, the prefrontal cortex, is turned off. When you have entered this sort of fight/flight response, you need to bring the volume down again, soothing yourself so you can take in what your partner is saying.

Some partners react differently to the stress of conflict, leaving the window of tolerance by becoming *hypo-aroused*. They might feel numb, spaced out or paralysed, shutting down and withdrawing from their partner.

If the temperature rises too much, it can be helpful to call a *time out* in your interaction. This gets your parasympathetic nervous system a chance to cool you down, to soothe the threat and regulate your emotions to make them tolerable again.

The vicious cycle of withdraw and demand

A very common pattern seen in couples is that of *withdraw and demand*, where one partner pulls away and the other pursues. It may be initiated by one partner becoming aggressive or critical, leaving the other person feeling overwhelmed, thus pulling away as an act of self-preservation. It may be initiated by one partner being generally avoidant or secretive, not expressing very much in the relationship, leaving the other partner feeling threatened by the lack of communication and thus having to push the withholding partner for more answers or interaction.

This pattern arises from a threat system activation in either partner, and the response is selected from the menu of protective strategies: fight, flight, freeze and appease. These responses are automatic, and they can be subtle. It's easy to notice the withdraw and demand pattern in a couple where one person gets off the sofa and *physically* leaves the room, slamming the door, and the other person opens the door to follow them and continue the argument. It's harder to spot when they both remain seated on the sofa, but one partner has stopped listening, and has *mentally* withdrawn as the other person continues talking. The silent partner has gone into shutdown due to feeling overwhelmed by threat.

Reflection & Connection

Sit down with your partner to reflect on what puts each of you in your threat system, where you might withdraw or attack to keep safe, or why either of you might have a narrow window of tolerance.

> *What triggers you to withdraw from your partner?*
>
> *What triggers you to be demanding of your partner?*

Use your compassionate communication to make space for your differences here.

From the sofa

Jo and Andrew were caught in a strong withdraw and demand pattern, and both struggled with their self-esteem. Andrew often felt insecure about Jo's love for him. When Jo was upset with Andrew she would walk away, withdrawing. This activated Andrew's threat system, feeding his story that he was worthless in her eyes. He would respond with anger and accuse Jo of not loving him and not making enough effort. This fed Jo's story that she was failing as a wife, so she withdrew more. Their respective low sense of self triggered this reactive withdraw and demand pattern, making them flammable and disconnected. They were so deep in their threat systems that they showed contempt for each other through non-verbal clues, such as rolling their eyes, crossing their arms or sighing ostentatiously when disagreeing.

Somewhat paradoxically, they both spoke warmly about each other, especially when the other partner wasn't in the room. Their problem wasn't so much that they were different or didn't love each other – it stemmed from where they were very similar (their negative view of themselves taking them away from the values they had about how to be as a husband or wife). Strengthening Andrew's self-esteem and soothing his threat helped him make less aggressive bids for Jo's love and affection, whereas Jo practised showing Andrew in practical ways that she loved him when he wasn't asking for it. Jo strengthened her confidence as a mother and wife by stepping into the more nurturing version of herself, which had been there all along. Both of them were recommended personal therapy for low self-esteem to help them reduce their flammability. It took some hard looks in the mirror for each of them to realise how they had both contributed to the pattern they had got stuck in.

The magnifying glass, the spotlight and the mirror

Couples often point a *magnifying glass* onto each other's flaws, highlighting all the ways the other person is to blame. They zoom in so much on what is going wrong that they miss what is going right. If you zoom out a bit more you can get some perspective on your relationship. For instance, you may be going through lots of irritability and tension, but you're still able to make decisions together as a team; or you're struggling with sexual intimacy, but are still close friends and share emotional intimacy.

Instead of zooming in on each other as the problem, make it a team effort to shine that *spotlight* of attention onto the relationship patterns as the problem – illuminating what's going on between you. You'll also need a *mirror*, to understand how your own behaviours feed into the vicious cycles in your relationship.

Couples where both partners are willing to reflect on themselves are more able to change for the better. Without this, improving the relationship is an uphill struggle. Sometimes one partner is willing and on board and the other one isn't, and this resistance can be really frustrating for them as a couple. *Rolling with resistance* helps the resistant partner realise what's in it for them to commit to the process of change; how could they benefit from looking at their own actions and changing them? Often, the way in lies in clarifying their values in life, exploring what motivates them and how they want to be as a person and a partner. Especially if they have children, for whom they will be a role model – how do you want your children to grow up and behave in loving relationships?

What you're doing too much of

Take a look in that mirror now: what *negative things do you do* in your relationship, which contribute to the negative climate between you? Do you have a go at your partner when they make mistakes? Do you end up shouting or threatening to leave? Perhaps you use harsh words about them when you're angry? Do you mock your partner for their opinions, or make fun of them in front of their friends? These behaviours are likely to increase the negative heat in your relationship. This can be hard to tolerate, and will likely encourage your partner to withdraw.

Your unhelpful behaviours may be much less aggressive than that and instead take on a cold, icy nature; you may withdraw and stop talking to your partner when they have upset you, or you might make important decisions without consulting them first. These negative behaviours will shake your relationship, and if you aren't careful, can shatter your connection completely.

> *What are you doing too much of, which either freezes your relationship or threatens to make it go up in flames?*

What you're not doing enough of

Continue to look in the mirror: what *positive things don't you do* in your relationship, which could improve it? Do you ask for forgiveness when you've made a mistake? Do you forgive when your partner has messed up, and focus on moving forward? Do you make efforts to repair? Do you listen to your partner's viewpoint? Do you share the softer feelings behind your anger, being vulnerable enough to say if you're scared or sad? Do you make your partner feel valued and special? Do you bring kindness and compassion to your partnership?

> *What are you not doing enough of, which could either thaw a cold relationship or lower the flames in an overheated relationship?*

What you're doing well

Taking one last look in the mirror now: what *positive things are you doing well* with, which you don't acknowledge enough? If you struggle to notice what you're doing well, or are particularly hard on yourself, revisit Chapter 10 about softening self-criticism. You might need to ask your partner to help here.

> *What relationship skills have you got which help you deepen the connection with your partner?*

Compassionately soothing the negatives

Remember the second part of the compassion definition? The commitment and dedication to do something about the pain you have found, wanting to be helpful and not harmful. Once you've become aware of the vicious cycles contributing to the negative emotional climate in your relationship, you can do something about it by using your compassionate tool kit.

Your compassionate tool kit for the couples apocalypse

Gottman's 'four horsemen of the apocalypse' are those factors which create negative heat in a relationship and can make it go up in flames. You need to let go of these four apocalyptic riders in order to reconnect and rebuild trust, promoting that lasting connection.

Letting go of: criticism

Remind yourself of the compassionate teacher being the most likely to facilitate change. Raising a complaint in a compassionate way is not about letting your partner get away with murder – you can still hold them accountable and express how you feel about what they have done.

Try this

Use your compassionate self to point out an issue in a corrective rather than critical way. Use your compassionate self to ask your needs to be met, instead of criticising when the needs haven't been met.

Letting go of: contempt

Remind yourself of the jigsaw puzzle you've drawn out for your partner, understanding why they do what they do instead of treating them with contempt for their actions. Remember the non-verbal clues you send out with your facial expression, tone of voice and posture, and remind yourself of the compassionate motivation to collaborate with rather than to beat each other.

Try this

Write a compassionate letter to your partner to better keep in mind what you know about them. Ask for time out when things get heated, to enable you to step into your compassionate self to send kinder non-verbal clues when in conversation, instead of eye-rolling or sighing.

Letting go of: defensiveness

Remind yourself that living in a frantic modern world makes it harder to step into compassionate rather than competitive motivation. You can gently set a boundary by expressing that you don't want to be spoken to like that, but also understand that it's about your partner's threat activation too.

Try this

Use mindfulness, soothing breathing rhythm and safe place imagery to soothe your threat system when you feel attacked, putting your compassionate self in the driving seat. Put yourself in your partner's shoes and try to soothe them, instead of focusing on defending yourself.

Letting go of: stonewalling

Remind yourself how tricky our brains are, and how quickly they turn to self-protection from threat, like withdrawing. It's not your fault, but it's your responsibility to do something about it.

Try this

Use your compassionate inner mentor to soothe you so you can tell your partner how you feel, instead of pulling away. Let this wise inner part of you remind you of the values you hold for yourself as a partner, and help you find the strength to consistently behave in line with those values.

Be aware that the next section could be upsetting for you to read if you've gone through traumatic experiences.

Healing the threat from trauma

Some people are particularly quick to enter their threat systems because of what's happened to them in life, as difficult or traumatic experiences can leave us being on high alert for danger. We know that touch is important for regulating your physiology, as it brings down your heart rate and slows down your breathing. However, if you don't feel *safe* being touched, your body and brain chooses to activate the threat system *for you*.

If you have experienced things in your past making touch difficult, *it's not your fault*. Childhood sexual abuse is estimated to have affected 1 in 20 children in the UK,[37] so there's a chance that you or someone you engage with intimately has experienced being taken advantage of at a young age. Be sensitive as to how touch can be perceived.

Abuse isn't the only reason why touch might be threatening. Those who have experienced difficult rejections, or lack of nurture as a child, can feel that touch is challenging. It might be linked with a fear of it being taken away again, or that it's not given without a hidden agenda. Remind yourselves of your attachment styles, of your experience of care when you were younger. Some families and some cultures are more tactile than others, so be respectful of your differences.

If touch is difficult for you, start becoming mindfully aware of how your body responds when you give or receive touch. If it doesn't feel safe, back off and use your soothing skills to settle yourself. Trauma shapes your nervous system, your wiring, but it can also be treated and soothed. If you've gone through something traumatic, Deborah Lee's book *The Compassionate Mind Approach to Trauma* is a good place to start.

The healing of trauma comes from understanding, compassion and nurture. Work with your compassionate self for both your partner and yourself and be willing to get creative and playful as a way to get yourself back into that window of tolerance.

My story

If you feel overwhelmed while fighting with your partner, chances are that nothing good will come out of it and you'll struggle to resolve the disagreement. I'm more emotionally reactive than my husband, having a broader emotional range. We've learned that the hard way, as arguments about essentially nothing have blown out of proportion. Let me present Exhibit A, *The hat rack fight of 2014*, where deciding how high on the wall the new hat rack would sit resulted in me getting so angry that I slept on the sofa that night. Ridiculous, I know.

That fight – which occurred in the context of me experiencing burnout at work – taught me that I have a need for calling 'time out' on a fight to help me get back into my window of tolerance. Using a healthy form of distraction can take the edge off. After a few minutes of somewhat angrily playing a card game such as Go Fish, focusing my attention on the game rather than on my inner stuff, I can return to the problem with slightly less threat activation and might be able to hold my partner's perspective more in mind, and reach a solution together. It also helps me receive compassion, accepting a hug from my husband and allowing us to repair whatever hurt was caused in the heat of the moment.

Mind you, this is not a strategy to throw in when your partner is deeply upset or needs you to physically and emotionally be there to soothe them. It's *not OK* to shout, 'You're crying so let's play Go Fish to make you feel better!' This small strategy can be helpful at times where you're butting heads on a problem which you both agree needs to be solved but the conversation is getting too heated, and your threat systems are blocking your drive systems. It can be really hard to jump straight into the soothing system and give each other a hug and apology at that point, without first bringing down the heat somewhat.

Looking after flammability

When you don't look after yourself, or stretch yourself beyond your limits, you're more likely to snap. You therefore need to manage how reactive you are, how flammable you are in your relationship. You on a good day might be able to resist the urge to make that passive-aggressive comment to your partner when they make a mistake, but you on a day without much sleep or with a looming work deadline may act completely away from your values.

You can soothe your own threat system and engage in self-compassion to be less reactive and flammable day-to-day. Make your own well-being a priority.

Struggling against what is

What you're going through in life right now – *it is what it is*. You can focus on doing something about it, but not without first accepting the problem exists. You need to let go of the struggle against your problems, say illness or financial strain, perhaps wishing them away or to be not so bad. By non-judgementally observing what is going on you can see how you can help yourselves in a difficult time. You can't wait until the person who is sick is no longer sick, or until your financial problems have got better, before you do something to look after your relationship. You may be able to bring your connection back, but for some the connection may have dwindled beyond the point of repair.

Why take that risk? You can still take action to value your relationship in the midst of something challenging. The global crisis of COVID-19 has shown us that acceptance is key in order for us to keep functioning day-to-day.

Try this

Stop the struggle

Try to do this exercise together with your partner.

1 Take an A4 piece of paper each and decide together which couple of words to write down to describe a problem causing friction in your

relationship right now. You might write 'money problems', 'intimacy issues', 'in-laws' or 'coronavirus'.

2 Hold your paper with both hands, pushing it as far away as possible from your face. Notice how that feels after a little while. Are you feeling that tension? Notice how much you can see beyond the paper. Is it blocking your vision? Notice how much else you can concentrate on, when firmly holding on to the paper. Is it taking up all your attention? It's occupying your hands, leaving you unable to do much else. This is probably what you've been doing in your relationship, spending all your effort trying to get rid of the problem, or firmly holding on to it, not wanting to back down on your viewpoint. You and your partner have drifted apart, as you can't do much else but hold this problem in mind (and in hand).

   How has that been working out for you?

Your struggle against the problem has become the problem.

3 Now try something new. Rather than pushing the problem (the paper) away, gently lay it down on your lap. The problem hasn't gone away, but by choosing to sit with it, allowing it to be there without fighting against it, you can liberate both your mind and your hands to engage with things which are important to you. You can engage better with your partner and turn down the heat in your relationship coming from the tension and exhaustion of struggling against the problem.

This too shall pass

One lesson from Eastern philosophy relates to the impermanence of things, of how everything changes. This is a hard pill to swallow in the Western world, where we focus so much of our time and effort on chasing after and clinging onto happiness. If you're going through hard times, with fear, worry or uncertainty around the future, reminding yourself that 'This too shall pass' can be helpful. Like the ebb and flow of the ocean, you can't make it stop or make it move faster.

Sadly, the good times will also pass. The initial romance and exhilarating desire of the early days of a relationship will pass – we can't cling onto that or make it stay. We can only accept that all good things and all bad things will eventually pass, like waves on the ocean. *You can't stop the waves, but you can learn to surf*, as Jon Kabat-Zinn says.[38]

Summary

- To reconnect with your partner, you need to turn down the volume on the negatives in your relationship first.
- If you constantly argue and criticise each other, it doesn't matter how many date nights you go on; the threat will block the opportunity to feel close.
- You can't fully eradicate threat and negativity from your relationship, but you can equip yourself with the compassionate tool kit to keep the couples apocalypse at bay.
- Using compassionate mind training skills you can soothe the threat between you to be less reactive and flammable day-to-day.

We can now move onto increasing the positives in your relationship, to help you foster an emotional connection and get closer together.

19 Surviving and thriving

Connecting emotionally through good times and bad

There will be times in your relationship when you're just surviving, barely keeping your heads above the surface of the stormy water. Ride out the storm together – when it has passed you can focus on thriving again, by being joyful, playful, grateful and fun as a couple. Reconnect and increase the positive feelings in your relationship by doing more of the things you value together. Emotional connection comes through surviving hard times as well as enjoying good times together.

Intimate connection

What do you think of when you hear the word '*intimacy*' – does your mind go straight to sex? Intimacy is much broader than sex, and as a word, it can be synonymous with togetherness, affinity, closeness, familiarity. I work with both *emotional intimacy* and *physical intimacy*, helping couples who have drifted apart in their busy modern lives to get closer together through both mind and body connection.

Emotional connection from surviving together

All *relationships* go through hardship and stressors, as *life* is full of hardship and stressors. All couples have to navigate choppy waters at times. Relationships aren't linear, just getting better and better the longer we're in them. They're more like a heartbeat on a monitor, constantly going up and down. Relationships take commitment and work. People often think that if you have to work at a relationship, it isn't 'right' or 'meant to be'. Some relationships take more work than others, depending on personalities and temperaments and external stressful events.

Turning towards each other for support and strength, and keeping an open dialogue about how you're both affected by what you're going through, can really help you connect more deeply through periods of hardship. You can create meaning from the most horrendous things happening to you in life, with an open mind and acceptance around how 'It is what it is'.

Keeping your head above water

We delude ourselves that we don't need to work on a relationship when it's going well, then panic that the connection is lost when we hit a rough patch. To thrive as a couple, you have to accept that there are times where you'll simply just survive, barely keeping your heads above water – times which are simply just a bit sh*t. Letting go of the fairy-tale perfection and focusing on reality can, paradoxically, make you happier than chasing dreams. Fighting against having hardship in a relationship expends more energy than just settling in and dealing with it. That includes the ability to allow an argument.

Allowing an argument

Never fighting isn't an indication that you'll have a healthy and long-lasting relationship together. You may simply not have hit any hardship yet – the curveballs life throws you. Or you may not have hit upon any major and challenging decisions, like about how to raise children or whether to even have children. Never having arguments can also mean that one or both partners self-silence, not expressing how they really feel and instead going along with whatever the other partner wants.

If you lean into your relationship with trust and commitment, you can allow an argument. If you act with respect and compassion towards your partner, you can dare to express how you truly feel and think about something, by making space for both of your views.

> *To ultimately thrive in your relationship you need to allow and survive arguments and still be there for each other afterwards.*

Turn to your 'village'

There is a saying *'It takes a village to raise a child'*, meaning that the entire village or community has the shared responsibility for the child's wellbeing and happiness. The wellbeing of a relationship also is dependent on a 'village' of support, to get through rough patches without falling apart. Think of all the guests who came to your wedding and celebrated with you on the day, for example, wishing for you to both flourish in your relationship.

Hold in mind those around you who, for instance, helped you move into your first home or attended your wedding day – can you seek support from them? Do you know any couples who have been through hardship, who you could turn to for wisdom and advice? If you're a parent, are there any other couples who could offer you some baby-sitting for a chance to go out on your own as a couple?

Couples who have support tend to do better in times of crisis, partly because of feeling less alone in their struggles and partly because of any practical advice and help offered. The outside support can also be for just one partner, to take the pressure off the other, or to complement the partnership. It's unrealistic to get all your needs met at all times by just one person, so couples who get some needs met outside the partnership tend to weather a storm better.

My story

The hardest challenges to my marriage have come through my mood, when tough times leave me feeling stressed, low and anxious. The transition we had into parenthood tops that list of hard times, as we had challenging and traumatic experiences with our child's physical health. The irritability which came from sleep deprivation was a threat to our partnership, giving rise to criticism and defensiveness. There was constant threat activation, as we had to be vigilant about how to keep our baby safe and comfortable. This presence of negativity made it difficult to do the things together which we had previously enjoyed, and to recognise what drew us to each other initially, such as witty banter and caring supportiveness. All our efforts were directed towards our baby, and just getting through. It's common to go through hard times, regardless of how much you love each other or how many relationship skills you have. Now that we've survived these tough times, we've seen the strength of our team and know how much adversity we're capable of weathering together.

Reflection & Connection

There's a fascinating concept called *post-traumatic growth*, which means to achieve personal growth from the adversity you have been through. Couples have this capacity too, if willing to learn from the tough times they've survived together.

> *What hardships have you survived which have helped build strength, togetherness and interdependence, and the ability to take turns leaning on each other?*

Emotional connection from thriving together

Once you go past the initial romance and infatuation of a relationship, you build a deeper emotional connection through friendship and mutual respect. That's difficult if you're constantly fighting and criticising each other. After you've worked towards decreasing any negative exchanges you can increase the positive interactions, helping you move from surviving into thriving.

Mending the ship after a storm

If you've been together for a few years, odds are that you've survived some tough things together, having got through a few rough storms – but the ship may have become a bit battered. You need to repair the ship so that your relationship can thrive and flourish. One way to build your emotional connection is by doing more of the activities you enjoy, or used to enjoy, together. This might feel like a challenge; your interests will have changed compared to when you were dating, as people grow and develop with age and maturation. The things you used to do early in your relationship may not feel that enjoyable any more, so you might tell yourself 'Treasure hunts are too silly' or 'There's no way I can go climbing now, I did that when I was young and fit.' Try this with an open mind, using brainstorming and problem-solving if you can't settle on an activity to try. The beauty of the partnership is getting to see the world through another person's lens. If you have a *willingness* to try new things your partner enjoys, you can discover things about yourself you didn't know.

Being well, doing well

Wellbeing in your relationship is not just the absence of sarcasm or hostility, much like mental and physical good health is more than just the absence of illness. Relationship wellbeing is also the presence of something positive.

Baucom, Epstein and Sullivan define a 'healthy relationship' as one which contributes to the growth and wellbeing of both partners, working well together as a team, and being able to adapt to their physical and social environment over time.[39] That reflects the importance of flexibility – being able to adapt and bend, to not break.

Flourishing together

How do you know if you're flourishing together as a couple? Partly it's to do with what's happening within each of you, *how you feel*, but also between you, *how you feel about each other*. Being well as a person means it's more likely you'll be doing well as a couple, so make sure to take care of and increase your overall wellbeing if necessary.

If you flourish as a couple, you're interested in the direction of your relationship, looking forward to your future together, wanting to improve your relationship and help it develop further. You feel like your life together has meaning – it's purposeful to be with one another. You can get through your daily responsibilities as a couple, who does what in your household. Flourishing in your relationship reduces your risk of depression, as the wellbeing of your relationship affects the wellbeing of both partners.

Compassion isn't just about alleviating the pain we're in; it's also about the prevention of suffering. If you can identify what your partner needs, and they can do the same for you, then you can meet each other's needs without getting caught up too much with your own ego. *Doing* good literally *feels* good.

Thriving through joy and play

When we're engaging in something which stimulates us, which we think is fun, we're lit up with joy. This can help us to focus on what we're doing in that moment. One definition of 'play' is to 'engage in activity for enjoyment and recreation rather than a serious or practical purpose'. Play is not only fun enjoyment in the moment, but also facilitates our movement in the *direction* of our serious or practical purpose. Playing helps us feel robust and restored so we can take all the hardship of working to make a living. Life is hard enough – why not add in some more of the light and joy, on *purpose*?

The word purpose comes up again – doing something deliberately to take ourselves in the direction of what is meaningful in our lives. If it's meaningful for you to work, achieve and perform, then great – you have ambition. Play and joy can also facilitate being ambitious and driven, without burning out in the process. So, dance like nobody's watching, chase your kids around, lose yourself in a game of badminton, laugh at silly jokes . . . whatever floats your joy boat. Living life in a more flexible way and giving yourself the permission to pause can help you still reach those goals and perform better.

To connect in play with your partner can be tricky, as it requires a degree of matching your states or emotional systems. One of you might be more in your threat system (feel too tense, stressed or angry to play) or in your drive system (want to get things done, not having time for games). This disconnect can result in bickering between couples and missed opportunities for connection. You need to pause and slow down first, soothing yourselves before you can play.

Permission to play

Why don't we all just play more then, if it's that joyful? For some, play itself can be connected to the threat system, as it may trigger memories of shame for being told off for being playful or silly as a child. That's why you need to give yourself and your partner the *permission* to play, to make it a safe thing to do. If your soothing system is activated, you feel safe, secure and relaxed. You can then get into the more energetic drive system, to play.

Playing is associated with positive feelings such as joy, pride, satisfaction and meaning. You might also be pursuing a shared value of having fun together, regardless if the activity is tickling each other, racing each other to an imaginary finish line or trying to win at a game of chess or tennis. Play can give you that direction of walking in line with values such as fun, connection, creativity, spontaneity and light-heartedness.

There are many ways to play – just watch a child for a bit and see what they do. That doesn't mean you have to pretend to be an astronaut. You can adapt it to adulthood, but to be honest only your own embarrassment puts a stop to how you play. Use the list below for inspiration.

The Pause – Purpose – Play buffet of activities

Here's a *smörgåsbord* (buffet) of options you could choose from: a mix of drive and soothing system activation. Some activities are related to eating (people often enjoy preparing and consuming food together). Some involve being active and doing exercise (stimulating endorphins, increasing your sense of joy). Some are related to slowing down and taking it easy (stimulating your soothing system, facilitating closeness). Some are about *hedonistic* wellbeing (doing things just for pleasure and fun), and some are about *eudaimonic* wellbeing (doing things which are linked to your values and giving you meaning and purpose).

Essentially, it's about slowing down to *pause* for long enough to figure out what is important to you both, what fills you with *purpose*, and then taking some time to *play*, to increase relationship satisfaction.

Try this

Joint activities for increased joy and fulfilment together

Pause

Go for a massage/massage each other
Meditate together
Take a nap, cuddled up together
Relax in a café, chatting
Have a picnic and watch the clouds
Go for a walk, holding hands
Watch people go by
Drive or hike through nature
Breakfast in bed
Look at photos of joint memories
Sit chatting in your garden
Take a yoga class
Go to a spa
Doodle or draw together without aim
Stare out into space, wonder what's out there

Purpose

Help an elderly person
Visit an animal shelter
Redecorate your home
Volunteer at a shelter/soup kitchen
Babysit for a friend together
Set up a savings plan for a dedicated aim
Learn to cook a new dish
Take a class to learn a new hobby
Build something for your home
Plan a trip or holiday
Create a vision board, with magazine cut-outs
Read the same book and discuss impact on your life

Play

Play a racket sport
Watch an uplifting film
Listen to music you love
Go to the gym or run together
Go to a comedy gig
Go to the ballet/theatre/cinema
Try a random new restaurant for dinner
Listen to your favourite music
Dance like nobody's watching
Jump in puddles in the rain
Take silly photos in a photo machine
Go fishing or climbing
Play a board game/cards
Blow bubbles and try to pop them
Create a treasure hunt
Go exploring on holiday
Complete crosswords
Tickle each other, pillow fight or wrestle in bed
Host a murder mystery party with dress up
Get messy – foam party, mud jumping, finger painting

Reflection & Connection

Before What was it like to choose an activity together? If you started arguing, use compassionate communication to share thoughts and feelings better. Be respectful of your differences – you won't feel soothed, excited or threatened by the same things. What is important is the *willingness to try*, to step out of your comfort zone to try something together with your partner.

During Use mindfulness skills to pay attention to what's happening around you in the here and now, with your partner, catching yourself when you drift off in your mind. Notice how you're *feeling* together, allowing yourselves moments of tenderness or excitement and really being present with it. Put your phones away.

After You've finished the activity, that's all done. Or is it? Here we use *savouring* to stretch the experience further, as if slowly eating a delicious piece of chocolate instead of just scoffing it down. Chat about the best moments you had together, remembering the laughter or the tenderness. Look at photos if you took any, reliving the experience.

> *Spending time together, building friendship and closeness, will not only help you mend any broken parts of your ship from past storms, but also help strengthen your relationship boat for the rougher seas ahead.*

From the sofa

Suffering from sleep deprivation after having had their third baby, Marcie found it difficult to spot when her husband Billy made bids for joy and playfulness. They were both fatigued from the emotional strain of having three young children under five, so he missed her attempts as well. It just didn't feel safe enough to play, when they were both often wound up and irritated. When Marcie was shattered and would grumpily storm into the kitchen after trying to get their overactive child to sleep, Billy would try to 'cheer her up' through making jokes or making the situation more light-hearted. Marcie would stare at him in disbelief and storm out of the kitchen, and they would spend the rest of the evening in separate rooms. Later on, Marcie would try to hand Billy an olive branch by being playful and tickling him in bed, but Billy would roll over and turn out the lights, still angry about how he had been rejected earlier.

Marcie and Billy missed opportunities for connection through play, as they were in their threat systems. They hadn't created a safe space where play could occur. They needed to really see each other and validate each other's emotions about the lack of sleep and the new baby. That would have helped create a place of calm and safeness, where they would naturally gravitate more towards each other. Billy's jokes *could* have been met with a laugh and a head tilt; that tender tickle *could* have turned into something more intimate like a warm hug.

Try this

Tuning into what you each need

- Ask yourself how *your partner* might feel in this moment, before you make a joke or try to 'lift the mood'.
- Ask yourself how *you* might feel in this moment, if you feel uncomfortable with negative feelings and try to lift the mood for your own sake.
- Ask your partner what they need in this moment when they seem irritable, sad or worried – perhaps make an agreement of how you signal to each other when it's OK to try to cheer up and distract away from it, and when you need the space to talk it through and offload.

Summary

- All relationships go through hard times, storms, and brighter times, sunshine.
- A relationship which has only experienced sunshine isn't necessarily a 'better' relationship than one which has experienced strains.
- Storms give you a chance to practise skills in protecting your connection and can bring you closer together through surviving hard times.
- After the storm has passed, you can relax and mend the broken parts and find playfulness again, to really thrive together.

After learning how emotional connection works, let's move on to physical connection and intimacy through touch and sex.

20 Turning up the heat

Connecting physically through intimacy and touch

We move on to getting physically close and being playful, using mindfulness and compassion in the bedroom. Learn the difference between performative sex and connected sex, and use compassionate communication to make sex meaningful to you.

Physical intimacy

What's the first thing you think of when reading 'physical intimacy'? Probably sex. How does it make you feel, emotionally and physically, to read about sex? Perhaps a bit cringey? You're in good company – lots of us find this challenging. Especially with partners. Sit with that discomfort for now, because physical satisfaction does have a bearing on your overall relationship satisfaction.

Physical connection and intimacy are more than sex

It's important to emphasise that a lot of the physical closeness between partners is not sexual in nature. Holding hands, cuddling up, stroking a cheek – those non-sexual touches are key to your social joy and emotional connection. In the everyday hustle and bustle it's easy to forget to hold each other close, to hug, to kiss – especially if you also have children. Try to make space for these little acts of affection, as drawing close for a snuggle can deepen your moments together, bringing more magic to the mundane.

Why is physical closeness important in intimate relationships? We know that oxytocin, 'the cuddle hormone', can soothe and calm you and your partner. This hormone is released in a long hug, rather than a quick brush against each other. If you have experienced sexual trauma in the past, physical touch may feel triggering for you and you may need professional help. If you never touch each other it's difficult to spark desire and passion.

Myths about physical intimacy and desire

In this section I lean on the expertise of a 'sexpert': Dr Karen Gurney, Clinical Psychologist and Psychosexologist, author of *Mind the Gap.*

The most common misconception about physical intimacy in committed relationships is that 'Everyone is having more sex than we are'. The British National Survey of Sexual Attitudes and Lifestyles (Natsal) showed that, on average, adults aged 16–74 years in the UK have sex about three times a month. However, 29 per cent of people under 44 had no sex at all in the month prior to the survey. If you have sex four times a week, or haven't had sex for four years, that's OK. How often you have sex isn't an important metric by which to measure your relationship satisfaction. Quality is more important than quantity when it comes to sexual intimacy and a lasting connection.

One partner often wants to have sex more often than the other, and this difference in level of desire is the norm. We need acceptance and compassionate communication around this discrepancy – it's not anyone's 'fault' that they experience less desire than their partner, nor does it mean that they're broken. Natsal established that both men and women commonly experience a lack of interest in sex (34 per cent of women and 15 per cent of men), and that sexual difficulties affect as many as 51 per cent of women and 42 per cent of men aged 18–80.[40] If you're experiencing sexual difficulties seek out advice from your GP for a referral to a specialist psychosexual clinic.

If lack of desire is this common, and if sexual difficulties affect this many, couples really need to get talking about sex.

Compassionate chats about sex

Why should we talk about sex? If you have no particular interest in sex, and it seems OK as it is between you and your partner, why would you make the effort?

Good sex (quality, not quantity) is linked with short-term positive effects on your mood, and long-term positive effects on relationship satisfaction and stability. According to Dr Gurney, communication about sex is the strongest predictor of long-term sexual satisfaction in relationships, much more than how often you have sex, or how often you orgasm, or how much pleasure you take from sex, or liking the same things as your partner.

Talking about sex is no different from talking about how to live and love, or from talking about your values. You might just be out of practice, or have never had these conversations, perhaps because sex worked well for you in the past – but now it might not be as satisfying. It's better to be proactive rather than reactive, so bring up the subject of sex every so often to just check in or show appreciation, rather than only bringing it up when it's a problem. All things worth having are worth working for, so you need to make some concerted efforts to get your sex life back on track. Use compassionate communication around any differences in preferences around sexual intimacy as well, and handle your incompatibilities with compassion.

With these blocks around physical intimacy, in a society which is more and more physically disconnected, how do we make space for desire? How do we create opportunities for pleasure in a performance-driven world? How do we focus on quality over quantity in sex, and let go of comparing with others? And how do we stop looking for quick fixes to something which takes effort? Your emotional systems of threat, drive and soothing follow you into the bedroom as well as everywhere else in your life.

Desire – it's a drive thing

Desire, both a verb and a noun, means to wish or long for; to crave; to want. You can desire something, but you can also *be desired*. If you don't feel desired by your partner, you don't feel wanted or longed for.

No wonder that so many couples feel upset about dwindling desire in their relationship, given that it can feel like a rejection, to be turned down. To understand lack of desire in a compassionate way, we need to see which system is activated for you – threat, drive, soothing, or a blend of all three?

Within Compassion Focused Therapy, we think of desire as corresponding to the drive system. Desire can be split into two parts: *pursuing* and *consuming*. The first part is the motivation to pursue something rewarding and feeling excited about it. You feel excitement, joy and lust when wanting to get close to your partner, or when finding someone sexy and wanting to get with them. The second part is when you get what you desire, then really savour and take pleasure from it, losing yourself in the moment.

How does that resonate with your relationship at the moment?

Do you each feel motivated to pursue intimacy with one another?

When you have intimacy, do you enjoy it fully or get distracted by other things?

So what gets in the way of desire?

Desire blocked by threat

We're acutely aware of our own bodies when we're naked – it's a vulnerable thing to take your clothes off in front of someone and be intimate with them. Animals don't get caught up in these loops when they have sex, as they're following their drives and instincts. We, on the other hand, are very open to self-criticism.

If negative thoughts and feelings show up when you consider getting it on with your partner, your *threat system* is being activated and might block you entering your drive system. You no longer feel like making out or having sex; the mood has been lost. You might not even be consciously aware of it, but it could be to do with self-critical thoughts or shame, or stress in your life.

Here are some of the things getting couples into their threat zones:

- Body image issues, feeling flawed and unattractive
- Pressure to perform and be perfect as a lover, to have an orgasm
- Fear of being left, getting too close or getting hurt, not feeling safe
- Distraction, thinking about the to-do list, work, children or life stressors
- Shame, not allowing oneself to feel pleasure, or for liking particular kinds of sex
- Worry about children waking up or something going wrong in the sex act
- Resentment, feeling angry around other issues in the relationship
- Pain, anticipating that sex will hurt and tensing up in anticipation

Common thoughts blocking pleasure and desire:

- I'm not good enough in bed, I'll mess it up
- I'm not attractive enough, I'm ashamed of my body
- I don't have time for this, I can't concentrate
- I'm not feeling it, I feel low/anxious

The way you think and feel about yourself and the world around you has an impact on your physical sensations. If you're feeling nervous about having sex, tension in your body will make it difficult to relax into intimacy. For men, that might mean struggling to get or keep an erection, or being unable to have an orgasm or ejaculate, and for women it might mean experiencing vaginal dryness, feeling turned off, feeling pain or not reaching an orgasm. Our bodies get blocked by what's going on in our heads.

> *How do you feel about yourself when you're having sex?*
>
> *What do you focus on?*
>
> *What gets you or your partner into threat?*
>
> *Do you struggle to be in the present moment with your partner?*

Shame around sex

What has shaped how you express what you want sexually? Do you tell your partner what you're into? There are so many taboos around desire, even though sex is completely natural. The shaming around asking for our needs to be met starts early. Young children express very loudly what they want and don't want, and it's crucial to teach them to act with kindness towards others, to share and ask nicely instead of just taking what they want. But have we thwarted a natural tendency to express our wants, our desires, and saying no, in order to be polite, well-mannered and please others? No wonder that asking for what we want from our partners can be tricky. Lots of people would self-silence needs or hold back sexually out of a fear of being rejected or shamed if showing their true desires. This level of self-control can be difficult when it comes to sex, as you might resist losing yourself in the moment for fear of judgement.

My story

Noticing my own shame around pleasure has been important in my work as a couples therapist, understanding the journey of socialisation I've been on. If there was anything raunchy on TV when I was a teenager, my parents would awkwardly turn off the TV (bless them). This reaction is common – and not their fault – but it's made me reflect on how adults make sex a taboo, especially for girls. I try to change the shame-based narrative by having an open dialogue about this with my own child, in an age-appropriate way. Children are curious and explore their bodies, but if we from an early age tell them that it's 'disgusting' to touch themselves, no wonder they grow up with blocks around giving themselves permission for pleasure.

Expectation vs reality

Often couples expect to have regular sex throughout their relationship, and might panic around a lack of intimacy. They may interpret it as incompatibility; that they should have married someone else; or that it will always be this way. In reality it's common for sexual interest to slow down between partners who have been together for a while. That doesn't mean that long-term relationships are by definition boring and destined to be sexless and unfulfilling.

The stories you tell yourself about intimacy (or lack thereof) can keep you stuck in the threat system. When you're in fight or flight, your body doesn't want to focus on closeness and desire but focuses on protecting you – the brain fixes on *'better safe than sorry'*. Hence why a lot of couples avoid sex when they don't feel satisfied, happy or safe overall in their relationship, or they engage in having sex anyway, perhaps out of duty, but don't take much pleasure from it. This actually threatens relationship satisfaction, if the sex isn't connected and meaningful.

Putting on a show or enjoying the play?

We can be self-critical about how we're performing sexually, so let's consider the difference between *performative sex* and *connected sex*.

Putting on a show, a 'performance', can be how it feels in the earlier stages of dating – you want it to be good so they'll like you. The drawback is that you lose focus on the here and now, being so focused on 'getting it right'. Like the opening night of a new play, the actors are nervous about missing their lines or receiving a critical review. They probably won't enjoy that show as much as they will the next few, when they start to relax and settle into the rhythm of the play. The more they try to be perfect, the less authentic and enjoyable the result might be.

Sometimes sex becomes performative simply out of habit. Imagine those actors delivering the same play for two hundred nights. The actors know the lines by heart and feel secure in the character they're playing; but the magic, the spark, might have gone. They might need to reconnect with the character again, to find new energy in how they engage with the play.

Who's watching your 'performance'? Is it your inner critic, judging you? Is your partner likely to criticise you in the same way? Does beating yourself up help you connect with your partner in this moment, or block it? Does sex become more or less enjoyable when you've focused intensely on your bodily flaws?

Imagine that you could let go of the pressure to be perfect, not putting expectation on yourself or your partner to 'get it right', but instead tolerating that sex is messy and not at all as pretty as it is in the films. Real people tend to be hairier and sweatier – and films rarely depict people needing the toilet or falling asleep during sex . . .

> *What would sex be like for you if you could calm your inner critic and let go of that pressure? Could you relax into it and be more curious and playful, more connected?*

Feeling safe enough to play

A lot of people need emotional connection with their partner to engage with them sexually. They want to feel loved and validated before feeling safe and secure enough to be physically intimate. You need to soothe your threat system to be able to enter your drive system (desire and reward), where you can have pleasure, fun and excitement. By softening self-criticism through self-compassion, you activate the soothing system (calm and connection) with your partner, to feel safe enough to *play*.

What would your inner mentor say? Possibly that you're not alone in feeling shame about your body, or in having those sexual preferences, or in having difficulties in bed. Soothe yourself using your compassionate inner team to find what action to take to alleviate this pain and to tolerate the difficult conversations with your partner. When you create a compassionate climate of being non-judgemental and accepting of each other and of yourselves, you can explore your sexuality and broaden your repertoire.

Long-term connection isn't always sexy

Monogamy, long-term relationships and sex are a problematic mix. The brain loves familiarity so it gives a sense of comfort and security to deeply know your partner and your relationship. Paradoxically, we're attracted to excitement and new things, and over time a long-lasting settled relationship can feel boring instead of exciting and sexy. There *can* be a decline in desire over time in committed relationships, but it isn't always the case. We need to sit with that paradox, of wanting to have safety, but not the boredom coming from comfort.

Some couples find that talking to new, engaging people, or even having a flirtation, boosts their overall drive and passion in life; they feel more desirable and inclined towards initiating something with their partner. This can turn up the heat if you're stuck in a rut, but also be a threat to your lasting connection in your relationship. Be clear on what is and isn't OK within your partnership – what your boundaries are.

Some couples find that sexual fantasy gets them into the mood. If you fantasise about people other than your partner, don't worry about it; what you do in your mind is not the same as what you do in the outside world. It's common to feel drawn to people outside the partnership – the important thing is what we do about the attraction and what meaning it might hold.

Are you fantasising about someone else because you've fallen in love with them, and you're deeply unhappy in your current relationship? If so you need to decide whether to not work through the dissatisfaction to try to reconnect, or to leave the partnership.

Or are you fantasising about someone else simply because they're good looking and you fancied a release? Do you still love your partner as well, and find that you also turn towards them for intimacy? Then it's an innocent spice, like biting into a chilli, to turn up the heat in your sex life.

Reflection & Connection

Sit down with your partner to discuss what you've read so far about physical connection:

Using your jigsaw puzzle, what blocks or promotes your desire?

Using your values, how do you want to show up in your relationship when it comes to expressing your desire?

Using your compassionate communication, what do you want to ask your partner about how they experience your sex life? What do you want to tell them about how you feel?

From the sofa

George, a young gay man, wanted help with insecurities and blocks around expressing his desire in sex. Through individual therapy, he felt the answer was the 'C word' (compassion). He understood that his struggles came from feeling different from other boys growing up, and the shame he experienced around coming out as gay. This gave rise to key beliefs over the years ('I'm not good enough', 'I can't be honest about who I am'), which helped him make sense of the strategies he'd used to make himself feel better (using social media for external validation from other men; engaging in sexual acts he didn't take pleasure from; and second-guessing his identity as a gay man).

In the short term these strategies made him feel good about himself, confirming that he was 'good enough' and attractive, but made him feel low and empty in the long run. After working on the shame he felt around sex and intimacy, he was able to be more vulnerable and authentic, to connect more deeply with his new boyfriend on both an emotional and sexual level. George felt the ripple effects of his new behaviours in his relationship, with his partner responding with more affection, trust and connection. Often working on one partner can help to unlock the potential in the relationship overall, soothing the threat.

The buffet of intimate connection

You can create a buffet of physical intimacy activities to engage in to help you out of a rut or routine of following the same script. Kiss, kiss, clothes off, intercourse.

If you think that sex equals penetration, you're missing out on all the other dishes on the buffet. This pressure of penetration affects hetero couples as well as lesbian and gay couples, and the media has a lot to answer for here. Even in romantic films (and not just in porn), the couples go from 0 to 100 very quickly, rarely showing much lead up to the penetration part. No wonder sex can become limited, with rigid rules or scripts around what 'sex' is.

> *We need to prevent the all/nothing trap of seeing sex as synonymous with intercourse and that anything else doesn't count as 'proper sex'.*

Often these scripts emphasise male pleasure and neglect female pleasure, ignoring the fact that the majority of women struggle to reach climax through penetrative sex alone, and need stimulation of the clitoris as well. We need to be sensitive not just to each other's pain and problems, but also pay attention to each other's pleasure, adding all kinds of touches and intimacies.

Try this

Creating your intimacy buffet

> *What kind of physical, sexual intimacy do you find exciting?*

Write down all the kinds of activities you're into, creating your own 'buffet of intimacy', to expand your sexual repertoire.

Mindful compassionate sex

Mindful and compassionate sensuality doesn't just involve feeling each other's bodies. It involves using your five senses for a heightened sensory experience, both of you being *right here, right now*, experiencing pleasure. It also involves noticing your inner world and compassionately unhooking from the thoughts and feelings getting in the way of you connecting with your partner. Lastly, it involves compassionately holding their experience and body in mind too, noticing what's going on for them without judgement.

Try this

Mindful compassionate sensuality
Use your soothing breathing rhythm to slow things down and calm your body and mind so you can enter into play and excitement through feeling safe. Then let the spotlight of attention wander over your partner.

Sight
Take in the sight of your partner with your eyes, drawing a map of the ridges and valleys of their body. Be mindfully aware of the flaws and imperfections. Notice with compassion the new curves and lines to a woman's body after becoming a mother, or the physical wear and tear of someone engaged in physical work, or the signs of ageing. Our bodies are amazing to explore and discover; appreciate the journey they have travelled.

Hearing
Tune into the sounds around you – perhaps there's music playing – then steer your attention onto the sound of your partner's breathing. That may even slow or speed up your own breathing rhythm through the power of *synchronicity*; couples can synchronise their heartbeats and breath. Put your head on your partner's chest and listen to the steady sound of their heartbeat – does that make you feel safe or grounded? Listen to the soft sound of your hands running over your partner's body.

Smell
Draw in deep breaths to notice and appreciate your partner's scent – perhaps freshly washed hair, or perfume or aftershave. What does your partner smell like just as they are, that pillow smell? Experiment with nuzzling into the nape of their neck and see what that feels like, what memories awaken. We smell our babies' heads as it helps aid the connection between parent and baby, but smelling your partner can also do this.

Taste
Use your sense of taste to heighten every moment of a kiss. Feel the warmth of your partner's breath, slowly see what it tastes like when

your lips meet theirs. Much like when we try a ripe strawberry from our garden, approach the kiss with longing and curiosity, even though you have eaten many strawberries before. Try to turn off autopilot to fully devote your attention to the warmth and flavour of the kiss. Experiment with the pressure of the kiss, increasing and decreasing the intensity and fervour. Does this make any difference to how much you enjoy yourself?

Touch

Curiously let your hands be your spotlight of attention as you're exploring your partner's body, using different parts of your hands to vary the sensation for both of you. What does it feel like if you rest the palm of your hand on them, generating heat, versus lightly letting your fingertips dance up and down their back? Alternate the pressure from light to firm and back again, seeing how that feels. Pause to let your partner take over, closing your eyes and visualising their hands wandering over your body. See how the sensation of being touched is heightened by you visualising the same thing in your mind's eye.

What was it like to slow things down like this, in a sensory and sensual exploration? Bring a curious rather than self-critical mind to any blocks getting in the way of fully engaging with it.

Given everything you know about yourself and your partner, does it make sense that either of you might struggle with this? If yes, what can you now do to soothe yourself or your partner, to be helpful and not harmful?

Body autonomy – the courage to set boundaries

Your body is *yours*. Try to find the courage to express what touch you like and want more of, and what doesn't feel good and you want to stop. Listen intently to your partner's signals around what they like and dislike, around what works for them. Share thoughts and feelings around how you build compassionate intimacy, on equal terms. This can be really challenging if you've experienced trauma in the past, so get additional support if you need it to help you set boundaries around what's OK and what isn't.

From the sofa

Jessie and Dwayne had been married for nine years and struggled with sexual intimacy for most of that time. They still loved each other and were good friends, but the lack of intimacy was weighing on their relationship. Jessie still wanted to be with Dwayne, but really struggled to get in the mood for sex. When attempting intercourse, she felt a burning sensation and had to stop – penetration felt impossible. She had experienced this with previous sexual partners and felt very ashamed of how her body 'failed' her. She worried that Dwayne would fall out of love with her and leave, ruining her chances of having a family. Every time they started making out these thoughts of fear and pain ran through her mind, making her lose focus, and she didn't feel turned on.

Jessie and Dwayne were referred to a specialist sexual health clinic for a physical examination. Jessie was diagnosed with vaginismus, a condition creating fear of penetration and an automatic and uncontrollable tightening reaction during vaginal penetration. Jessie and Dwayne could then build a compassionate understanding of how this had limited not just their sex life, but also Jessie's ability to feel pleasure and lose herself in sex.

They broadened their sex buffet with intimate actions other than intercourse to take the pressure off, and set realistic expectations around how female desire works differently from male desire (less likely to be spontaneously triggered and taking longer to 'heat' up). Jessie's threat response was calmed with mindfulness and the soothing breathing rhythm. She established boundaries of what she was OK with and when to stop, so that attempts at intimacy would feel rewarding and not like failures, making them more about connection and closeness than about a box to tick (intercourse, done). Over time, together with physical help such as lubricants and intimate moisturisers, she eased into the intimacy and had rewarding intercourse again. A few months later, they conceived their first baby.

Summary

- The three emotional systems of threat, drive and soothing affect desire, either facilitating or blocking it.
- Using mindfulness and compassion you can calm your threat and be curious about the shame and self-criticism getting in the way of you connecting physically with your partner.
- Feeling safe and soothed helps you to be more playful, allowing yourself the permission to experience pleasure in a connected way, rather than worrying about putting on a good performance.

Now you need to consider the stormy seas ahead. Preparing for rupture helps you be better equipped in dealing with them, managing these risks to your connection before they make your connection snap.

21 Stormy seas

Managing threats to your connection

Many things can stretch the connection between a couple, sometimes to the point of that bond snapping. Some strains are dramatic and instant, like the betrayal and hurt from an infidelity, and some are a slow burn, like the everyday wear and tear from becoming parents or experiencing long-term illness. Learning to spot these high-risk situations will help you take compassionate action to manage any threat.

Threats to your connection

Relationships are far from smooth sailing, and although life stressors can blow up like a hurricane on the water, they are also an opportunity to practise what you've learned about compassion, to keep you afloat. If you can weather a storm together, you can grow stronger as a couple.

Let's start with the most hazardous threat to your connection: *infidelity*.

Infidelity – a fire hazard

Infidelity in your relationship can threaten to burn your house down. It's impossible to completely fireproof your house, but you can take precautions to protect your connection.

Take note of these potential *fire hazards*:

- Making close friends with a colleague you could be attracted to
- Spending time confiding in a friend you could be attracted to
- Working closely with a colleague and celebrating success together
- Office parties or social settings where alcohol might lower your inhibitions

- Sending text messages late at night to someone you could be attracted to
- Physical touch with someone you could be attracted to

Having an emotional connection with someone for whom you could feel desire could be risky – the next level (adding physical intimacy) may not seem such a big step up once a bond is established. Professor Don Baucom, founder of Behavioural Couples Therapy, calls this a '*slippery slope*', as you may not even notice yourself gradually slipping past boundaries. If you've finished a difficult project with a colleague, staying late in the office, you may go for a drink or hug each other to celebrate. The release of finishing the project and alcohol lowering your inhibitions . . . you may end up crossing a boundary you hadn't planned to.

A fire needs fuel, heat and oxygen to ignite. If you know that you find this particular colleague attractive, that is your heat. If you've been unfaithful before or recently gone through a challenging patch in your relationship and feel starved of positive attention, your fuel is dry. Add alcohol and a celebration and you're blowing air into your co-working relationship to go beyond the combustion point and ignite. When the heat of the moment is gone and the fire has been put out you may be left with the cooling ashes of betrayal. There's no taking it back once you've crossed that line.

Whose fault is it?

The partner choosing to stray outside the relationship boundaries holds the responsibility for that. It's not your fault if your partner has cheated on you. There can be contributing factors, however, leading up to the partner being unfaithful. If you've participated in an extra-marital affair or infidelity, you can make efforts to repair and reconnect with the person you've hurt, if they give you the opportunity. We don't tend to learn from our mistakes through blaming and shaming ourselves, so each partner needs to take a careful, but compassionate, look at what's contributed to this derailing of the relationship.

From the sofa

Joel and Petra needed help after the breakdown of their relationship. It had come to light that Joel had had a series of infidelities during the years they'd been together, having had brief sexual encounters with strangers and some female friends. Joel had not had any ongoing affairs – he didn't feel any emotional connection to the other women. When Petra found out, her world fell apart. Joel experienced deep remorse, bewildered over *why* he'd hurt the love of his life – he couldn't imagine being with anyone else. It turned out that Joel suffered from low self-esteem and placed high demands on himself – he never felt good enough. The infidelities served as confirmation of his worth – being seen, validated and appreciated for a brief moment. Petra felt that she didn't know her partner any more and everything in their home served as a trigger for the trauma she had suffered – Joel had brought women home to their bed. She also felt a sense of shame in front of friends and family, who were judgemental of her decision to try to work it out with Joel. She was older than Joel and wondered if she'd led him into a commitment before he'd been emotionally ready. Joel had put Petra on a pedestal and felt he couldn't live up to her 'goodness'.

They spent a year in therapy, making sense of the infidelities and communicating about their needs, making space for Petra's anger and sadness as well as Joel's fear of failing to meet Petra's standards. Joel had individual sessions as well, to prevent himself entering into any high-risk situations again.

This couple decided to continue their relationship and also go through the strain of fertility treatment. They had their first baby and moved forward into their future together. They learned about their own needs and triggers, about how their relationship functions and what they each need to thrive. It isn't perfect and the triggers for the trauma are bound to upset Petra from time to time, for a long time. They decided to choose each other again, and again, reaffirming their commitment to each other. Through the couples therapy, their connection was stronger than ever, facilitating living well together as a family of three.

The trauma of infidelity

The impact of an infidelity or affair is vast – to both partners. The brain of the injured partner has a similar reaction as going through a traumatic experience, like having survived a car crash. This is why infidelity is seen as a *relationship trauma*. The injured partner loses a sense of identity and security, no longer feeling safe in their own home and relationship, and can experience flashbacks. The participating partner is often also deeply affected and may be overcome by guilt, remorse, shame and self-hatred. On the other hand, they may not feel bad at all, which means it's likely to happen again. Only by discovering the reasons for *why* it happened, paired with appropriate remorse and regret, can we try to protect the couple from another infidelity. The scary thing about life is that there are no guarantees that we won't be hurt again.

There are three tough phases in working through an infidelity (from *Getting Past the Affair* by Snyder, Baucom and Gordon):[41]

1 **Establishing safety** by restoring normality and doing damage control. Who stays where, how to manage daily tasks and contact, and who finds out about the infidelity, to not polarise friends and family into taking sides.

2 **Creating meaning** by understanding why the infidelity happened. How had the relationship been? Any high-risk situations which the participating partner should have navigated differently? Imagine you have a thorn in your shoe: you take off the shoe to remove the thorn and assess the damage. We need to sit with the pain of cleaning the wound out so it can heal, but also be aware of the thorn causing the friction in the first place. This is done without blaming or shaming, being empathetic about the experience of both partners.

3 **Moving forward**, together or apart. Once the couple has created a shared understanding of why this happened, they can choose to work on forgiveness and rebuilding trust, or to go separate ways. Either way, this phase is about healing and repairing after the rupture. If you find the shoe still not fitting well, and you think it's

going to give you blisters again, you may decide that you don't want it any more.

Now let's move on to another challenge for the couple relationship – becoming parents.

The pain points of parenting

Parenting is hard. The first few years after becoming parents is the most challenging time for couples across the lifespan of their relationship. Research suggests that couples' happiness ratings drop successively during the early years, picking up again once the children grow older and go to school, with increasing satisfaction through the teenage years, as shown in Bee and Boyd's marital satisfaction through the family life cycle illustration.[42]

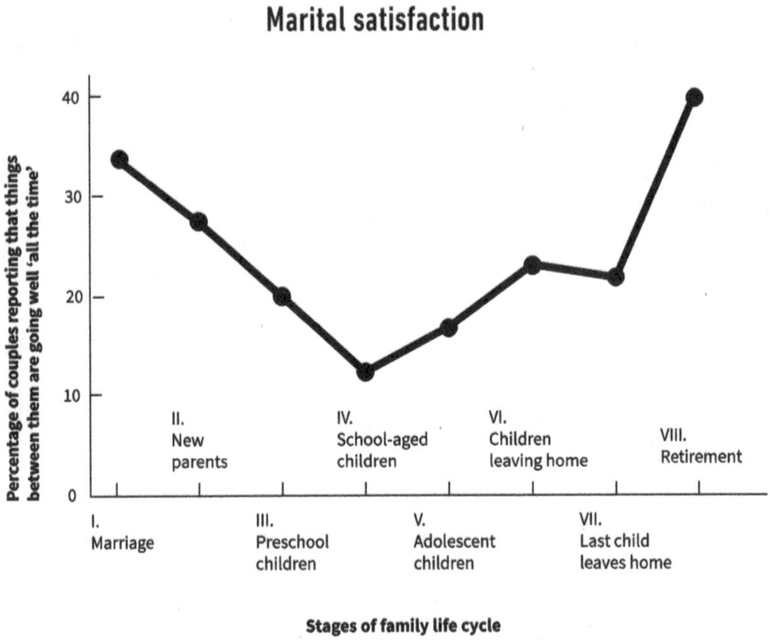

Sleep deprivation

Disturbed sleep is a huge strain on the relationship. You're likely to be impatient, irritable, snappy and frazzled to the point of putting your car keys in the fridge – you struggle to focus. Not only will it be harder for you to take your partner's perspective, you might also lack the energy to *care* about what they're going through. It's just that much harder to be compassionate when you're sleep deprived. The early days of parenting might mean being a grumpier version of yourselves, so do what you can to be reasonably kind and pleasant towards each other. Set realistic expectations and be prepared to forgive each other for goblin moments.

Remind yourself of how hard it is to function without sleep, to have realistic expectations during this life stage.

Discuss how you can help each other and take turns to rest – being kinder to each other when exhausted is more about 'paying it forward' than 'tit for tat'.

The pressure is on

The transition into parenthood can be a tumultuous life change, going from two in a relationship to three (or more) in a family. You might also be depleted from pregnancy, birth or a long adoption process, and while trying to recover and care for yourselves, you also have the responsibility of caring for a baby or child 24/7. This family can mean that your expressed love changes and one partner feels left out.

Regardless of how equal you felt before becoming parents, society pushes a lot of couples into more traditional roles with outdated gender expectations. Mother looks after baby; father earns the money. A mother is seen as having a 'natural maternal instinct' and should self-sacrifice everything for the baby while also 'bouncing back into shape' after giving birth; the father is described as 'daddy day care', an incompetent babysitting facility who should just hide at work rather than be a capable equal part in the child rearing.

These factually incorrect stereotypes are damaging to the couple relationship and put pressure on the individuals to conform to the stereotype. They can leave you both depleted, and your relationship polarised.

Families come in many different formats – two mums, two dads, single parents, adoptive parents, a trio of a couple and sperm/egg donor or surrogate. Compassionately discussing your family structure and what you want these roles to look like before becoming parents can prepare you for stormy seas and threats to your connection as *partners* as you navigate your life as *parents*.

Changes in roles and identity

After bringing a child into the partnership, the partner being the secondary caregiver can get pushed further down the pecking order and may receive less love and affection than previously. On her podcast *Where Should We Begin*, couples therapist Esther Perel talks about how caretaking blocks desire, as the energy is directed away from the couple and onto the children. There might be a mismatch in connection and a withdraw/demand pattern may establish: the person working might come home and want to reconnect with their partner, whereas the person caring for the child might want to be left alone, feeling 'touched out' from the constant demands.

This can mean feelings of rejection, creating deeper rifts between the couple. If the rejected partner can understand the reasons why, and support the caregiving partner through this phase, they can reconnect soon enough. Looking after a helpless infant is just hard, but so is being the sole breadwinner in a growing family. Both roles are challenging. Resentment can be avoided by focusing more on collaboration rather than competition, showing appreciation and gratitude for what each partner brings to the table.

Parenthood brings a shift to your identity. Some partners on parental leave or as stay-at-home parents miss the mental stimulation and professional identity from the workplace. Others find themselves pushed back into work, feeling torn away from their caregiving role. Women are more likely than men to take parental leave and work part-time, so this again affects the roles in the partnership. It can be hard to wear all those hats at once – partner, parent, worker.

I came across one lesbian couple who decided to take turns conceiving, birthing, breastfeeding and taking maternity leave for their two children. Each taking a turn at being either the primary caregiver or the main breadwinner had helped them develop empathy for the other partner's responsibilities. Stepping into the shoes of your partner is crucial if you're going to survive the days of young children without letting your connection snap.

The mental load

It's common for new parents to feel resentment towards each other. An unfair amount of childcare falls on women, who also tend to carry a heavier *'mental load'* – juggling household tasks and telling the other partner what to do, rather than them taking the initiative. So even in heterosexual relationships where the man does his 'fair share' of the household chores and parenting, the woman may be mentally exhausted from delegating tasks or giving reminders (often seen as 'nagging'). This can create vicious cycles, stemming from the pervasive myth that men are less capable as caregivers, and so they step out of it. If the woman then keeps doing more of the childcare tasks, the male partner misses out on the parenting learning curve and the myth becomes a self-fulfilling prophecy.

On the other hand, the partner who is solely responsible for making an income for the family can feel immense pressure and risk burning out under the weight of that responsibility, being resentful about not getting enough sleep when having to get up to work. Looking after children is also 'work', and both partners need sleep.

One partner rarely 'wins' in the early days of parenthood; both partners tend to struggle with the weight of parenthood, but in different ways. It can be very difficult to communicate what we each need in these new roles.

The 'who has done more' game

Parents often get into a competitive mindset – who's been up more times with the baby, earned more money, changed more nappies, done more school runs, helped with more homework, been to more swimming lessons . . . the list is endless. This stops you from seeing what your partner actually *is* doing; it's hard to be compassionate and appreciative when we're stuck in this.

If there's a genuine imbalance you need to hear each other with compassion to address the inequality through problem-solving, negotiation and decision-making. To help you share the mental load, take a look at Eve Rodsky's book *Fair Play.*[43] It's hard to make space for appreciation if you're really fed up – but it's quite normal to have mixed emotions towards your partner.

Blast from your past

Few phases of the couple relationship require as much negotiation around decisions as parenthood. How will we raise our children? You might feel strongly about bringing up your children like you were brought up, or you might want to do things very differently. Use your jigsaw puzzle to reflect on how your past experiences might influence you. Perhaps your parents argued, treated each other badly or divorced; or didn't split up when they might have been better as parents if they'd been apart. You've got no control over how you were parented, but you can prevent those patterns from being replicated. Clinical Psychologist Emma Svanberg's online course *Breaking Past Patterns*[44] may be helpful, as well as Philippa Perry's *The Book You Wish Your Parents Had Read.*[45]

Surviving parenthood

These practical suggestions will help to reduce the risk of the ripple effect from the early days of parenthood becoming established for years to come:

- Have a weekly check-in with each other, asking what each partner wants or needs for themselves that week. Try to plan together as a team to negotiate your needs.
- Educate yourselves on 'mental load' and 'emotional labour', to understand the societal pressures on women to take on the caring role and managing of the household. If you don't want your daughters to grow up thinking that they're worth less than men, or

your sons to grow up thinking that they're worth more than women, work on balancing the load and modelling this to your children, to help them pick up the values you want them to hold. Children do what we do, not what we say that they should do.

- Identify when you're mind reading or wanting your partner to guess what you want and need. Use compassionate communication instead. Expressing yourself in 'I' statements can help, e.g. 'I would like you to make food for us for tomorrow' or 'When you come home late I feel upset as I have been alone coping with the baby all day, I would like you to come home earlier to help me and so we can spend time together', to focus on what you need to happen, but also the positive aspect of it.
- Make space for expressing the things you're grateful for. We can easily get into the habit of being critical and stop recognising the good things our partner does. You might not always get it right, so it's OK to ask for forgiveness when you get it wrong.
- You can't change your partner, but if you endeavour to bring more kindness and compassion into your partnership, you'll not only have a greater chance of reaching your partner so they can hear you, but also model that way of being to your child.
- Discuss how desire, sex and intimacy has been affected by parenthood and try not to put pressure on each other about any particular method which may be challenging postnatally. Educate yourselves on pelvic floor and postnatal sex.
- Have realistic expectations for how life will be while you have young children and accept the mess instead of putting pressure on your relationship to be perfect. It's already hard – don't make it harder.

Expressing needs

Have you and your partner had the sort of upbringing and life experiences where you've practised expressing what you want and need? Or have you learned that expressing needs is demanding or selfish, and you might be punished for it? If so you might experience blocks to self-compassion. It's important to be aware of this in parenthood, as the partner who's blocked in expressing their needs might end up bitter and resentful over time, from not being looked after and not practising enough self-care.

Try this

Weekly wants and needs check in

1 Sit down with your diaries at a good time (after bedtime or during TV time for the kids).

2 Partner 1 asks partner 2: *What do you need this week?*

Needs are essential to cope better, feel better, restore and nourish ourselves, e.g. sleep, alone time or social connection, good food, exercise.

3 Partner 2 chooses one or two things, and then uses negotiation skills to compromise on how to make that happen, so that partner 1 doesn't feel put upon. Both partners have to let go of some control to fully support each other in parenting.

Example If one partner gets a lie-in to catch up on sleep, the other partner has to take the children in the morning. The resting partner needs to be able to let go of responsibility for that time and let the other partner manage the children. Plan it into your diaries (or make it happen organically in the moment if you wake exhausted after a tough night). Following through on your promise to your partner will build trust and deepen connection, and they're more likely to give you a morning off in return, or something else you need.

4 Partner 1 asks partner 2: *What do you want this week?*

Wants are still important for our wellbeing but not as crucial as the basic self-care needs, and can include doing something fun, going out with a friend, engaging in a hobby, seeing a film. Negotiate on how this can happen and what partner 1 needs to do to facilitate it, plan it in and promise to make it happen.

Swap and repeat the process for the other partner.

If arguments around unfairness or your parental roles arise, try sharing thoughts and feelings in a compassionate way. It can help to spend five minutes in separate rooms first, each using your compassionate self to express yourself in a way your partner can hear. Once this weekly check-in is established, it will turn down the heat and friction in the family as a whole, and once the children are old enough they can also join in. It's important that you both are looked after as parents, to help keep you well and healthy.

In sickness and in health

We know one thing for sure in life – *we will all die*. We just don't know when or how, or what sickness we'll experience across our lifespan. Hence why most marital vows include a promise to stand by your partner 'in sickness and in health', or 'for better, for worse': supporting each other if you're going through hard times.

Physical health problems

Sickness in one or both partners changes the dynamic between the couple. One partner may be left with an unfair share of the responsibilities, as well as experiencing worry about the pain the loved one is going through. There may be uncertainty around the future, whether the sick partner will recover or get worse, or even pass away. This can be hugely traumatic for the whole family. There may be financial worries from reducing to one income or paying for adaptations to the home e.g. for mobility access. The physically well partner may have to stop work to care for the ill partner, meaning an even greater financial strain. These are life-altering stressors and ones which we can't predict. Use your compassionate communication to each share how you feel about the illness, to make space for both the sick partner being in anguish, and the well partner worrying about losing their loved one. Find support outside the partnership, such as counselling specific to the condition you or your loved one has, and use self-care strategies.

Some long-term health conditions and disabilities may not be life-threatening but affect your day-to-day life together through friction and frustration. If one partner is able-bodied and the other needs physical support, this will impact the range of activities you can do together. You'll need more planning and adaptations; the disabled partner may experience discrimination and alienation, or a lack of understanding from the able-bodied partner. Compassionate communication is key here, to truly listen and understand each other's experience and frustrations, to create a meaningful life for both of you. What are your deal-breakers? What do you absolutely need to have in your life to each feel fulfilled, and how can you compromise around the rest?

Mental health problems

Feeling mentally unwell can contribute to relationship problems, and vice versa. If you feel unhappy and dissatisfied with your relationship, you and your partner are 2.7 times more likely to develop mental illnesses such as depression. Equally if you or your partner is experiencing depression, your relationship is more at risk of being distressed as well.[46]

If you're often arguing with your partner, or discussing a divorce or separation, no wonder you'd feel low, sad or down. Ending a long-term relationship is frequently listed as one of the most stressful life events we can go through. Although the experience of depression differs from person to person, it can consist of a combination of the following: low mood, lack of motivation, no pleasure in doing things you previously liked, irritability, sleep problems, lowered sexual libido, lack of concentration, hopelessness. No wonder the relationship will be impacted. Furthermore, if your relationship is in distress, it's 3.7 times more likely for either of you to develop alcohol abuse or alcohol dependence. Some people drink to cope with negative life events and distract themselves from the pain of having issues in their marriage or relationship.

If you experience depression, anxiety or other common mental health problems, it's important to seek help from a trained health professional. Behavioural Couples Therapy is a method of relationship support which can also effectively treat depression or anxiety in one or both of the partners at the same time as addressing issues in the relationship. If the low mood was linked to issues in the relationship, couples therapy for the depression provides a lower risk of relapse into depression than having individual sessions.

Reflection & Connection

Sit down with your partner to discuss the impact of physical or mental illness.

If one of you were to fall physically ill, how would that affect your relationship?

If one of you were to feel mentally unwell, what could you do to provide non-judgemental support and compassion for each other?

What have you experienced thus far together, around physically or mentally tough times, and what did you do to survive those threats to your connection?

My story

I grew up with a mother suffering from a chronic pain condition, which meant that she was ill for large parts of my childhood. She tried very hard to keep strong for the family, but eventually she had to stop working because of the pain and the brain fog the condition brought with it. At that time, there wasn't enough awareness of her condition and she wasn't given the interventions she would have received today. Our family was also left without support, so we didn't understand it. What I know as an adult today is how it shaped my parents' relationship and my own awareness of 'in sickness and in health'. For some couples, there will be no recovery, no return to the 'health' part. It just is what it is. Although it saddens me to think of how my mother has lived her life in so much pain, my parents have created a lasting connection through both light and dark times, having just celebrated their fortieth wedding anniversary

Giving and receiving care requires compassion

To be able to keep caring for the person you love, draw on the strength and courage of compassion. Caring for someone else is hard, so there's a risk of you burning out and feeling exhausted. If you're caring for someone with physical or mental health needs, it's important that you *look after yourself as well.*

If you're the person being cared for, notice any blocks to receiving that care, for instance guilt around it not being fairly balanced between you. Not wanting to accept your partner's care may lead to more frustration – you might need to work on closing the umbrella and letting the raindrops of care shower you. This is hard, so use your compassionate inner mentor to support you.

> *What compassionate actions of self-care could you use from your tool kit if there was a caring responsibility within your relationship?*

Summary

- Infidelity, the crossing of boundaries and betrayal of trust, may be repaired and used as a point of deepening the connection, by making sense of what led up to it and preventing it happening again.
- Parenthood can divide a couple if not taking steps to meet both partners' needs – work through any resentment in a compassionate way.
- Physical or mental illness changes the dynamic between the couple, with imbalance of responsibilities, financial strain and uncertainty around the future.
- Compassion both for the sick person and for the carer is essential to not burn out and drift apart.

Any ruptures in a relationship need to be repaired with forgiveness. Next we'll explore what forgiveness is and practise giving it both to your partner and to yourself.

22 Forgive and let go

Letting go of blame to move forward together

You can use your new communication skills and compassionate actions to help you decide if you want to forgive any mistakes your partner has made and let go of your pain, to move forward together, or decide to go your separate ways. Learn how to forgive yourself if you've been the one causing the hurt in the relationship.

Forgive, not forget

Forgiveness is a difficult subject. Firstly, there's no definitive answer as to how to do it, and secondly, it involves pain. It's understandable if you struggle with the idea of forgiving someone who hurt you.

Let's be clear on one thing: the expression *'forgive and forget'* doesn't apply here. We tend not to forget the ways we've been wronged. We have the capacity for remembering a time in the past where the hurt happened, or imagining a time in the future where it might happen again. You can, however, make peace with the injury and move forward from it, letting go. Let's look at what forgiveness is – and what it isn't.

The vulnerability and courage of forgiveness

Forgiveness is a vulnerable process requiring *courage* – daring to express how you were hurt by someone. If they don't listen and take it on board, it takes tenacity to keep bringing it up until you can trust that they've understood the impact of their actions. Letting go and moving forward with your life also takes a lot of *strength* – it's easier to lash out and retaliate than to forgive and let go. You might also be reluctant to share how angry you are for fear that the relationship might end.

Forgiving isn't about letting someone off the hook and *not* holding them accountable; on the contrary, being able to soften and let go of blame helps you have the tenacity to *keep* holding someone accountable. Using your compassionate communication, tell your partner that what they did wasn't OK, that it hurt your feelings, and how it's left you feeling about the future of your relationship.

Forgiveness doesn't mean that what happened was OK – it means moving forward *in spite of* it happening. It means making sense of *why* it happened and not holding it against the other person (or yourself) for the rest of your life, even when it still hurts. It means letting go of what you *can* control, like blaming and shaming.

The blame game

Researcher Brené Brown discusses blame as a discharge of energy, such as anger and pain, with a negative impact on accountability – people cannot hold themselves or others accountable when they're focused on whose *fault* something is.[47]

It's easier to be compassionate towards someone you like than someone you dislike. If you're very angry with your partner and now really dislike them for what they've done, it's a much bigger ask to show compassion and forgive them – but it's not impossible.

How easy has it been to forgive yourself, when you're the person who's caused the hurt or betrayal, and you don't like *yourself*? Self-blame activates your threat system, and you'll be less likely to do the things necessary for repair. In some ways, it then becomes more about *your* pain than about your partner's pain. You can't hear how badly your partner is hurting if you're busy beating yourself up for what you've done.

Reflection & Connection

Consider these questions around forgiveness:

> *What happens in your relationship when you make a mistake? How does your partner react?*
>
> *What happens in your relationship when your partner makes a mistake? How do you react?*
>
> *Do you blame and shame each other, struggling to forgive?*
>
> *How do you each feel about yourselves when you make mistakes?*
>
> *Do you blame and shame yourselves, struggling to forgive?*

Let's start by learning how to forgive *your partner.*

Forgiveness for your partner

What would it mean for you if you were to forgive your partner for the hurt they've caused? You might fear that they'd do it again. A word of caution: if you're convinced that they *will* do it again, perhaps your decision isn't about how to forgive and let *it* go, but how to let *them* go. Forgiveness isn't about letting someone 'get away with' treating you badly. You also need to separate your partner's actions from who they actually are and understand that even kind, generous, loving people make mistakes; good people do bad things.

What's in it for me to forgive?

You might be in a lot of pain, struggling to move forward with your life together because of what's happened. You might find it difficult to see a *future place* you can feel comfortable in, because of the *past place* you've already been in. The only place you can do something about is *this place right here* – in the here and now.

Ask yourself this:

> *What's in it for me if I forgive my partner?*
>
> *What do I need forgiveness to do for me?*
>
> *If I was able to forgive my partner, how would that free me up?*

From the sofa

Harry found out that Luisa had been having an extramarital affair for years with an ex-boyfriend. Harry was confused, angry, sad and incredibly hurt by Luisa's actions, yet he showed a willingness to hear her out and understand why this had happened. They had a young child together, and part of what made Luisa vulnerable was the postnatal depression and anxiety she developed after the birth. She felt too ashamed to share how difficult she found bonding with the baby, and her sense of failure was cemented by her husband shouldering most of the baby care and finding their baby 'easy'. As she didn't express how she really felt, she started to feel more resentful towards her husband. She missed her home country and felt completely unsafe in her role as a mother. After a while she started the infidelity with her ex from back home, despite not feeling any happier from this. The depression made her feel so bad about who she was that she didn't think she deserved the love from her husband and child, and engaged in the affair as self-sabotage.

When working on the meaning-making stage of the couples therapy, Harry felt torn between his compassion for Luisa's deep depression and self-hatred, and his fear of it happening again if he was to comfort and forgive her. Understanding what she'd been through as an *explanation*, rather than *excuse*, he was able to meet her emotional needs, without promising to forgive her in that moment. He saw that she wasn't a bad person because she had done some bad things. Luisa had individual therapy to lift her depression, and showed her husband remorse and that she was actively working on it not happening again. They agreed to hold off any decisions about marriage until Luisa's depression lifted, so they could see how she really felt about her husband when feeling mentally well. So much of her resentment and lack of joy and desire within the relationship had come from her depression.

After having stabilised Luisa, it was clear that what mattered most to her were her husband and child, and she worked tirelessly to show Harry this through committed actions of love. Harry made space for his feelings: anger about what she'd done, fear of it happening again, shame around 'not being enough of a man' and sadness around how it took this much pain for them to properly talk to each other. They slowly rebuilt trust and closeness, moving back in together with better relationship skills and more open and honest communication than ever before.

Try this

Imagining forgiveness

Warm up with your soothing breathing rhythm, close your eyes and perhaps sit with your inner mentor in your safe place. Imagine a time in the future where you forgive your partner:

In this imagined scenario, how did it feel to reconcile, to come back together after the hurt?

How did it affect your connection – could you move forward together?

Validation of the softer core

It's important to use compassionate communication when working on forgiveness, to truly hear and understand what the pain is about. Often there are softer, more approachable feelings underneath the hard shell of the expressed anger from the injured partner towards the participating partner. We tend to protect this *soft core*, not sharing our feelings of sadness, fear or shame, as it can make us more vulnerable than when expressing emotions such as anger, rage or disgust.

Perhaps you feel sad that all that you've built in your relationship could be lost, so you're angry and blame your partner for 'ruining it'. Maybe you're really scared that you'll get hurt again if you move forward together, so you protect yourself by attacking your partner and pushing them away. Maybe you feel ashamed for 'having let yourself be treated this way', worrying about what other people will think of you if you forgive. To not risk that humiliation, you hold onto the pain.

Although these more vulnerable emotions of sadness, fear and shame are hard to feel and *express* they're often easier for the other person to hear and *tolerate* than just anger – it's an easier ball to catch. If you are vulnerable enough to show your soft core it's more likely your partner can understand the damage they've done and validate your feelings. When we don't feel heard and validated, we tend to 'ramp it up' – we shout louder. This expends even more energy and increases the 'stuckness' – your partner doesn't understand why you're so angry about something they did in the past, perhaps even years ago. Are they asking you to just let it go? To move on? It's hard to move on without making sense of things first.

Making sense of the seemingly senseless

The couple that have experienced one partner significantly hurting the other need to make sense of what has happened. When you're in your threat system, the parts of your brain which help you think things through in a clear and concise way are blocked. Soothing yourself, independently of your partner, can help you make wiser decisions about whether you want to stay or leave, whether you want to forgive this mistake and how to increase the odds of it not happening again. Even if you do all that, there are bound to be some gremlins still lurking around in your head. If you've experienced infidelity, also explore the forgiveness practices later in this chapter.

The gremlins of hurt in the past

Consider the stream of consciousness which hooks you and pulls you away from being who you want to be. Let's call that mind chatter *gremlins*. The gremlins point out all the ways someone has hurt you, and why you shouldn't forgive them. They can be quite scary, like monsters, and sneaky. Are they controlling your life and deciding the direction you move in?

Try this

Gremlins on the bus

Imagine that you're driving along nicely in your own bus, heading for 'Close Connection City'. Suddenly you hit something in the road, smash your head on the steering wheel and stop the bus. There's a horrible noise coming from the back – you look around to see a pack of gremlins snarling at you and shouting things like 'You weren't careful enough, it's all your fault!' and 'It'll happen again and then you'd be even more of an idiot!' They're blaming you for hurt someone else has caused, or something which may even have been unintentional.

Consider how this leaves you feeling. You've just had a terrifying experience getting hurt and the gremlins make you feel even worse, adding insult to injury. When you try to get rid of them by shouting at them to get off the bus, or telling them why it wasn't your fault, you find yourself really wound up as they have a reply to everything. When you're turned around in your seat to deal with the gremlins, you've taken your eyes off the road and nobody is going anywhere.

What's happening with your bus journey? Has it come to a standstill?

Can you clean your wound and dress it, preventing infection and things getting worse?

Once you're patched up, can you start the bus and continue towards your destination of close connection, even with fierce gremlins screaming at you?

It's important to *pause* to take stock of one's injuries after hurt has been caused. If you ignore your wounds and just get going again as if nothing has happened, you might be in more pain long-term. You need to process it. Once you're clear on what's happened and why, mending any issues in your relationship and reminding yourself about the *purpose* of this journey (close connection), you can press *play* again and choose to start driving your bus forward. Those gremlins are going to tell you over and over that it's a bad idea – perhaps that you can't trust your partner. In a way, they're trying to prevent you from making a mistake or getting hurt again, much like your inner critic, but the way they go about it adds more pain than it prevents.

Entering into the unknown to rebuild trust

One of the trickiest parts of forgiving and letting go is rebuilding the trust after you've been hurt or betrayed, because of the fear of what it will mean if you do forgive. 'How can I trust that you won't just do the same thing again?' If you knew without doubt that your partner would never, ever hurt you again, why would you need trust?

> *Trust means tolerating that there's no guarantee against hurt.*

Trusting someone means you tolerate the risk that they *could* do it again, hoping that they've learned enough to not make the same mistake. It took a lot of courage for Harry to give Luisa compassion after what she did, driven by his deep love for her and wish to keep their family together. The partner who's betrayed the trust or made the mistake can't give a guarantee, but needs to *make their best efforts* to show the hurt partner that they're a '*safe bet*'; that it will be worthwhile investing more time and emotion into continuing together. The injured partner also can't guarantee that they will be able to trust again, or not leave, but can give it their best shot. Trust rests on a foundation of honesty, not more lies. If being honest will cause pain, try to express yourself in a way which your partner can hear.

Fool me once, shame on you, fool me twice, shame on me

This expression implies that we somehow deserve to suffer if we've forgiven someone who then hurts us again. We don't. It's *not your fault* if you give someone a second chance and they betray that trust. It's more about developing wisdom and insight – possibly you're drawn to people who don't treat you well. Has there been a pattern of you being on the receiving end of hurtful behaviour? You'll need clarity around what's harmful, rather than helpful, in how other people treat you. Don't allow people to treat you badly without setting a boundary, finding the courage to say that this just cannot continue. This is where fierce compassion comes in.

Fierce compassion

Have you ever heard of a mother bear defending her young from danger, like roaring fiercely at a human getting too close to her cub? The strength with which she asserts herself can be astounding, and we see this in humans too – parents protecting their children or partners defending their spouses can gain almost superhuman strength.

Because it takes a lot of strength and courage to stand up for yourself and what you believe to be right in life, it's understandably also hard to do this in relationships. If your partner has treated you badly, you might feel very capable of saying 'NO! You can't treat me this way!', but you might also struggle to set that boundary. You might silence yourself and let unfair treatment carry on. Forgiveness is not about allowing abuse or degrading treatment, it's about moving beyond hurt and heartache towards a more meaningful life together, learning and growing from the mistakes made. Forgiveness serves *you*, even if you choose to move apart from the person who hurt you.

Greta Thunberg, teenage environmental activist from my home country of Sweden, uses *fierce compassion*. She stands up to some of the most influential people in the world, telling them they need to do better – that this *just can't carry on*. She facilitates change, through holding people accountable. Can you embody some of that courage before sitting down to write a letter to your partner, if they've hurt you?

Try this

Fierce compassion letter to your partner

You may wish to say things around why and how you're still wanting to work on things together, but also put in a boundary around what is and isn't acceptable going forward. Make space for all your emotions – like sadness, anger, anxiety. Express why it makes sense that you both feel the way you do, and what you need for forgiveness and reconnection.

Warm up before you start – the soothing breathing rhythm and safe place enables you to step into a version of yourself which is strong and brave, still keeping clarity and your caring commitment towards yourself and others.

> *To N,*
>
> *I want to be with you, as I still love you. I want to find a way to trust you again, but it's going to take time. I feel so hurt by what you did, and it scares me that this was going on without me knowing. I get that you're very sorry for what you did, but I'm still really angry. You can't treat me like this ever again, or I WILL LEAVE. I get that we had problems in our relationship – you struggled to talk to me about your feelings after we lost the baby. I suppose you found an escape with her, with no talk of babies or loss. I reminded you of your grief. I'm very hurt by how you betrayed me at a time when I needed you the most; it will take time to work through that. I still have nightmares about you being with her instead of me while we were grieving our baby. It's made me wonder if I really know you at all. But this process has helped me understand how much you were grieving as well, and that you made this mistake because you were lost, and I was so caught up in my own grief that I couldn't make space for yours. We need to turn to each other in times of struggle, you need to work on this, opening up to me more. I don't want this to happen again, it just CAN'T happen again. You need to show me that I can trust you again. It isn't OK to spend that much time with another woman, even if it's a colleague. You can't stay out late drinking and not tell me when you're coming home, it makes me feel like I'm worthless to you. If we're going to make it through, we both have to value each other more, and get to know each other again.*

Try to write your own letter now, going easy on yourself. It's bound to hurt, so sit with your compassionate inner mentor next to you. It's also powerful to read it out loud to your partner.

Forgiveness for yourself

What if you've been the one causing pain? The process of forgiving yourself for something you have done within your relationship can be very difficult. You can have fears, blocks and resistances, as giving yourself forgiveness is an act of self-compassion. You might *fear* that if you forgive yourself you could do the hurtful thing again, and that's not who you want to be. You might *resist* forgiving yourself, thinking that you don't deserve forgiveness after the way you've acted. You might have a *block*, as you might not know *how* to forgive yourself. Perhaps you were never taught that as a child, or never practised it as an adult. If you've done something to hurt your partner, you'll need compassion for your dark sides.

Eliciting forgiveness from your partner

How can you show your partner that you're a safe bet? Use compassionate communication to really listen to what hurts them the most, to validate those emotions. When they're upset about what you did, can you get a feel for which part of them you're having the conversation with? The angry version of them may want you to be sorry for what you've done, or to hurt you back (for revenge). The anxious part may think they had a part in it and want to hide away from the conflict. It may worry about the future of your relationship. The self-critical part might *blame them* for *your actions*. Your partner's sad part may feel like it's all hopeless and the relationship has been lost and may just want to hide away and cry. Your partner may also have a compassionate part, giving them some solace, soothing their pain.

Eliciting forgiveness from your partner is not about you smoothing things over and them not talkng about it any more. You need to show your partner that you understand the effects your actions have had, really empathising with the hurt you've caused. You'll need your compassionate self and inner mentor to help you tolerate the strong emotions emanating from your partner. All that hurt, all those threat emotions flying at you – rage, disgust, sadness, fear – can result in them swinging between accusing you, threatening to leave, crying, begging you to stay.

The more flammable they are, the more of this heat you'll feel. The trickier the mix of your attachment styles, the bigger the flame will be.

Pouring petrol on the fire is going to cause one giant explosion, so be careful to proceed with support and empathy – but also allow yourself to stand tall and strong and not be treated like a punch bag because you've made mistakes.

Try this

Compassionate letter of eliciting forgiveness from your partner
Drawing upon your compassionate self put yourself in your partner's shoes and validate how they're feeling – what are they scared of? Express what you're doing to be helpful, and not harmful, and find the strength and tenacity needed to rebuild your connection.

To L,

I know I've hurt you more than words, I can't tell you how sorry I am for what I've done. I understand that it's left you feeling insecure and thinking that you're not worth anything to me, because I treated you badly. Which isn't true, I've realised how much you mean to me and what a mistake I've made, but I understand why you feel that way. I know you were hurt in your last relationship as well, and I'm very sorry for causing you to go through that again. It was never my intention to hurt you, but I wasn't acting with you in mind, I wasn't showing you that you're what's most important to me. I get that you'll continue to feel angry, disappointed and sad for a long time, that's OK. And also really worried I'll hurt you like this again. I can only promise you that I'm doing my very best to ensure it never happens, I've learned my lesson. I've tried to show you the changes I've put in place, it's not the kind of person I want to be, and I feel ashamed of myself. But I also know that I'm really hard on myself and I can't keep showing you that I'm sorry by beating myself up, I need to instead keep showing you through my actions of now being there for you. To rebuild what we had, not by saying that I'm a horrible partner. It won't make you feel any better or make our relationship any better. So, I want to stop with the name calling. If you get angry with me, I want to hear it, but also I want to hear what you would want from me now. There's no excuse for what I did, but we've learned what the explanations were, and I want to improve our relationship, so we remove those risk factors. Just talk to me, don't hide away from me. You've got every right to be upset and there's no pressure for you to 'get over this' and not get to talk about how you feel. I still love you and still want to make this work, and I'm ready to do what it takes.

Eliciting forgiveness from yourself

Who's mostly holding the blame over your head right now – you or your partner? If it's your partner, it may be most important to focus your efforts on the reparation with them, writing them a letter first. If it's you, focus on yourself first, writing yourself a letter. Otherwise there's a risk that you make your attempts at reconciliation with your partner be about your own pain or guilty conscience. It's not their job to make you feel better for what you did, or help you forgive yourself. You're responsible for working through your feelings. Guilt can help you work on repair as that emotion tells you 'I DID something bad', whereas shame tells you 'I AM bad'.[48] Work on your self-compassion and use your inner critic if you're plagued by feelings of shame, as you'll otherwise struggle to hold yourself accountable. Sometimes the injured partner is able to move towards forgiving the partner who has hurt them, but that participating partner can't move towards forgiving themselves.

Warm up first, using your soothing breathing rhythm and stepping into the compassionate version of yourself. You're likely to also be joined by your inner critic, so gather up your strength to soothe yourself even if you receive a barrage of harshness about your actions.

Try this

Compassionate letter of forgiveness for yourself

Dear Me,

This is the hardest thing I've ever gone through, no wonder I'm feeling awful as I really hurt the person I love the most. What kind of person does that?! It makes sense that I'm blaming myself right now, this is what I do when I mess up. But it might not be so helpful to blame myself, as I need to figure out why I did this. No wonder I'm struggling to sleep, sleeping in the spare room and can't switch off from thoughts about what I've done. I feel so bad, it's almost impossible for me to listen to L talking about what I did. I just want to disappear and make this go away. I understand that's my shame – my inner critic telling me I'm a horrible person who doesn't deserve forgiveness or for this relationship to work. Whenever I hear that voice, I feel so low, so disgusted with myself, that I can't move forward even if L wants to. I think I need some help to work this through. My friends have been so kind and understanding, it might help to think of myself like they do: an essentially nice person who messed up, but who's learning from this and wanting to make amends. I'll try to remind myself of this when I speak to L next time, and I know that my inner mentor agrees. Maybe I DO deserve forgiveness, even though I don't feel like it right now. I'll keep trying; with time it will get easier, and with the support of friends who still believe in me. I know I've learned from this, and I'm trying my hardest to show L that too – I'm not like my parents, I won't replicate their patterns. I'm doing the best I can.

Moving forward, letting go

Remember the multiple parts of us? The compassionate self was the only one focusing on reconnecting and moving forward together. It wanted to rebuild the trust and learn from the mistakes, whereas the threat-based emotional parts of us focus on the fight/flight reactions. In order to move forward together and truly let go of our past mistakes, remind yourselves of what you really value. That's the function forgiveness can serve for you – to release you and your partner from that emotional anguish and help you continue as a loving couple who may or may not make that same mistake again.

If forgiveness is so good, why does it hurt so much?

Forgiveness is based on compassion, which sits in the middle of threat, drive and soothing. In order to forgive, you need to consider how much pain you've experienced (or caused). This activates your *threat system*, experiencing unpleasant emotions such as anger, fear and disgust. Forgiveness is also about wanting to move towards a better relationship, perhaps pursuing a resolution to your problems. This activates your *drive system*, as you may want to experience joy and satisfaction again, to move past problems and reconnect. Forgiveness also activates the *soothing system*, from tending to that close bond between you two, if you allow the time and space to heal and feel safe again. Draw on compassion to tolerate all that distress, having the *willingness* to sit with the hard feelings instead of pushing them away.

My story

My motherhood journey was incredibly hard in the first two years, especially the first ten months, and this took a toll on our marriage. We were in survival mode. Our son, our beautiful and beloved baby, was unsettled from the word go. Something was wrong, but it took some time to understand the pain he was in from silent reflux, tongue ties and multiple severe allergies. Sleep was non-existent, as baby woke up distressed every fifteen minutes. We were a shell of our former selves – 'the compassionate self has left the building; only shadow selves live here'. We were both stressed from managing a sick baby and living off one income from my husband's job with long working hours and little flexibility. I'm still working on forgiving my husband for what emotionally felt like an 'abandonment'. It wasn't his fault – he simply had to go to work so we could survive. I was left alone all day with a distressed infant I couldn't soothe and who wouldn't sleep, so I couldn't recover from the birth.

I've had to work very hard at forgiving *myself* for the version of me who was present in those long days of sleep deprivation, not always having been the parent I had envisioned: *calm, caring, connected.* Instead I had to embrace reality: *frantic, caring for others at the expense of my own wellbeing, connected through repairing my mistakes*. It took me travelling to a compassion retreat in Thailand, then seeing a perinatal psychologist, then having EMDR therapy for trauma, to reach a point where I was able stop beating myself up. We did the best we could, given the context. We're still carrying the memories but spending less and less time in the versions of ourselves we were then. Forgiveness is helping us move forward together, slowly, reconnecting again step-by-step. We're able to weather any storm after what we went through, remembering that connection comes from both light and dark times and that relationships are a long end game with many bumps in the road.

When forgiveness is impossible

If you can't forgive, and decide to go separate ways, you'll still need to consider the questions around how holding onto the pain is serving you, how not letting go is affecting you. Is it helping you to go forward when you rehash the past? Even if you split up it's important to make sense of why this happened, becoming wiser from experience, to avoid it affecting you as you move into another relationship. Remember that *Wherever you go, there you are.*

Summary

- Forgiveness is not about letting someone off the hook – it's about holding them gently accountable for what they've done, moving towards repair and reconciliation.
- What kind of life could you lead if you could forgive and let go? Could you get peace and calm, feeling free?
- Blaming yourself is less likely to help you learn from your mistake, compared to gently holding yourself accountable in a compassionate way.
- By doing that you can become aware of what led you to do what you did, so you can prevent it from happening again.

Coming to the surface to breathe after a deep dive, we'll move into the last part of the book – looking after yourself and continuing to live a connected life together.

Part IV

Maintaining your connection

- Understand why self-care is couple care, as you cannot give what you haven't got
- Incorporate strategies for looking after yourself into your self-compassion tool kit, for sustainable compassion
- Start rituals around kindness and gratitude, to maintain your progress and a lasting connection
- Map out the road ahead, looking at road blocks to practising and continuing the journey on your own

23 Self-care is couple care

Look after yourself to look after your relationship

Why is self-care and self-compassion so important to your relationship? Because you cannot pour from an empty glass – you cannot give what you haven't got. You deserve to take better care of yourself to also be there for your partner by being your compassionate best. If you want longevity in your relationship, you need to prioritise sustainability for yourself and be the best version of yourself: being who you want to be.

You at your compassionate best

There's a saying – *'You cannot pour from an empty glass'*. Imagine that a glass of water represents your energy levels. When you wake up in the morning, sleep has refilled your glass. If you have problems sleeping, the glass isn't topped up fully and you start your day a bit depleted. During the day you focus your energy on things which matter to you –'work', 'family', 'friends' and 'relationship'. Every time you make efforts in those areas, some of the water in your glass drains out.

If you don't look after yourself – if you don't keep yourself topped up – your glass will empty and you'll have nothing left to give. If you put work ahead of your relationship, your liquid will be all gone by the time you come home. You're then more likely to be irritable and snappy, as nobody can run on empty. It's common for burnt-out professionals to struggle in their relationships – they're too exhausted to give anything to their partners.

Running low on energy can also come from a pattern of *self-silencing*, pouring into your partner's glass without voicing your own needs and getting yourself 'topped up'. You'll gradually feel more hard done by, with festering resentment towards your partner. It's not sustainable – you'll only be able to do it for so long before things come crashing down.

Your compassionate best sees you balancing your needs with other people's needs, especially your partner's, and having the strength and courage to face your difficulties with perseverance and grit.

The oxytocin mask tops you up

We have to look after our own needs to be there for those we love, as an act of wise compassion for yourself and others. In Chapter 10 I mentioned the metaphor of putting on your own oxygen mask first in an aeroplane emergency, before helping others; if you pass out from lack of oxygen you cannot help them, and they may well die too.

Using the example of the *oxytocin* mask, you need to make yourself feel safe and soothed, in order to be calmer and more connected overall in your relationship. This tops you up when you're depleted, when your glass is empty. Soothing your own threat system puts you in a much better place to be mindfully present in conversations with your partner, less reactive to what they say, and able to think clearly when attempting problem solving. When you're overwhelmed the parts of your brain needed for clarity and reasoning are turned down low, and you'll focus just on survival, defending yourself rather than focusing on the connection with your partner.

Self-care isn't supposed to be selfish

It's not compassionate to consistently choose your own needs at the expense of others. Self-care under the umbrella of self-compassion is not about caring for oneself as a block to caring for others or making them happy, nor is it about being selfish or self-entitled. Quite the opposite: focusing on the happiness of our partner tends to make us happy too. Research has shown that those low in self-compassion were good at caring *for* others, but not at seeking care *from* others; those high in self-compassion cared for others AND could seek care from others.[49]

So self-care and self-compassion doesn't make you focused just on yourself – it provides you with a bit more balance.

Suzy Reading, psychologist, yoga teacher and author of *The Self-Care Revolution*, emphasises the importance of dividing your care between yourself and others, to make it 'one for you and one for them' – not 'me first', but 'me as well'.[50] Psychologist Laura Silberstein-Tirch uses warmth and non-judgement to show how you can manage your emotions and practise self-compassion in her book *How to Be Nice to Yourself*,[51] and researcher Kristin Neff highlights the importance of talking to yourself as you would talk to a friend in her book *Self Compassion*.[52]

Beyond pampering

There's a common myth that self-care is an indulgent, lovely thing to do for yourself, like having a nice bath or pampering session at the spa. Now, there's nothing wrong with wanting to draw yourself a bath and let the warm water cover your tired body – that can be an act of self-care. There's also nothing wrong with treating yourself to a spa day, perhaps with your partner – but self-compassionate care is not exclusive to those activities.

Turning up for yourself is not necessarily a comfortable, relaxing thing. Take going to a dental hygienist: that's an act of self-compassionate care, but is it comfortable to have the cleaning, scraping and polishing done? No. Is it relaxing to lie there with someone working inside your mouth, sometimes inflicting pain? No. Is it selfish to look after your teeth, so that you don't get bleeding gums or tooth decay? No, it takes a caring commitment with yourself to keep cleaning and flossing. Is it weak to tolerate the pain? No, it requires strength to endure the treatment. Caring for yourself requires you to tolerate some discomfort at times, for a healthier and happier long-term outcome.

Self-care is health care – a necessity

Next time you think about giving your teeth a quick brush, reflect on what it would be like to slow down and mindfully brush them, noticing the sensations and allowing yourself to spend a few extra minutes on flossing too. Notice what blocks or resistances might come up – I don't have time to floss, I can't be bothered, it's not important etc. Flossing is an act of self-compassion as it meets your dental needs and prevents future pain – it's not pampering.

This is where the two parts of the compassion definition meet: firstly turning up for yourself by being *sensitive* to how painful it is to have bleeding gums, but also to how challenging it is to create healthy habits; secondly making a *commitment* to take small steps today to reduce that distress in the future. Self-care is health care, preventing further suffering and illness.

The ripple effect

To have a lasting connection, you need to nurture not only your partner, but also yourself, even if it's uncomfortable in the short run. When you care for yourself, you have more to give when your glass is full. Self-care is couple care. That's the ripple effect – throwing some stones of self-care will spread positive wellbeing like rings on the water in your relationship.

To keep the couple connection strong, partners can:

- Exercise regularly to keep mentally and physically healthy, and in good shape
- Eat regularly to avoid getting 'hangry' and snappy with each other
- Ensure good sleeping habits to reduce irritability and low mood
- Rest and relax to be less frazzled and calmer and kinder with one another
- Follow your respective passions, to make life meaningful and bring joy to the partnership
- Keep good social connections for fun and support, taking the pressure off each other to meet every social need
- Set boundaries with yourselves and others, to not spread yourselves too thin

These self-care factors are promoted by many researchers and speakers on longevity, happiness and life satisfaction, such as Dan Buettner, author of *The Blue Zones*. Tune into the amazing interviews with Dr Rangan Chatterjee on the *Feel Better, Live More* podcast for more inspiration.

Your compassionate self-care kit

The following seven self-nourishing practices make up your *compassionate self-care kit*. Taking care of yourself isn't the full picture of self-compassion, but it's one very important part. It's hard to implement these habits for ourselves, and it may be even more important for you to explore *what's getting in the way* – your fears, blocks and resistances around self-compassion – than learning what it is you *need to be doing*.

1 Move your body

Regular exercise helps keep us healthy and well, strengthening our immune system and improving our mood. *Not enough* movement increases risk of injuries and low mood. Moderate levels of exercise can improve libido, as our overall energy levels and dopamine levels go up. All good things in moderation, though. *Too much* exercise in a regimented fashion creates stress on the body, reducing both the time and energy you have available for your partner. What's behind your urge to train: threat, drive or soothing? There's a difference between pursuing something for vitality and enjoyment, and striving for something as a way to escape the threat of rejection, criticism or disappointment.

If your motivation for going to the gym is burning calories and getting rid of 'disgusting fat', you're likely to be driven by threat emotions such as fear, shame and disgust with your own body. You might be scared to gain weight and not be attractive enough. Compare that to going to the gym to build a stronger body, feel healthier and manage a challenge such as climbing Mount Snowdon with your partner, running a 10k race or catching the kids in a chase. That's linked with vitality and meaning, doing something important to you and bringing you joy.

In what way will you commit to moving your body more as a way to look after yourself?

How would getting fitter and stronger improve your connection with your partner?

2 Eat real food mindfully

If you're hungry, you might get 'hangry' – angry, irritable or aggressive from lack of energy. Refuelling regularly may keep some of the minor 'quakes' at bay in your relationship. When I was pregnant, my husband routinely had a snack bar in his coat pocket, to wave in front of the goblin I would turn into when blood sugars dropped. Make sure you're eating enough to help level out your mood, and improve your overall wellbeing through a balanced weight and food intake.

Lots of us in this busy society eat mindlessly, distracted by mobile phones or computers, leading to issues with indigestion, overeating, skipping meals or eating comfort foods to manage our emotions. Try to eat *mindfully* by purposefully paying attention to your food and your body signals.

It's important to also be mindful if you're following fad diets aimed at punishing and restricting *short term*, as there's no evidence for that supporting a healthy weight and lifestyle *long term*, nor do they hold compassion for you. Intuitively respond to hunger signals, choosing healthy options of 'real food' (as few ingredients as possible on the packaging). There's plenty of inspiration available on these topics, like The Medicinal Chef (Dale Pinnock) and The Mindful Cook (Josie Buck).

Try this

Mindful and intuitive eating

1 Focus on your food without distraction – put down your phone and your work

2 Use your senses to enjoy food – really tasting what you eat to fully appreciate it

3 Listen to your hunger signals – eat when hungry and refuel to avoid irritation

4 Don't override your 'full' signals – eat in moderation, not 'must finish my plate'

5 Eat real, nutritious food – have a healthy balance of varied food groups, not fad diets

6 Breathe to aid digestion – slow down the pace of eating instead of rushing

7 Drink enough water – do not confuse thirst signals for hunger

8 Appreciate the food source – where it was grown, made or cooked

9 Pay attention to your partner – have food as a point of connection and conversation

> *In what way will you commit to eating more mindfully as a way to look after yourself?*
>
> *How would improving your eating habits improve your connection with your partner?*

3 Get better sleep

We need rest and sleep to recharge our batteries and clear our body and mind. Mindfulness or meditation at bedtime can serve as a 'beditation', helping you switch off and prepare for sleep. Meditation can have a calming, soothing impact on your body and mind, even if you're unable to sleep. If your mind is really distracted, doing mental gymnastics and not letting you switch off, it can be helpful to jot down a few words about whatever you're struggling to let go of, trusting that it will be there for you the next day. 'Nothing good comes out of 3am' – don't attempt to solve your problems then.

Experiencing the impact of sleep deprivation on my own body and mind has been terrifying. If you're frequently woken by a baby or child, can you rest at other times or get support? If you're a shift worker, get proper blackout blinds to get good rest in the daytime. If you're woken by needing to go to the toilet, which happens more as you progress into older age, try a calming meditation or counting breaths to come back to rest afterwards.

Try this

Counting breaths if you can't sleep

'If you can't sleep, count breaths and rest' advises psychologist and ACT author Professor Kelly Wilson. If you're tossing and turning when you're trying to go to sleep you actually make yourself more awake (it creates tension in the body). Instead, stop trying and just count breaths in and out. One for in, two for out, three for in, four for out, and so on. When you get to ten, start again. If you get distracted and start thinking about something else, start over from one. Don't try to force it; use your soothing breathing rhythm to calmly breathe in and out, focusing on this breathing anchor.

What small changes can you make to promote better sleep every day?

How would improving your sleep strengthen your connection with your partner?

4 Rest and relax to recharge

People often save their relaxation for holiday time, hoping to recharge their batteries. Now, reality hits when you go away – you get a dodgy tummy, you fight with your partner after a long journey and the kids have gone feral. Relaxing? Maybe less so. Sometimes going on holiday is just a *change of scenery*, rather than a *break*. Try not to put so much pressure on going away as your respite; find downtime where you are, right now, in everyday life. Take three deep breaths and slowly release the air, or take five minutes to do nothing at all, like looking out the window or just sitting down. Look at your working pattern and see what you can let go of – which of the balls you're juggling can you put down? Resting is an art form, one which we've neglected in the Western world, where being 'busy' is hailed as a measure of success.

One of the most common disruptors to downtime in our modern society is people being on their smartphones. Mindlessly scrolling isn't downtime, even if it's a pocket of time and space for yourself. If you do something purposefully on your phone for a few minutes, like using a breathing app leaving you feeling calm and rested, that's fine. Most people instead find themselves having got lost down a rabbit hole, spending more time on their phone than intended, and then not having time for things they actually find restful, like listening to music, going for a walk, having a bath or stretching out on the sofa. Rest and downtime are more about *being*, instead of *doing*, having mindful moments of not focusing on productivity.

Try this

Park your phone for a mental break

Put both your phones in a box – a mobile phone parking lot. The whole family can join in, if appropriate. Agree on when the phones go in, to remove that distraction and block to more restful and recharging ways of being, and when they're allowed to come out. You wouldn't forget to plug your phone in to recharge the battery – so how about plugging yourself in to recharge yours?

In what way can you create some downtime for yourself, having rest and relaxation?

How would slowing down and doing less improve your connection with your partner?

5 Find your passion to give you purpose

Walking in line with your values will give you a greater sense of purpose and meaning, so find out what you're passionate about and engage with it on a regular basis. Perhaps it's that pottery class you long for every week, or being alone in nature with your camera. Perhaps it's when you volunteer at the local homeless shelter, or when you write your blog. This kind of self-care is more about nourishing your soul, or your heart if you like, with *eudaimonic wellbeing*.

What do you love doing which you can commit to doing regularly as an act of self-care?

How would doing more meaningful things for yourself improve your connection with your partner?

6 Nurture your social connections

Couples with outside social support tend to manage the hardship of intimate relationships better; it takes the pressure off your partner to have to meet your every social need. So what if your partner doesn't like dancing? Go with your friend instead. Nurturing those other social connections will help you thrive and flourish, as you get to have fun and feel close to others, and not 'put all of your eggs in the partner basket'. Being with others makes us feel good, but better one close friend you can *belong* with than ten superficial friendships where you bend over backwards *fitting in*. The former is restorative; the latter is exhausting.

Try this

Radiators or drains?

Consider who in your life is filling up your glass with energy. They might be a *radiator*, keeping you warm and safe with their positive energy. Consider who drains away energy from you, emptying your glass by taking more than they pour in. They might be a *drain*. Reflect together with your partner which social connections fill up your respective glasses and which empty them. Be open and curious rather than aggressive about the other person's friends and family.

How can you spend more time with the people who recharge your batteries?

How would honing your social connections with others improve your connection with your partner?

7 Set boundaries with fierce self-compassion

One way to protect your time and energy is to be careful when you say 'yes'. Setting boundaries in a compassionate way means considering your own needs and balancing them with the other person's needs, not sacrificing yourself for the sake of others. *Fierce self-compassion* means standing tall, saying 'No, I'm afraid I can't do that right now', as a way to protect yourself. If you can set a boundary to your partner, saying no to things which will max out your metaphorical energy credit card, you're less likely to feel resentful over time. The fierceness is about engaging strength and courage, daring to say no and to draw a line and not crossing it. It's not about being selfish or inflexible in a way which blocks caring and compassion ever flowing out to others. Setting a boundary is not an excuse for treating others badly.

> *Who or what do you need to set a boundary with, to not deplete yourself?*
>
> *How would setting boundaries towards others improve your connection with your partner?*

Reflection & Connection

Self-care habits

Sit down with your partner and consider the practices above. Notice self-limiting negative beliefs or objections, such as 'I don't have the time', 'It costs too much money' or 'It's too hard'.

> *What could you do more or less of this week, to look after yourself?*
>
> *How could this help you manage the triggers in your relationship?*
>
> *How would you be in your partnership if you made yourself a priority as well?*
>
> *What's getting in the way for each of you to improve self-care? What are your blocks?*
>
> *Which domain can you choose first and what small steps can you take this week?*

From the sofa

Ravi and Tahani were looking for support for their mental wellbeing, having children with additional needs. Ravi worked long hours to provide for the family, whereas Tahani was a dedicated mother shouldering more of the household responsibilities, on top of working. Tahani was very clear on her values as a mother, of how she wanted to be with her children when they were in distress. Ravi felt overwhelmed and stressed, and would use his smartphone as an escape, realising he'd become addicted to it and it was impacting on his family life. They both felt they struggled in their own self-care but found that their relationship was actually doing OK. They had navigated how to divide up the responsibilities, so that they both contributed to the wellbeing of the family. Although it wasn't a 'like for like' equal division on paper, what made it sustainable was that they each felt that the other was doing their part and expressed gratitude for their contribution. They were focused on surviving, not thriving, and needed help to each look after themselves to be able to keep giving to those who mattered the most to them – their children.

My story

I've always struggled with self-care, as it wasn't modelled so well to me as a child. Remember that I'm not perfect, that I haven't 'got it all figured out' – I'm human too! Being *aware* of the fears, blocks and resistances to self-care, as well as the shaping of me, helps me to choose wisely and remind myself why it makes sense that I neglect self-care. It took me travelling halfway around the world to a compassion retreat – twice – to look after myself properly. I'm sad to say it also took two episodes of burnout from working too hard in an environment which was fertile soil for overachieving.

My husband supported me through the tough period a few years ago where I sat on the stairs at home, crying and not wanting to go to work. I was depleted. Learning to have appropriate self-care and working to live instead of living to work helped me continue to follow my ambition instead of drowning in it. I now make space for me as well as others, working on my own terms in my own private practice. I have fewer client sessions per week, working from home half of my time and take time for rest, walks or yoga during the working day. I enjoy my hobbies outside of work, like my Dancehall/Afrobeats class. When I come home and my husband can enjoy seeing me being lit on fire, passionate and light-hearted. What I do for me ripples out to him, and reduces any resentment of motherhood, as I can be there for others in the way which fits with my values. My supervisors, friends and husband also help me be kinder and more caring of myself than my inner critic would like to allow me. My glass isn't always full, as life with a young child is still hard, but I know how and when to top it up.

Summary

- Truly care for yourself through moving your body, eating real food in a mindful way, having downtime with rest and relaxation, and finding your purpose through your values.
- Self-care isn't a competition or race to a finish line.
- Self-care is a marathon over a lifetime of looking after yourself, so that you can be well in your relationship as well.

We're almost at the end! The last chapter focuses on tying it all together and looks at pitfalls in the journey ahead, with kindness and gratitude practices to help you.

24 The journey from here

Moving forward with compassionate intention

Compassionate actions can help you feel happy, content and fulfilled. Focusing on what you feel grateful for, in your relationship or otherwise, can help you move from surviving to thriving. Learn how to take steps towards what matters to you, by being kind and compassionate to your partner and others. Know when to ask for help for yourself or your relationship and use the concept of gentle returns when you drift off course.

Kindness

Compassion includes kindness, but compassion isn't the same as kindness. Compassion is about noticing suffering in others and wanting to help. Kindness rests on that same motivation to be helpful, not harmful, but might not have that same awareness of the pain in others. Kindness relates to being friendly and deliberately doing good unto others but is also related to the word 'kin' (family). Being kind to others is a basis for our connection with others, not just those we like and love, but to anyone – hence 'random acts of kindness'. So what's going on when partners are unkind to each other in a way they wouldn't be to strangers?

Letting it all hang out

If you feel safe and comfortable with your partner, you might have a tendency to 'let it all hang out' after a stressful day, daring to show them your full range of emotions. The downside of this, of course, is the unpleasant emotions your partner has to face. If they only get to receive you on 'a really bad day' it can wear them down over time.

You need to show your partner you on a really good day *as well*, as that's probably the person they first fell in love with.

Think about what young children or teenagers are like after a long day in childcare or at school. After being told what to do and behaving themselves all day, they've got pent-up emotions needing to escape. If their home is their safe environment, they release and *misbehave*. Can you blame them? They've kept it in all day – now they're home they can let it all out.

Unfortunately, adults do this too. Partners coming home irritable, grumpy and distant – a long way from who they might be at work, cracking jokes with colleagues, or supporting someone with a problem. Which version is the 'right' version? Which one is your 'true self'? Well, neither and both. With our many different selves we can show up in one way at work and in a different way at home. It is not, however, helpful and healthy for your relationship if you consistently only show an unkind, irritated version of yourself at home as you have 'used up' all the good sides of you at work. Your partner deserves to see what others also get to see.

Making an effort

If you want your body to be strong and healthy, you have to make some efforts to exercise regularly and feed it with good nutrients. Intimate relationships are no different. When your motivation is low, and you're exhausted after work, you still need to make an effort to be kind and compassionate to your partner, or your relationship will weaken over time. It's the same with fitness and physical strength – if you don't use it, you lose it.

You know now that you can form new habits and contribute to a more compassionate climate in your relationship. Tending your relationship garden takes time, energy and commitment; you may not see the fruits of what you've planted until months or even a year later. Don't give up, keep making the effort – we're going for longevity rather than quick fixes.

Plants and humans both need nourishment in a non-toxic environment to thrive and grow. Making an effort to be kind to your partner at the end of a long day is like pouring fertiliser onto the soil of your relationship. It will do the partner plant a world of good, but also do your own plant good, as it *feels good to do good.*

The Kindness Jar

It's easy to forget to make efforts in your relationship – we need reminders to stay on track.

Whenever someone in your home does something kind, put a marble or pebble in the Kindness Jar – to highlight and appreciate when you're living in line with the value of kindness. The jar is placed somewhere visible where everyone can track its progress. Decide together what will happen when the jar is full, for example:

- You donate money, time or work to someone needing kindness and support
- You invest in some nourishing self-care
- You go for a special family day out (our favourite is the Dinosaur Park)
- You treat yourselves to something nice as a couple, like a hotel stay or dinner

If you want your children to grow up to be kind to others, you need to show them that through your own kind actions, practising what you preach to them, but also with your partner. The point is to make it rewarding; strengthening our natural tendency to be *kind* to one another in a world where humans often end up being *unkind* to one another. It can also help you to acknowledge and appreciate your partner's efforts and so keep compassion flowing in.

Gratitude

The act of writing things down has real value, giving space between us and our thoughts. Gratitude journals have become a popular way to bring attention to things we appreciate in life, in ourselves, or in other people.

Often couples get annoyed when asked to make space for gratitude for their partner, as they might be feeling resentful or angry with the other person. However, you can appreciate things about your partner AND be mad at them at the same time. It's common for partners to feel they love their other half dearly, but also feel furious with how annoying the partner can be. I once read on a wedding card that 'Marriage is promising to annoy each other for the rest of your lives'. If you make some space for the appreciation, you can soothe some of the annoyance.

My story

You've already read how hard it was for us when we had our child. My husband did everything he could to support us, but due to paternity leave regulations had to return to work two weeks after the baby arrived. Over the course of the maternity year, this led to resentment building towards the love of my life/father of my child, who would 'get to leave' every day; have a coffee break without anyone screaming at him; 'enjoy' going to the toilet uninterrupted. In the midst of sleep deprivation, I couldn't see clearly what I see now: we were both in pain. He felt the pressure from being the only one working to pay the mortgage, to make sure we could always put food on the table. I missed these opportunities for empathy for my husband in my haze of sleep deprivation and having the baby with me all day long. Whatever pain he was in, I felt that mine was greater. Being a couples therapist, I could see the resentment, so I introduced an attempt at holding in mind what we appreciated at the same time as making space for being angry or envious of each other.

Try this exercise below, but be aware that you won't magically feel love towards your partner – it can just make it easier to get through a rough patch. You can use the 'gratitude for your partner' audio from Chapter 9 to get you started.

Try this

Giving and receiving appreciation and gratitude

Consider what your partner has done or been for you today, however small and fleeting, which you've appreciated. Express it to your partner – we all tend to be more likely to express the things we're upset and annoyed about than the things we're grateful for. Use your compassionate facial expression and tone of voice to share this.

For instance, you might say 'I appreciated you picking up some food for dinner tonight, so I didn't have to think about what to cook', while also being annoyed that they didn't put their clothes in the laundry hamper. A negative behaviour does not cancel out a positive one, and the positives are the ones we want to strengthen to also strengthen our connection.

1 What three things have you appreciated about your partner today?
   *
   *
   *

2 Find a time to tell your partner the three things you've appreciated. Ask them to listen without interruption, encouraging them to take it in without batting the appreciation away, letting kindness flow in and accepting it. It can be quite soothing to do this before bed, and can strengthen that connection between you.

3 Swap, so it's your turn to receive. Notice your own tendencies to not acknowledge the actions your partner is appreciating. Remember that it's each person's subjective experience what they appreciate in another person, so try to take it in.

4 Thank each other for the kind words and go with what feels good here. Perhaps this has given you an emotional connection, so that a physical connection feels natural (cuddling up together to go to sleep or giving each other a hug before you carry on with your day).

5 Reflect together how this has made you feel, having spent a few mindful moments on telling each other what you've liked about the other. Has this lifted you up? If so, why don't you make space for this more often? It feels good to do good, remember?

The intention is to help focus your mind on the things your partner is doing *right*, and not just on the things you perceive them doing *wrong*. You also get to experience what it feels like to be appreciated yourself, and that may well make you feel like your actions are noticed and worthwhile.

'Thank you' vs 'I'm sorry'

There are many ways to express gratitude and appreciation for your partner, but couples often get caught up in their own shame and guilt by apologising for how they have behaved. Apologies are helpful and important, but it matters how we carry them out. We can also use an appreciation statement as a way to acknowledge that we're sorry for how we have behaved, without beating ourselves up.

Look at this example:

'I'm sorry I was so late home, I'm so rubbish, it's unacceptable.'

Feel the tension there. Yes, it's great that you acknowledge that you were late home, as your lack of punctuality may have upset or frustrated your partner. But how does it leave you feeling? Like you're worthless or not good enough, or that you have failed? How does it leave your partner feeling? Like they need to reassure you that you're good enough?

'Thank you for waiting for me when I was late home, I appreciate that you were patient with me even though I'm sure it was frustrating to wait. I'll really try not be so late again.'

Do you feel this statement is a bit long and clunky? Good communication often feels that way at first, as you're learning a new language and the sentence structure and vocabulary is unfamiliar. Practise this new language as often as you can, and you'll become proficient.

You're being specific about what you're grateful for, noticing what they've done for you (waited). You're making a guess at your partner's emotions there, which often is really validating and helpful, as you've acknowledged that your behaviour may have caused an upset. It also gives them a chance to correct you, or to soften into it a bit, by responding that they were worried about you rather than frustrated. By acknowledging what you appreciated, you reinforce their behaviour and they're more likely to be patient with you in future, as you also acknowledge how you'll try to not do it again. Furthermore, you're more likely to be kinder to yourself in future, as you haven't had a go at yourself for making a mistake. Win win.

Finding your way again

You will inevitably drift off course and act away from your values at times. As your relationship lifespan will mean a lifetime of gentle returns, it's important to keep in mind what you want to return to and how to find your way again.

We have a magnetic whiteboard on our fridge, serving as a visual reminder for one thing which I believe keeps us on track within our relationship: kindness. I find it incredibly easy to drift away from it, but that's no testament to how important the value is to me. It's just a sign that I've been too busy in my life and need to pause.

The whiteboard has three questions, stating 'Have I been kind to . . . today?' for each of our names in the family. These serve as reminders for the two adults to be kind to each other, as partners, and also to our child, as parents. They also help us remember to be kind to ourselves. Once our son can read, this will be part of our family mantra. My son does call me out when I haven't acted in a kind way, and he's only three. You can to some extent shape the values you want your children to grow up with, but it starts with you.

> *What mantra or visual reminder can you put on the fridge in your family?*

How can you gently return, to find your way again when you drift off course?

The pitfalls to come

Let's try to anticipate any stumbling blocks on the road ahead. Reflect on these possible pitfalls and use problem-solving skills to come up with some answers.

POSSIBLE PITFALLS	POSSIBLE ANSWERS
Too hard to remember ('I forgot to do what I promised my partner, even though I'd planned to')	Negotiate with your partner how to make this a priority, and how you can help each other remember without adding pressure or criticism. Decide on reminders or systems you can use to remember to read this book, do exercises from it or have connected time.
Too difficult ('I don't know what I'm doing, it's all new to me, I can't cope with this')	Remind yourself with compassion that anything new will feel difficult at first, before you become practised in it. It's about making progress, not getting it perfect.
Too busy ('We don't have the time to work on our relationship')	Remind yourself of your intention: ***why*** am I doing this? Consider how you're spending your time, whether you can let go of something to make space for improving the relationship.
Too silly ('None of this psychobabble compassion stuff is even going to work, what's the point?')	What does it bring up for you to own a self-help book for the couple relationship? – perhaps you feel embarrassed and don't want to tell others about the need to strengthen your relationship. Find someone who supports you making your partnership a priority, who won't mock you.

Too boring ('It's not exactly fun to sit down and talk about our relationship, so I avoid it')	Set some short-term rewards for doing the work, to increase the motivation, like doing something fun once you've finished a chapter or rewarding your partner with something when they've made an effort to talk about their feelings.
Too stressful ('I feel overwhelmed whenever we work with the book or try to talk, so I don't do it')	Break things down into more manageable chunks and use your self-soothing skills to cope with overwhelming emotions. Do what you can. Be honest with yourself about why you're not working on your relationship, without blaming and shaming yourself or your partner.

Putting it all together

I've introduced you to a lot of skills and exercises, which you might have found challenging. I want to show you that you're probably doing a lot of these things already, or parts of the skills, but perhaps inconsistently so. Making changes to how you act, in order to contribute to a lasting connection, doesn't have to be really complicated. Below I've used an example from my own marital life to show you how to use these skills in the moment. The last couple I'll show you is Robin and Michaela.

From the sofa

One evening after our young son had been particularly difficult to get to bed, I came into the kitchen and told my husband 'I'm so fed up with this, why won't he just go to sleep?' and slammed a few cupboards. My husband took a deep **breath** and watched me as he slowly released the air (**soothing self**), letting me get it out of my system by not interrupting or trying to 'fix' (using the **clarity** of knowing that when I'm angry attempts at fixing don't work very well). He waited with patience, **accepting** what I was feeling. After a little while I turned to him as I 'ran out of steam'. My husband moved closer to me with a concerned face and said softly 'I know, it's been like this for so long now, it's exhausting' (showing a **caring commitment** and **validating** my emotions with his **facial expression** and **tone of voice**). He held his arms out and let me choose to move into the embrace, not to fix, but to show me his **willingness** to be there. He let me ease into the hug and relax (soothing through **touch**). I started **breathing** more slowly, and really **noticed** the warmth of my husband's body next to mine (**mindfulness**) and let myself cry (**courage to be vulnerable**), understanding my frustration over the bedtime battles (**self-compassion**). We held each other for a while (**physical connection**), until my husband **gently** suggested we do something light to take our minds off the tough evening (**decreasing the negatives**) and have some fun together (**increasing the positives**). I decided to sit down to play even though not feeling like it, as we had planned board game night (**strength and dedication** to go in line with my **values**).

We focus on **surviving** the hard times and move towards **thriving** through our **emotional connection**. These skills build longevity for us, having **trust** that we can turn towards each other as a **team** and **tolerate imperfection**. We are each other's best **friends**.

If you need more help

Well done for getting to the end of the book! If you've learned new concepts and started to apply the skills practice into your life, then great – but sometimes self-help is not enough. Your relationship might have gone through too many ruptures for you to be able to repair them on your own, or you may be under too much strain at the moment to think clearly regarding the major decisions you have to make – or perhaps struggling with your mental health. If so you might need more help.

I help people all over the world in my private practice, but I can't know what services are available near to where you live or help you in an immediate crisis. If you feel in any way unsafe or that you're going to hurt yourself or your partner, contact the emergency services in your area.

If you want to arrange a free chat about how I can best support you, go to my website for The Thomas Connection:

www.thethomasconnection.co.uk.

If you want to dive deeper than this book, but don't feel the need for one-to-one therapy as such, I run retreats, courses and workshops for couples and individuals to cultivate compassion for themselves and others. I'm especially passionate about helping people let go of the pressure of perfection, so they can find their purpose and create a more meaningful, balanced life. I would love you to join my Facebook groups; search for 'The Lasting Connection' for couple-related discussions and free resources, or for 'Pause * Purpose * Play' for a group aimed at high-striving, ambitious people wanting to let go of the pressure of perfection.

I've also started a podcast called *Pause Purpose Play.* Here I'll cover some of the psychology concepts you've read in this book, with guest interviews as well as solo episodes.

Summary

We've come to the end of the journey.

My hope would be for you to continue to practise these skills throughout the lifespan of your relationship, to keep working on that lasting connection. Should your relationship end, for whatever reason, my hope is that these insights will help you choose wisely the next time you meet someone. You now also know what to do should you need more help.

Do me a favour? Gift this book to someone you think needs it. It takes on average six years before people seek help for their relationship – don't let it be too late for them to develop more love and compassion for themselves and each other. Thank you, dear reader.

On that note, I bid you farewell and good luck on this continued journey through life and through love, through both light and dark times.

References

1. Gottman, J. M., & Silver, N. (1999). *The Seven Principles For Making Marriage Work* New York: Harmony Books.
2. Buettner, D. (2012). *The Blue Zones* National Geographic.
3. Fisher, H. (2004). *Why We Love* New York: St Martin's Griffin.
4. DeKoven Fishbane, M. (2013). *Loving with the Brain in Mind* New York: Norton.
5. Gottman, J. M., & Silver, N. (1999).
6. Wax, R. (2018). *How to Be Human* Milton Keynes, UK: Penguin Life.
7. Levine, A., & Heller, R. S. F. (2010). *Attached* New York: TarcherPerigree.
8. Funk, J. L. & Rogge, R. D. (2007). Testing the ruler with item response theory: Increasing precision of measurement for relationship satisfaction with the Couples Satisfaction Index. *Journal of Family Psychology, 21*, pp.572–83.
9. Gilbert, P. (2009). *The Compassionate Mind* London: Constable.
10. Gottman, J. M., & Silver, N. (1999).
11. DeKoven Fishbane, M. (2013).
12. Eisenberger, N. I., Lieberman, M. D., & Williams, K. D. (2003). Does rejection hurt? An FMRI study of social exclusion. *Science* (New York, N. Y.), *302*(5643), pp.290–2.
13. Doyle, G. (2020). *Untamed* London: Vermilion.

14. Murphy, K. (2020). *You're Not Listening* London: Harvill Secker.
15. Hari, J. (2018). *Lost Connections* London: Bloomsbury.
16. Curran, T., & Hill, A.P. (2019). Perfectionism Is Increasing Over Time: A Meta-Analysis of Birth Cohort Differences From 1989 to 2016. *American Psychological Association, Psychological Bulletin 145,* No. 4, pp.410–29.
17. Harlow, H. & Zimmermann, R., 1959. Affectional Response in the Infant Monkey: Orphaned baby monkeys develop a strong and persistent attachment to inanimate surrogate mothers. *Science 130*(3373), pp.421–32.
18. Gottman, J. M., & Silver, N. (1999).
19. Matos, M., Duarte, C., Duarte, J. et al. (2017). Psychological and Physiological Effects of Compassionate Mind Training: a Pilot Randomised Controlled Study. *Mindfulness 8*, pp.1699–1712.
20. Meevissen, Y. M., Peters, M. L., & Alberts, H. J. (2011). Become more optimistic by imagining a best possible self: effects of a two-week intervention. *Journal of behavior therapy and experimental psychiatry*, *42*(3), pp.371–8.
21. Breines, J. G., & Chen, S. (2012). Self-Compassion Increases Self-Improvement Motivation. *Personality and Social Psychology Bulletin*, *38*(9), pp.1133–43.
22. Weng, H. Y., Fox, A. S., Shackman, A. J., Stodola, D. E., Caldwell, J. Z., Olson, M. C., Rogers, G. M., & Davidson, R. J. (2013). Compassion training alters altruism and neural responses to suffering. *Psychological science*, *24*(7), pp.1171–80.
23. Crocker, J., & Canevello, A. (2008). Creating and undermining social support in communal relationships: The role of compassionate and self-image goals. *Journal of Personality and Social Psychology*, *95*(3), pp.555–75.
24. Gilbert, P., McEwan, K., Matos, M. & Rivis, A. (2011). Fears of compassion: Development of three self-report measures. *Psychology and Psychotherapy: Theory, Research and Practice 84*, pp.23–55.

25. Hibberd, J. (2019). *The Imposter Cure* London: Aster.
26. Gilbert, P., Clarke, M., Hempel, S., Miles, J. N., & Irons, C. (2004). Criticizing and reassuring oneself: An exploration of forms, styles and reasons in female students. *The British Journal of Clinical Psychology 43*(Pt 1), pp.31–50.
27. Dweck, C. (2017). *Mindset* London: Robinson.
28. *Compassion for Voices* – animation by Charlie Heriot-Maitland, available on YouTube.
29. Harris, R. (2019). *ACT Made Simple* Oakland, CA: New Harbinger.
30. Gottman, J. M., & Silver, N. (1999).
31. Winnicott, D.W. (1956). Primary maternal preoccupation. In *Collected papers, through paediatrics to psychoanalysis* (pp.300–5). London: Tavistock Publications, 1958.
32. Kabat-Zinn, J. (2004). *Wherever You Go, There You Are* London: Piatkus.
33. Brown, B. TED talk *The Power of Vulnerability.*
34. Francis-Tan, Andrew and Mialon, Hugo M., 'A Diamond is Forever' and Other Fairy Tales: The Relationship between Wedding Expenses and Marriage Duration (15 September 2014). Available at SSRN: https://ssrn.com/abstract=2501480 or http://dx.doi.org/10.2139/ssrn.2501480
35. https://luminalearning.com/personality-dynamics
36. Epstein, N. B., & Baucom, D. H. (2002). *Enhanced cognitive-behavioral therapy for couples: A contextual approach* American Psychological Association.
37. Radford, L. et al. (2011). *Child abuse and neglect in the UK today* London: NSPCC.
38. Kabat-Zinn, J. (2004).
39. Baucom, D. H., Epstein, N., & Sullivan, L. J. (2004). Brief Couple Therapy. In Dewan, M., Steenbarger, B., & Greenberg, R. P. (eds), *The art and science of brief therapies* (pp189–227). Washington, DC: American Psychiatric Publishing.
40. Gurney, K. (2020). *Mind the Gap* London: Headline.

41. Snyder, D. K., Baucom, D. H., & Gordon, K. C. (2007). *Getting Past the Affair* New York: The Guilford Press.
42. Boyd, D. & Bee, H. (1994). *Life span development* Pearson.
43. Rodsky, E. (2019) *Fair Play* London: Quercus.
44. Svanberg, E. *Breaking Past Patterns* Online course accessed via www.mumologist.com
45. Perry, P. (2019). *The Book You Wish Your Parents Had Read (and Your Children Will be Glad That You Did).* London: Penguin Life.
46. Whisman, M.A., Uebelacker, L. A. (2003). Comorbidity of Relationship Distress and Mental and Physical Health Problems. In Snyder, D. K., Whisman, M. A. (eds), *Treating Difficult Couples* Guilford Press.
47. Brown, B. *Brené Brown on Blame* (3 February 2015). RSA short animation of original talk, *The Power of Vulnerability*. https://www.youtube.com/watch?v=RZWf2_2L2v8
48. Brown, B. (2015). *Daring Greatly: How the Courage to Be Vulnerable Transforms the Way We Live, Love, Parent, and Lead* Penguin Life.
49. Hermanto, N., & Zuroff, D. C. (2016). The social mentality theory of self-compassion and self-reassurance: The interactive effect of care-seeking and caregiving. *The Journal of Social Psychology, 156*(5), pp.523–35.
50. Reading, S. (2017). *The Self-Care Revolution* London: Aster.
51. Silberstein-Tirch, L. (2019). *How to Be Nice to Yourself* Emeryville, California: Althea Press.
52. Neff, K. (2011). *Self Compassion* London: Hodder & Stoughton.

Resources

Downloads

All audios for the practical compassion exercises can be downloaded by logging in here:

www.thethomasconnection.co.uk/thelastingconnection
Login: TheLastingConnection
Password: COMPASSIONBOOK

Questionnaires

Fears of Compassion Scale
https://www.compassionatemind.co.uk/uploads/files/fears-of-compassion-scale.pdf

Forms of Self-Criticising/Attacking and Self-Reassuring Scale
https://www.compassionatemind.co.uk/uploads/files/forms-of-self-criticising-attacking-and-self-reassuring-scale-fscrs.pdf

Functions of Self-Criticising/Attacking Scale
https://compassionatemind.co.uk/uploads/files/functions-of-self-criticizing-attacking-scale-fscs.pdf

Watching

The Space Between Self-Esteem and Self-Compassion, TED talk with Kristin Neff on YouTube
Brené Brown on Empathy – short animation available on YouTube
Brené Brown on Blame – short animation available on YouTube
Compassion For Voices – short animation by Charlie Heriot-Maitland on YouTube

Listening

The Pause Purpose Play podcast with Michaela Thomas

I'm Not Your Shrink podcast with Dr Tracy Dalgleish, Season 2 Episode 8: Growing Compassion and Kindness in Your Relationship with Michaela Thomas

Connection

Free Facebook group for high-striving ambitious people wanting to be kinder to themselves, search `Pause Purpose Play' on Facebook groups.

Acknowledgements

Without my husband Robin, none of this would have been possible. Without our strong, deep connection, I wouldn't have known how good love and life can be. Without our life experiences of parenthood, I wouldn't have known the depths of compassion. The support, negotiation and decision-making around me writing this book showed me that we truly work as a team. Thank you for helping me make my life-long dream of writing a book become a reality.

Without Prof Paul Gilbert, Prof Don Baucom, and Steve Hayes and Prof Kelly Wilson, the originators of Compassion Focused Therapy, Behavioural Couples Therapy, and Acceptance and Commitment Therapy respectively, this book wouldn't exist. My clinical work is resting on the theories of these wise humans, influencing my practice. I am forever indebted to the pioneers ahead of me, paving the way. One special note also for Russell Kolts and Dennis Tirch, for your kindness and sharing your wisdom and experience of blending ACT and CFT.

Without my fantastic supervisors, my own inner critic would have stopped me in my tracks and this book never would have seen the light of day:

Thank you Chris Irons, for believing in me even when I didn't. For so freely sharing your work and allowing me to adapt and blend, to come up with innovations. Attending your compassion retreats has been life altering. You are an inspiration, a pioneer and role model.

Thank you Sarah Corrie, for being part of my journey in CBT and Behavioural Couples Therapy from the moment I landed in the UK. Your supervision keeps me on point for my clients and kind to myself.

Thank you Mary Welford, for your compassionate supervision, mentoring and feminist perspective, helping me step up and play big even with my inner critical voice present.

Thank you Joe Oliver, for our mentoring sessions in the NHS, and for being part of my self-compassionate decision to take the courageous step of leaving the NHS and building my dream.

Thank you Annie Lapsley, for guiding me through burnout in a kind, caring and compassionate way, starting me on my journey towards compassion.

Thank you Marianne Lundahl, teaching me so much about how to trust my own instinct, how to step into the role of the psychologist whilst also being human. Your positive feedback still to this day keeps the imposter syndrome at bay.

My book writing coach, Deborah Taylor, for helping me believe in my voice and to have faith in my offering to the world. You helped me fall in love with the writing process, and nourished this book baby together with me.

My editorial director, Andrew McAleer, and his whole team at my publishing house Little, Brown. You saw something big in this book, I'm forever grateful for the handholding into completing it.

My sister, for being so older-sisterly and always there for me, especially supporting me on my journey into motherhood and into marriage.

My parents, for believing in my writing from a young age (told you that the writing camp was a good idea!) and for showing me how to parent and partner across the lifespan of a marriage. Happy 40th wedding anniversary, Mamma and Pappa!

My old and new friends, cheering me on through this process. My connection with you has kept me going.

All of my clients and couples over the years, you teach me more than any textbook ever could. You keep me on my toes and make me feel eternally grateful for getting to do what I love – helping you survive and thrive.

Last, but most importantly, this book is for my son. My beautiful, bright, bold Henry. You are my world and I want to change the world for you. I wish for you to find love and connection as deep as the one I have with your father.

Index